Kitchen Culture in America

Kitchen Culture in America

Popular

Representations

of Food, Gender,

and Race

Edited by

Sherrie A. Inness

University of Pennsylvania Press

Philadelphia

Copyright © 2001 University of Pennsylvania Press
Printed in the United States of America on acid-free paper

10 9 8 7 6 5 4 3 2 1

Published by
University of Pennsylvania Press
Philadelphia, Pennsylvania 19104-4011

Library of Congress Cataloging-in-Publication Data
Kitchen culture in America : popular representations of food, gender, and race /
edited by Sherrie A. Inness.
        p.cm.
    Includes bibliographical references and index.
    ISBN 0-8122-3564-9 (cloth : alk. paper). —
ISBN 0-8122-1735-7 (pbk. : alk. paper)
    1. Food habits — United States — History.   2. Women — United States —
Psychology.   3. Women — United States — Attitudes.   4. Kitchens — Social
aspects — United States.   5. Sex role — United States.   6. United States — Social
conditions.   7. United States — Race relations.   I. Inness, Sherrie A.
GT2853.U5 K57 2000
392.3′7′0973 — dc21   00-039286

For Patricia Reynolds Smith

Contents

Introduction

Thinking Food/Thinking Gender

SHERRIE A. INNESS

Chocolate fudge brownie. Vanilla caramel fudge. Chocolate chip cookie dough. Mint chocolate chip. After scanning all the flavors in the Ben and Jerry's ice cream cooler at my local grocery store, I select a pint of coffee Heath bar crunch. I have just finished my grocery shopping, picking up household staples such as milk, broccoli, couscous, tomatoes, onions, and garlic. I have also purchased a few treats: a bar of Lindt chocolate, caramel wafer cookies, and, of course, ice cream. As I have done on innumerable shopping expeditions, I wait until I reach the end of my grocery list before picking up the ice cream — knowing the "correct" pattern of a grocery shopping trip, a pattern deeply engrained in my mind. I toss the ice cream into my cart and head for the checkout lines, searching for the shortest line, but they all appear crowded today. I push my cart in the line with only a few women.

As I wait, I notice dozens of other women, all making similar trips; a few men stand in the lines, but they are greatly outnumbered by women. The three women in line in front of me push carts heaped with meats, vegetables, fruits, frozen meals, gallons of milk, cartons of juice, bags of chips, boxes of cereal, cans of soda, huge bags of dog and cat food. The carts are monuments to conspicuous consumption that these women push much as though they were Sisyphus — forever doomed in Hades to push his boulder up the hill, only to have it roll back to the bottom, needing to be pushed up yet again. Knowing the line will move slowly, I pick up a copy of *Woman's Day* to flip through — finding it a more attractive choice than the tabloids proclaiming "Mutant Baby Born to Nun" and "Lose Thirty-five Pounds in One Week on Top-Secret CIA Diet." On nearly every page attractive women flash gleaming white smiles. Most of them clutch a food product. Some are shown whisking together the many recipes that fill the magazine; others tout everything from peanut butter to fish filets in advertisements that trumpet the miracles of extra-creamy peanut butter and new and improved fish sticks with a batter guaranteed to stay crunchy even during Noah's flood. As the line inches forward, I put down my magazine, noticing that many of the other magazines on the rack feature images of women and food; not a single magazine depicts images of men and food.

My turn arrives. I purchase my supplies, wheel the shopping cart to my car and unpack, drive home, unload the groceries, and put each item away in its respective home. The broccoli goes in the crisper so it won't grow limp. The ice cream gets put away quickly in the freezer so I won't have a soggy, sodden carton of goo. The onions belong in the bowl on the counter along with the garlic. The cookies go in the cupboard. Everything has its place.

After shopping and putting away the groceries, I still have work to do. A friend is coming over for dinner, and I am the cook. My menu is planned. We'll start with garlic bread and a tossed salad, followed by a main course of angel hair pasta mixed with pine nuts, tomatoes, olive oil, garlic, and basil. The ice cream will serve as dessert. Not a complex menu — it's one that I can prepare without much thought because I have prepared thousands of similar meals for friends and family. Preparing this meal (or any other) is a process involving numerous small tasks: peeling the garlic and putting the cloves through a garlic press for the bread and the pasta, taking the butter out of the refrigerator to soften and mashing it with the garlic, cutting up tomatoes, toasting pine nuts, heating up the olive oil and sautéing the garlic, boiling a pot of water for the pasta, cooking and draining the pasta and mixing it with the other ingredients, tossing a bag of prepared salad (I love this invention) along with a healthy amount of freshly ground black pepper and a vinegar-mustard dressing, which I made in the morning.

As any cook recognizes, however, the battle is only half done. I will have to make sure that the garlic bread is hot and crispy (but not burned) when it is served, and I'll have to prepare enough, as my friend consumes an inordinate amount of garlic bread. I'll have to make sure that I don't cook the pasta too long or too little. I will also have to make sure that I prepare the courses at just the right moment — neither too early nor too late — so they will be finished when my guest arrives. All cooks must juggle a dozen tasks at once, knowing that they must complete all of them or the whole edifice of the meal could crash to the ground. To someone not familiar with cooking, this meal might seem complex, but I don't believe it is. Preparing a meal is as familiar as tying a shoelace. Both activities are part of the daily and weekly rituals that compose my life.

My experiences with shopping and preparing meals are hardly unique. Millions of women perform similar activities on a daily basis. They shop for groceries, flip through women's magazines for recipes, and prepare breakfasts, lunches, after-school snacks, and dinners for hordes of men, women, boys, and girls. I mention women, not men, because women still do most of the domestic cooking in the United States. It continues to be an activity coded as "women's responsibility."[1] Like me, most women probably give little conscious thought to grocery shopping and cooking. Some time is devoted to deciding what to offer to family members: to the teenager who doesn't eat meat, the husband who hates fish, the four-year-old who accepts only cereal, the cousin who doesn't eat lima beans.

But there is a difference between such food-related planning activities and thinking critically about how food, cooking, and women are linked in America and how this connection influences women and their roles. The complex web of interrelationships among women, food, and cooking must be untangled by anyone wishing to understand American culture, whether in the 1700s or today. The goal of this book is to explore a few of the ways that food and cooking culture have shaped women's gender roles over the past century. I hope that *Kitchen Culture in America* will give its readers a better understanding of the important role that food plays in helping to constitute the lives of American women — whether rich or poor, old or young, black or white — and all of American society.

As I use the term, "kitchen culture" refers to the various discourses about food, cooking, and gender roles that stem from the kitchen but that pervade our society on many levels. Kitchen culture influences advertising, cooking literature, and our daily meals, wherever we might consume them. Whether we are reading an advertisement for peanut butter that depicts a blissful woman preparing sandwiches for a bunch of ravenous teenage boys or going to the restaurant down the street that offers "mom's cooking," our culture is filled with values and notions about gender that stem from cooking and food. The pervasive nature of kitchen culture will become clear as we venture from candy advertisements to marital sex guides to juvenile cookbooks, trying to fathom how kitchen culture shapes our society — in the kitchen and beyond.

The goals for this book are threefold. First, the authors seek to show how women's roles have been shaped by kitchen culture, whether found in advertising, articles in women's magazines, cookbooks, or many other sources. They argue that kitchen culture accomplishes far more than merely passing down Aunt Matilda's recipe for Swedish meatballs. Kitchen culture is a critical way that women are instructed about how to behave like "correctly" gendered beings. If we are to understand women's gender roles in the United States, we need to study food. All of the chapters here seek to show ways that kitchen culture, in its many forms, passes down lessons about gender roles at the same time it conveys lessons about how to prepare yeast rolls.

Second, the authors demonstrate that kitchen culture is influenced by race, ethnicity, social class, and regional location. Not all women are affected by American food culture in identical ways. Instead, many factors shape the relationship between women and food. A woman living in rural Alabama for her entire life will have a different experience than a woman residing in urban New York City. If a woman is black, she will have a different experience of food than if she were white, Hispanic, or Asian. If a woman is on welfare, she will have a different experience of food in the United States than if she is wealthy. Of course, food culture — dominated as it is by a handful of multinational conglomerates whose tasteless products appear everywhere — sometimes seems as though it is something that changes little over the American landscape. Wherever a woman lives in the United States, she will encounter many of the same foods and restaurant chains that she would encounter anywhere else in the country, but women still maintain food cultures that are distinctly shaped and influenced by region, ethnicity, and social class.

Third, *Kitchen Culture in America* reveals the importance of recognizing that food culture is composed of much more than cookbooks, television cooking shows, and women's magazines. We need to recognize the importance of studying less commonly analyzed areas, such as the gender-coding of particular food items like candy or TV Dinners. We also need to acknowledge the importance of studying texts (marital sex manuals, for instance) that might appear to have little to do with food studies. Food appears everywhere, and we are only beginning our study of the omnipresence of food culture's messages. The authors of *Kitchen Culture in America* hope to broaden our understanding of the vastness and variety of food culture over the last hundred years.

Why Study Food?

Why study food in the first place? What can we really say about the Pop Tarts we consume in the morning or about the frozen dinner that we warm in our microwaves in the evening? Eating is such a mundane part of our lives that we dismiss it and food-related experiences as trivial. Who pauses to think about the origin of the potato chips purchased at a vending machine? What we need to acknowledge is that eating is an activity that *always* has cultural reverberations. Food is *never* a simple matter of sustenance. How we eat, what we eat, and who prepares and serves our meals are all issues that shape society.

Scholars across many disciplines, including anthropology, history, literature, sociology, and nutritional studies, have examined the symbolic and social meanings attached to food. In *The Raw and the Cooked* (1964), Claude Lévi-Strauss helped bring food studies to a broader audience. Roland Barthes and Pierre Bourdieu were also influential. In essays such as "Operation Margarine," "Wine and Milk," "Steak and Chips," and "Ornamental Cookery," all contained in Barthes's *Mythologies* (1957), the French theorist explored the symbolism of food. Bourdieu's monumental work, *Distinction: A Social Critique of the Judgement of Taste* (1979), addresses how the French use their sense of taste to establish their place in society. Anthropologist Mary Douglas believed one must understand food in order to understand how society operates, and she claimed that food had been unfairly slighted by academe.[2] Lévi-Strauss, Barthes, Bourdieu, and Douglas helped to make food studies more acceptable as a field for scholarly research. None, however, focused predominantly on gender and cooking; women and gender concerns made only a limited appearance in their scholarship.

In the past few decades, an increasing number of scholars have acknowledge the importance of food studies.[3] For instance, in *Appetite for Change* (1989), Warren J. Belasco demonstrates how the countercultural revolution of the 1960s changed American eating habits. In *We Are What We Eat* (1998), Donna R. Gabaccia explores ethnic foods and their development in the United States. Neither Belasco nor Gabaccia, however, focuses exclusively on gender issues. In other scholarship on food, women and gender concerns are more central. In Carole Counihan and Penny Van Esterik's edited collection, *Food and Culture: A Reader* (1997), a number of essays focus on food and gender. Arlene Voski Avakian's anthology *Through the Kitchen Window* (1997) focuses exclusively on women, gender, and food culture. An ever greater number of scholars are acknowledging that gender is an essential component to analyze when focusing on food culture in the United States (and around the globe). Gender is moving into the limelight as a central issue of concern for anyone interested in food studies. As this field grows more popular in recent years, a greater number of scholars are exploring issues related to gender and kitchen culture.

Perhaps one reason for the growing interest in food studies is that, although food is often overlooked, it lies at the heart of the human experience. As Peter Farb and George Armelagos observe in *Consuming Passions: The Anthropology of Eating* (1980), "Cultural traits, social institutions, national histories, and individual attitudes cannot be entirely understood without an understanding also of how these have meshed with our varied and peculiar modes of eating" (4). Other scholars have noted the central role food plays in many cultures. In *Consuming Geographies: We Are Where We Eat* (1997), geographers David Bell and Gill Valentine suggest the symbolic complexity of food in human society: "For most inhabitants of (post)modern Western societies, food has long ceased to be merely about sustenance and nutrition. It is packed with social, cultural and symbolic meanings. Every mouthful, every meal, can tell us something about ourselves, and about our place in the world" (3).[4] Social anthropologist Nick Fiddes also acknowledges the complex roles that food plays in society, noting, "All over the world food means much more than mere nutrition" (38).[5] Counihan and Van Esterik write: "Food touches everything. Food is the foundation of every economy. It is a central pawn in political strategies of states and households. Food marks social differences, boundaries, bonds, and contradictions" (1). These scholars and many others are analyzing the myriad roles of food in our culture, both past and present.[6]

Kitchen Culture in America focuses on the relationship between women, food, and cooking culture because women and food have been deeply connected for countless centuries. What historian Susan Strasser calls "the central ritual of housekeeping" is still very much at the center of millions of American homes. In *Female Desires: How They Are Sought, Bought, and Packaged* (1985), Rosalind Coward observes that "how food is consumed and prepared has crucial implications for women in this society, because it expresses deeply held ideologies of provision and dependency. Where eating is no longer a matter of absolute survival, the preparation and contexts of food are laced with social symbolism" (109). Similarly, Sally Cline writes in *Just Desserts* (1990): "By looking at food we can get at the kernel of the political relationship between the sexes. For food is a crucial political area. Women's subordination is locked into food; an issue even feminists have not yet sufficiently investigated" (3). *Kitchen Culture in America* seeks to analyze the ways in which kitchen culture has confined women to traditional gender roles and the ways in which it has helped women to question and undermine such roles.

Candy and Campbell's Soup

Beginning our examination of women and food culture, Jane Dusselier analyzes the gender coding of candy in the Progressive Era. In the early twentieth century, candy manufacturers changed the way they advertised candy, shifting from perceiving it as a typically feminine pleasure to viewing it as a treat for women *and* men. Using a wide range of texts, from candy patents to turn-of-the-century advertisements, Dusselier reveals that studying a single food, such as candy, can reveal a great deal about how gender is constructed in the United States. In a similar fashion, Katherine Parkin focuses on one brand-name food in a single decade: Campbell's soup in the 1920s.[7] In *Perfection Salad: Women and Cooking at the Turn of the Century* (1986) food historian Laura Shapiro argues that a new image of the American housewife developed in this era: "an image suitable for a new age of material invention and consumption. The advertising industry, the manufacturers of household goods, the food companies, the women's magazines, and the schools all shared in the task of creating a woman who could discriminate among canned soups but who wouldn't ask too many questions about the ingredients: neither angel nor scientist, but homemaker" (221–22). Parkin studies the new homemaker whom Shapiro describes, arguing that traditional images of women and cooking helped to sell products to housewives early in the century. Focusing on Campbell's soup advertisements, Parkin demonstrates how the soup company used traditional gender images to encourage the consumption of soup by American families, reassuring housewives that they were following in the traditional footsteps of their grandmothers and mothers, even if they bought Campbell's soup instead of making soup from scratch. However, Parkin suggests, such advertising also encouraged its readers to perceive traditional gender imagery (i.e., mom in the kitchen) as socially desirable and "normal."

Like Parkin, Alice A. Deck focuses on food advertising and its messages to women about how they should behave. She studies images of African American cooks in advertisements from the first half of the twentieth century. Analyzing the popular Mammy figure that appeared on many food commodities, including bags of flour and packages of pancake mix, Deck asserts that these images served as a form of fetishism. White women cooks brought home not only a pancake mix but also the fetished image of the idealized southern black Mammy. Dusselier, Parkin, and Deck all reveal the importance of studying the messages contained in food advertisements — advertisements that reveal a great deal about how gender, race, and class are constituted in the United States.

Jessamyn Neuhaus examines marital sex manuals from forty years of American history — not a source that people typically consider when thinking about food in U.S. history. She demonstrates that food, sex, and gender roles were often intertwined concerns in such manuals and that this reveals a great deal about gender tensions in the United States after World War I and World War II. Sherrie A. Inness focuses on juvenile cookbooks to understand how cooking became gender-coded. She reveals how the juvenile cookbook — a popular genre for well over a century — taught generations of boys and girls not only how to boil an egg and but also how they were expected to behave when they became adults.

Neuhaus and Inness write about a few of the ways that cookbooks supported cultural stereotypes about how middle-class white women were behave. But did all cooking literature necessarily have a socially conservative role? This question is particularly intriguing because cookbooks are frequently thought to support a conservative ideology. Janet Theophano, however, argues the opposite, as she examines how two groups of women used cookbooks as a venue for social protest. Theophano is one of many scholars today who recognize that cookbooks are more complex documents than they have been given credit for. As Anne L. Bower astutely notes in *Recipes for Reading: Community Cookbooks, Stories, Histories* (1997), cookbooks "quietly or boldly tell of women's lives and beliefs. In community cookbooks women present their values, wittingly or unwittingly" (2). Theophano examines the beliefs that women "boldly" display in two cookbooks: the *Presbyterian Cookbook* (1886) by the Ladies Society of the First Presbyterian Church of Dayton, Ohio, and *How to Cook and Eat in Chinese* (1945) by Buwei Yang Chao. She discusses how women use cookbooks for social and political critique, going far beyond the limited confines of the kitchen. Chao used her book to critique the ethnocentrism of the United States at a time (World War II) when America suffered from tremendous xenophobia, especially in regard to Asians.

Theophano writes about the 1940s. The next three authors scrutinize the 1950s. Erika Endrijonas analyzes the cooking lessons passed on to women through cookbooks. Christopher Holmes Smith addresses frozen food at a time when the frozen food industry was booming. He studies the many ways that frozen food companies used women in articles and advertisements to assure women that frozen food was the best choice for their families. Jessica Weiss remembers a popular cooking column entitled "She Also Cooks" from Oakland, California. This column is an important source for studying how women working outside the home dealt with housework.

The final two chapters turn to more modern times. Doris Witt focuses on Vertamae Smart Grosvenor's *Vibration Cooking, or the Travel Notes of a Geechee Girl* (1970), showing how Grosvenor used the book to explore and critique the location of women within the Black Power movement and second-wave feminism. Moreover, Grosvenor used *Vibration Cooking* to question the dictates of the black soul food movement, for which she was an early champion. Traci Kelly studies how culinary autobiographies help women to investigate their own lives and those of other women. Culinary biographies, Kelly argues, are a way that women writers have explored a broad range of topics related to food, gender, and culture.

Food for Thought

After reading *Kitchen Culture in America*, readers will, I hope, have a better understanding of the importance of food culture. It is too easy to overlook food culture because it surrounds us. We need to stop and think carefully about what messages food conveys to us. We need to reflect on how and by whom the food items that we consume are created, as well as about how food serves as a marker of identity in our culture.

I also hope that *Kitchen Culture in America* will make its audience more critical of the gender-coded messages that food culture contains. Cooking provides more than a meal. Food culture contains messages about how women and men are supposed to act in our society and what roles they should play. Even today, millions of women are convinced that their place is in the kitchen; millions of men are convinced that their place is anywhere but the kitchen. To understand why food preparation is so strongly coded as a feminine activity, we need to explore the messages received about food from countless sources. To understand how men and women are constituted as gendered beings, we must recognize the role played by food culture. *Kitchen Culture in America* is one small step in the process of understanding the infinitely complex operations of food culture in American society.

Notes

1. Among her other chores, the housewife in the eighteenth century "did some back-yard butchering, . . . preserved the fruits and vegetables, salted and pickled the meat, churned butter, and baked enormous quantities of bread, pie, and cake" (Shapiro 12). The modern housewife's chores are quite different. She might make dinner by baking some frozen chicken nuggets, serving them with Tater Tots and grape Kool-Aid for the children. What has changed surprisingly little in the intervening years is that women continue to be primarily responsible for most kitchen tasks, especially shopping for, preparing, and serving food.

The research supporting this claim is vast. For instance, in her study of over three hundred households, Sarah Fenstermaker Berk found that the vast amount of household work was performed by women. Among her respondents, "the clear presumption existed that the wives were responsible for the work of the household. . . . This sort of normative structure — resting as it does on gender relations — lends a kind of solidity to the arrangement of work that, in principle, could be organized in many different ways or might be subject to substantial influence from pressures external to the household but is not" (198–99). For work that discusses the inordinate amount of food-related work that women perform today, see Charles and Kerr; DeVault; and Schafer and Schafer.

2. Douglas wrote: "The absence of serious research into the cultural and social uses of food is caused by a more fundamental separation between food sciences and social thought. It is the legacy of a process of intellectual compartmentalization corresponding to academic teaching and research divisions" (2).

3. For more information on the increasing popularity of food studies both in and out of academe, see Carlin; Little; Pogrebin; and Ruark.

4. Anthropologist Sidney W. Mintz shares the belief that food has a complex place in human societies: "Eating is never a 'purely biological' activity. . . . The foods eaten have histories associated with the pasts of those who eat them; the techniques employed to find, process, prepare, serve, and consume the foods are all culturally variable, with histories of their own. Nor is the food ever simply eaten; its consumption is always conditioned by meaning" (7).

5. See Tannahill.

6. In *Food, the Body, and the Self* (1996), Deborah Lupton points out, "Food and eating habits are banal practices of everyday life. . . . This apparent banality, however, is deceptive. Food and eating habits and preferences are not simply matters of 'fueling' ourselves. . . . Food and eating are central to our subjectivity, or sense of self" (1). Similarly, Anne R. Kaplan, Marjorie A. Hoover, and Willard B. Moore observe in *The Taste of American Place: A Reader on Regional and Ethnic Foods* (1998), "The things we eat can say a great deal about us — who we are, where we came from, our current social, cultural, economic, and religious circumstances, and what our aspirations might be" (121).

7. Dusselier and Parkin are not the first scholars to focus on a single food. Many others have, too, including Roland Barthes in *Mythologies* (1957), in which he mused on the importance of steak and chips, among other foods.

Works Cited

Avakian, Arlene Voski, ed. *Through the Kitchen Window: Women Explore the Intimate Meanings of Food and Cooking*. Boston: Beacon Press, 1997.

Barthes, Roland. *Mythologies*. 1957. New York: Hill and Wang, 1972.

Belasco, Warren J. *Appetite for Change: How the Counterculture Took on the Food Industry, 1966–1988*. New York: Pantheon Books, 1989.

Bell, David, and Gill Valentine. *Consuming Geographies: We Are Where We Eat*. New York: Routledge, 1997.

Berk, Sarah Fenstermaker. *The Gender Factory: The Apportionment of Work in American Households*. New York: Plenum, 1985.

Bourdieu, Pierre. *Distinction: A Social Critique of the Judgement of Taste*. Trans. Richard Nice. 1979. Cambridge: Harvard University Press, 1984.

Bower, Anne L., ed. *Recipes for Reading: Community Cookbooks, Stories, Histories*. Amherst: University of Massachusetts Press, 1997.

Carlin, Joseph M. "Reading about Food and Culinary History." *Topics in Clinical Nutrition* 13.3 (1998): 11–19.

Charles, Nickie, and Marion Kerr. *Women, Food, and Families*. Manchester: Manchester University Press, 1988.

Cline, Sally. *Just Desserts: Women and Food*. London: Deutsch, 1990.

Counihan, Carole, and Penny Van Esterik, eds. *Food and Culture: A Reader*. New York: Routledge, 1997.

Coward, Rosalind. *Female Desires: How They Are Sought, Bought, and Packaged*. New York: Grove, 1985.

DeVault, Marjorie L. *Feeding the Family: The Social Organization of Caring as Gendered Work*. Chicago: University of Chicago Press, 1991.

Douglas, Mary. "Standard Social Uses of Food: Introduction." *Food in the Social Order: Studies of Food and Festivities in Three American Communities*. Ed. Mary Douglas. New York: Russell Sage Foundation, 1984. 1–39.

Farb, Peter, and George Armelagos. *Consuming Passions: The Anthropology of Eating*. Boston: Houghton Mifflin, 1980.

Fiddes, Nick. *Meat: A Natural Symbol*. London: Routledge, 1991.

Gabaccia, Donna R. *We Are What We Eat: Ethnic Food and the Making of Americans*. Cambridge: Harvard University Press, 1998.

Kaplan, Anne R., Marjorie A. Hoover, and Willard B. Moore. "Introduction: On Ethnic Foodways." *The Taste of American Place: A Reader on Regional and Ethnic Foods*. Lanham: Rowman and Littlefield, 1998. 121–33.

Lévi-Strauss, Claude. *The Raw and the Cooked*. Trans. John and Doreen Weightman. 1964. New York: Harper and Row, 1969.

Little, Angela. "An Academic Ferment." *Journal of Gastronomy* 2 (1986): 24–29.

Lupton, Deborah. *Food, the Body, and the Self*. London: Sage, 1996.

Mintz, Sidney W. *Tasting Food, and Tasting Freedom: Excursions into Eating, Culture, and the Past*. Boston: Beacon Press, 1996.

Pogrebin, Robin. "More to Food Than Meets the Tongue." *New York Times* 31 Oct. 1998: A19+.

Ruark, Jennifer K. "A Place at the Table." *Chronicle of Higher Education* 9 July 1999: A17–A19.

Schafer, Robert B., and Elisabeth Schafer. "Relationship Between Gender and Food Roles in the Family." *Journal of Nutrition Education* 21.3 (1989): 119–26.

Shapiro, Laura. *Perfection Salad: Women and Cooking at the Turn of the Century.* New York: Farrar, Straus and Giroux, 1986.

Strasser, Susan. *Never Done: A History of American Housework.* New York: Pantheon Books, 1982.

Tannahill, Reay. *Food in History.* 1973. New York: Crown, 1988.

Bonbons, Lemon Drops, and Oh Henry! Bars

Candy, Consumer Culture, and the Construction of Gender, 1895–1920

JANE DUSSELIER

Life without candy is unfathomable for Americans living today. Per capita rates in the United States continue to rise with recent figures indicating that the average American consumed twenty-two pounds of candy in 1993 as compared to seventeen pounds in 1982.[1] Highlighting this hunger for candy, a front-page *New York Times* article on May 4, 1998, warned chocoholics that their "beloved bean" was in jeopardy due to crop failure and that a resulting shortage could develop into a "disaster of gigantic proportions."[2] A week later, another reporter offered a futuristic, tongue-in-cheek interpretation of this impending chocolate candy shortage. Writing as if he were living in the year 2098, the author reflected back on the "Great Chocolate Panic" of the previous century. In this account, refrigerator sales soared as candy lovers searched for space to store their cherished chocolate Easter bunnies, and with the resolution of this crisis in 2075, Israelis and Palestinians learned to live together peacefully.[3] Offering even more convincing evidence of candy's importance in the American diet, a Food and Drug Administration spokeswoman announced in 1994 that "candy is food" and followed up this declaration by stating: "We don't recommend shunning any food."[4] Such an endorsement of candy by a government agency and the intense desire that Americans express for this commodity raises several questions for scholars. Has candy always occupied a central place in the consciousness of Americans? What forces brought candy into the mainstream? How was the desire for candy created and shaped?

At the center of this present-day desire for candy are tensions surrounding shifting meanings of femininity and masculinity. Our everyday experiences confirm that most people enjoy candy, yet magazines and newspapers are filled with headlines that underscore a feminine fondness for Hershey's kisses, licorice, and truffles. Some articles encourage women to ignore feelings of guilt while eating chocolates and portray these cravings as biologically predetermined. Everything from low levels of endorphins and estrogen after ovulation to "premenstrual mood changes such as irritability, impulsive behavior, and anger" have been cited as reasons why women crave candy.[5] Other periodicals warn women that candy eating can become addictive, and they offer inspirational tips on how to "break the habit."[6] One woman was even reported to have a "dark obsession" with licorice as she "rummaged" through a Safeway store one afternoon in search of her favorite sweet.[7] Implicit in these discussions is the notion that candy eating represents weakness and reveals a cultural need to portray American women as incapable of controlling their own desires and impulses.[8]

Informed by current debates among cultural and gender historians, and the field of material culture, this essay argues that candy was a culturally constructed commodity. Of central importance will be how candy consumption became gendered between 1895 and 1920. For the purposes of this chapter, candy will be treated as a historical artifact embedded with the beliefs, ideas, and fears of those individuals who fabricated and consumed candy.[9] Although it would be shortsighted to argue that any artifact provides a complete cultural picture, candy does provide a window into the past. By utilizing candy as a historical document, my hope is to shed light on how Americans, living at the turn of the century, related to a material world filled with an ever-increasing quantity of factory-produced goods. This chapter illustrates how an ideology of gender became materialized in everyday life.

While candy has experienced an unwavering loyalty from Americans for over one hundred years, it has remained outside the realm of scholarly inquiry.

Culinary "experts" and historians who have studied the eating habits of Americans often ignored candy and at best mentioned candy eating as a childhood activity. Until recently, historians have taken a positivist approach, describing how a linear march toward greater abundance and quality of food sources has influenced the course of history and affected the health of all citizens.[10] Food critics have constructed narratives full of anecdotal information, producing accounts of how, when, and what foods were eaten. *Eating in America: A History*, the most exhaustive work of this genre, begins with a romanticized account of American Indians saving white settlers from sure starvation and ends by condemning the effects of modernity on eating customs in the United States.[11] Surprisingly, the authors never mentioned candy, even though they devoted an entire chapter to "the great American sweet tooth." Instead, America's thirst for Coca Cola and appetite for cakes, cookies, and pies takes center stage.

Although many Americans perceive their appetite for candy as natural and immutable, it was not until the Gilded Age, with the rise of a culture based on consumption, that candy emerged as a distinct product. Candy eating was initially viewed as a feminine activity best suited to women of better means. Images of white middle-class women as indulgent, seductive bonbon consumers aided in resolving tensions surrounding the clash between conventional Victorian ideals and hedonistic values associated with the Gilded Age. Once women had been converted into faithful and dedicated bonbon eaters, candy would be recast as a commodity that men desired. Candy as a substitute for alcohol and the portrayal of soldiers sustaining themselves on chocolate creams and lemon drops during battle would transform candy into an appropriate treat for men. Not surprisingly, during the second decade of the twentieth century, the popular press and advertisements directed at men began characterizing candy as a valuable fuel rather than a feminine indulgence. Soldiers, sailors, and businessmen would discover hidden power and stamina in Life Savers, lemon drops, and chocolate. As candy eating became legitimized for men, candy would acquire a new shape. Manly candy bars began to be marketed alongside round, voluptuous bonbons. Who was eating candy transformed not only the meaning attached to this commodity but also its physical properties.[12]

Candy's Beginnings in America

During the last half of the nineteenth century, America's primary association with sweetness began a slow, uneven transformation from "sweet dishes" made in the home to candy produced in factories. Before this time, candy was a luxury item and its consumption was limited even among the wealthy. In Victorian cookbooks and domestic economy manuals, the word *candy* rarely appeared.[13] Puddings, cakes, preserves, doughnuts, and popcorn balls made with molasses and maple syrup satisfied early nineteenth-century appetites for sweetness. However, during the late 1800s, domestic encyclopedias began including sections about candy, and books devoted exclusively to candy making emerged extolling the virtues and benefits of this product.[14] In 1875, a Philadelphia publisher acquired the rights to a British candy cookbook, which resembled a technical manual more than a collection of recipes. The author pleaded with readers to use the correct ingredients and to avoid "low class sugars," which could destroy the purity and value of the end product.[15] After having published a book on candy making for professional confectioners, George Frye "received letters of inquiry from ladies all over the country asking why [he] did not prepare a work especially adapted for the use of the housewife."[16] A lengthy book resulted, offering exacting instructions on how to make hundreds of candies from coconut and maple caramels to lemon comfits, chocolate logs, and cream mint drops. Echoing similar sentiments, an author who referred to himself simply as Perfecto promised readers perfect domestic candies if his instructions were carefully followed.[17]

To advertise the magical powers of sarsaparilla, C. I. Hood and Company published an eighteen-page candy recipe booklet in 1888. Each page of *Hood's Book of Homemade Candies* was divided in half with a line running down the middle. On one side the reader found candy recipes. On the opposite side was a list of diseases described in agonizing detail. Explicitly linking lemon taffy, vanilla cream sticks, and peppermint lozenges with the supposed medicinal and scientific properties of their own product, Hood and Company advised readers to purchase candy-making supplies from qualified druggists. Without the knowledge of a scientist, domestic candy makers risked "considerable difficulty and perhaps [even] failure."[18] Just like Hood's sarsaparilla, candy appeared to contain rejuvenating and mystical powers. More important, the sudden appearance of cookbooks such as Hood's served notice that candy was gaining acceptance in America. Providing evidence that only hindsight could produce, the *New York Times* reported in 1903: "Within twenty-five years the candy industry has increased from almost nothing to about $150,000,000 a year. A quarter of a century ago there was not an exclusive candy manufacturer in a large way of business."[19]

As candy became popularized, candy eating was an activity associated with girls and women. As early as 1874, young women from wealthy families were reported to be the "class of persons that, more than any other, purchase or have purchased for them, the most elaborate style of French candies."[20] New Yorker John Lewis, writing to family members in England, described the consumption of candy by women as "enormous" and stated that Americans thought of this behavior as a "great national failing."[21] A popular 1892 play, *Candy*, was billed as the "great American spectacular musical comedy." It depicted the birthday party of Kitty, a millionaire's daughter, "who is rather too fond of candy."[22] Her father informs a messenger delivering gifts of sugar sticks and chocolate drops that he would give "half his fortune to the man who would marry Kitty and induce her not to eat any more candy."[23] As the play progresses, Kitty is "cured of her candy craze" by a marriage proposal and reports to the audience that her fiancé's "kisses are sweeter than candy."[24]

An 1899 *New York Times* article reinforced this popular image: "Three-fourths of the candy made is consumed by women, and half the other fourth by children, leaving men a pitiable fraction of the total amount."[25] In that same year the Journeymen Bakers' and Confectioners' International Union of America issued a label to be found on boxes and wrappers of candy produced in union shops. Although the majority of candy workers under their jurisdiction were women, the union also chose to frame women as consumers of candy. In their announcement, the union leadership warned that they had "many friends among the fairer sex who would resent it as an insult" if a box of candy were offered to them without the union label. If men would buy only candy that carried this label, they could "open the road to [the] hearts of millions of proud beauties."[26] In Theodore Dreiser's novel *Sister Carrie*, well-to-do women in New York City were reported to be "spending money like water" on their candy habits.[27] According to the *Bakers' Journal*, even "Hindoo girls" exhibited an intense appetite for candy. "Like the American girls, Hindoo girls are passionately fond of sweet things. . . . [These] women pass most of their time eating candy and gossiping."[28] Candy eating was clearly depicted as a feminized activity in the popular press, and advertisers would soon begin national marketing campaigns that intensified the gendered quality of candy consumption.

Advertisements: Victorian Restraint and Gilded Age Indulgence

Before 1895, candy advertisements were rare and lacked expressive iconography. Arranged in small rectangular boxes, these advertisements consisted of unassuming typescript and were often hidden at the bottom of a page. Purity was the central message of candy companies advertising in mainstream publications. Philadelphia Crown Caramels and Plow's Candy of Chicago emphasized the "pure, fresh, delicious" qualities of their products with Acker's Candies claiming to be the "purest in the world!"[29] In African American newspapers, commercial representations of candy were often included with other services or products. Mrs. Sadie Reed's Restaurant and Confectionery advertisements proclaimed, "When you want a square meal or anything in the line of Confectioneries give me a call."[30] Miss Rosa Johnson of Cincinnati combined her skills, owning a business that advertised in bold letters, "Confectionaries, candies, bread and laundry office. Give her a trial."[31] Readers browsing through newspapers and magazines during the 1880s and early 1890s could find an occasional candy advertisement, but it would have been difficult for these same Americans to foresee what would happen in the summer of 1895.

Proclaiming a new age for candy, advertisements for chocolate bonbons appeared suddenly in May 1895. Lowney's placed ads for five consecutive months in the *Ladies' Home Journal* and presented provocative images of women as bonbon consumers. The iconography employed by Lowney's would endure and be widely used in other publications throughout the Progressive Era.[32] Just as with early candy ads, purity was a central component in Lowney's message. However, gender was employed in an explicit manner with candy companies using coquettish and flirtatious images of white middle-class women to convince Americans to indulge in this new commodity (fig. 1.1). Appearing with an opened box of candy, a conservatively dressed woman offered the public a "pure and wholesome" product.[33] Another ad presented a "Gibson Girl" properly attired with a flowing ribbon tied in a bow and hanging from her waist, resembling the wrapped box of candy she was holding.[34] Although to the modern reader these images do not appear provocative, for nineteenth-century women any acknowledgment or display of appetite was a sign of unbridled sexuality.[35] Portrayals of white middle-class women publicly satisfying their passion for candy signaled that a new social order was on the horizon.

Candy company advertisements significantly decreased during 1896, perhaps reflecting the effects of an economic depression that had engulfed most of the nation for three years. However, in ads placed by Lowney's and Huyler's during the last years of the century, the gendering of candy intensified. Candy consumption had been portrayed as a feminine behavior for over twenty years, and advertisers wasted little time reinforcing this link between

Fig. 1.1. Advertisements for Lowney's chocolate bonbons appeared in the summer of 1895 and pushed images of white middle-class women into the forefront of an emerging consumer culture. *Ladies' Home Journal*, August 1895, 18.

Fig. 1.2. By the winter of 1896, the gendering of candy advertisements intensified with this flirtatious white woman placing a bonbon to her lips. *Ladies' Home Journal,* February 1896, 30.

women and candy. For the first time Huyler's included a human image in advertisements and predictably the illustration depicted a white woman.[36] Lowney's presented a bare-shouldered woman peering seductively over her shoulder. With a box of candy in one hand and with a bonbon to her lips, this woman presented candy as a sensual, indulgent commodity. The caption read, "Delicious quality, dainty flavors, perfect purity" (fig. 1.2).[37] In a similar advertisement, we see the same woman facing us, holding an opened box of chocolates in one hand and presenting a bonbon with the other hand as if offering consumers the forbidden fruit (fig. 1.3).[38]

With these advertisements Lowney's and Huyler's challenged Victorian eating rituals, which dictated that human appetites be satisfied in private. In a nation undergoing profound change, rigidly defined and tightly scripted din-

LOWNEY'S
CHOCOLATE BONBONS
"Name on Every Piece"
Send 10 cents for Sample Package

P. S.—If you wish a pound or more and your dealer will not supply you, we will send, on receipt of retail price, 1-lb. box, 60c.; 2-lb. box, $1.20; 3-lb. box, $1.80; 5-lb. box, $3.00. Delivered free in United States.

THE WALTER M. LOWNEY CO., 89 Pearl Street, BOSTON

Fig. 1.3. In the spring of 1896, the same model is shown presenting a single piece of candy as if offering consumers the forbidden fruit. *Ladies' Home Journal*, April 1896, 24.

ing behavior provided a sense of tranquility among an increasingly anxious middle class.[39] A woman eating in public was a tantalizing image during the 1890s, with one etiquette manual warning that such activity indicated a lack of refinement and propriety.[40] Reflecting a new dialogue surrounding sexual mores, these candy advertisements broke with Victorian images of women as passionless and sexually restrained. Candy ads that pushed the image of white middle-class women into the forefront of an emerging consumer culture accompanied monumental social, demographic, and economic changes. Decreasing fertility rates, shifting occupational patterns, and new forms of heterosocial leisure helped construct new notions of sexuality for all Americans.[41] Food consumption was becoming explicitly linked with sexuality at the turn of the century, and candy eating by white middle-class women signified that indulgence was becoming increasingly proper.[42] Candy advertisements utilized the sexuality of women to communicate new emerging values rooted in the transformation from a production economy to one based on increased consumption.

Contrasted with the hedonistic quality of these ads was a wholesome, chaste style of advertisement that presented Lowney's chocolate bonbons perfectly arranged in a silver candy dish. Silver tongs were delicately positioned on top of the candy, suggesting that these confections be consumed in a restrained and orderly manner. Printed below this sophisticated image were the words "dainty — delicious — pure."[43] In this advertisement, potential consumers could be reassured that eating bonbons would not violate any nineteenth-century etiquette rituals. Indulging one's cravings was appropriate if this activity could be carried out in a disciplined, orderly atmosphere. Outlined in an eloquent frame, Lowney's chocolate bonbons appeared pretty as a picture, safe for consumption by even the most genteel members of society. Although candy ads were harbingers of new sexual attitudes, this Lowney's ad was clear evidence that Victorian values had not totally vanished.

Progressive Reform and Clean Candy

As America moved into the Progressive Era, old anxieties meshed with new expectations and commercial representations of candy reflected these tensions. Reacting to twenty-five years of unregulated, unchecked industrial capitalism, many middle-class Americans began to question the morality of laissez-faire economics. Intent on social, political, and economic change, progressive reformers campaigned for legislative and governmental intervention in solving the nation's problems. The Pure Food and Drug Act of 1906 was one of the legislative remedies that resulted from this reform movement, regulating the ingredients and process by which food, including candy, was produced. Candy companies were quick to respond to allegations of producing adulterated candies and became even more consumed with presenting their products as absolutely pure and wholesome. As the Confectioners' Association reported in 1910, candy companies made "purity their motto."[44]

The extent to which candy advertisements barraged consumers with messages of purity bordered on complete obsession. Taylor-Made Honey Comb Chocolate Chips proclaimed "Pure Candy for Every Woman" and declared their establishment "the model candy factory of the world, clean in every sense, flooded with pure air and sunshine."[45] Park and Tillford invited "ladies . . . to sample and test the purity and excellence of our candies, at any of our stores."[46] Heavenly images were employed in Whitman's ads with angels seated in a box of chocolates that appeared suspended in midair. Beneath this iconography was the slogan "Where Purity Reigns."[47] "Wholesome as bread and butter" was how Peter's described their chocolates, and Clark and Harris claimed that their butter cups could be recognized by a "clear, bright and glossy appearance which is a guarantee of purity."[48] Above the slogan "Pure Stick Licorice," the National Licorice Company presented three mammoth pieces of jet black licorice.[49] Compared with licorice manufacturers, U-All-No After Dinner Mints likely had an easier time convincing consumers of the morality of their product when they described their candy as "pure, wholesome . . . tiny snow-white sugary loaves."[50] Needless to say, candy advertisements during the Progressive Era were saturated with the words *clean*, *fresh*, and *pure* and images of virtuous candies abounded.

Manufacturers felt compelled to educate the public on the degraded production process of competitors while simultaneously highlighting the pristine conditions of their own factories. Necco (New England Confectionery Company) and the Loft Candy Company claimed to enforce stricter pure-food regulations than the United States government required and pledged to produce only "pure sugar candy."[51] Explaining to readers that most chocolates were dipped with the fingers, Bell's Forkdipt Chocolates promised candy untouched by human hands.[52] Stacy's Forkdipd Chocolates guaranteed "clean" candy made from the "purest materials" and urged candy consumers to "think of the impossibility of having the dipper's hands always clean, free from perspiration or abrasion."[53] A picture of a hand drenched in gooey, messy chocolate with the accompanying typescript reading "Not the Stacy Way" further advanced the idea of contaminated candy (fig. 1.4). A Silver

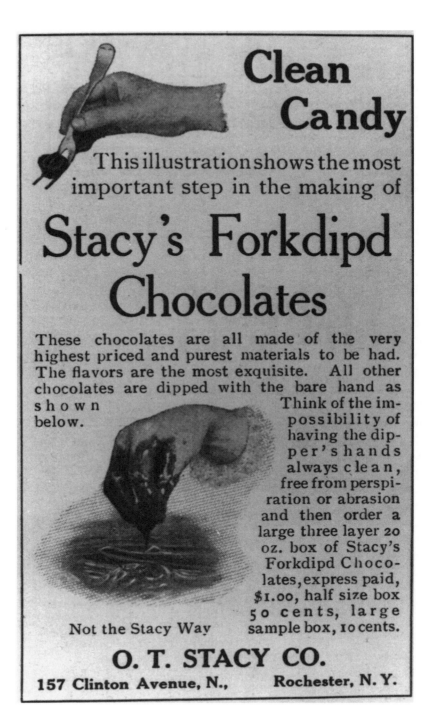

Clean Candy

This illustration shows the most important step in the making of

Stacy's Forkdipd Chocolates

These chocolates are all made of the very highest priced and purest materials to be had. The flavors are the most exquisite. All other chocolates are dipped with the bare hand as shown below. Think of the impossibility of having the dipper's hands always clean, free from perspiration or abrasion and then order a large three layer 20 oz. box of Stacy's Forkdipd Chocolates, express paid, $1.00, half size box 50 cents, large sample box, 10 cents.

Not the Stacy Way

O. T. STACY CO.

157 Clinton Avenue, N.,   Rochester, N. Y.

Fig. 1.4. During the Progressive Era, candy advertisements barraged consumers with images of purity. *Ladies' Home Journal*, April 1906, 57.

Springs, New York, pharmacy made certain everyone understood their candies were pure when they informed consumers they sold only "clean, fresh candy" manufactured in a "new, clean factory" and stored in "nice clean candy pails with covers."[54] Even Mrs. Stovall, who produced mail-order candies in her own kitchen, declared that the first requisite in candy making was to "make it pure."[55] Americans longing for purity and moral uplift in the social body could find solace in consuming candy that was marketed as unadulterated and chaste. Not only had immigrants created an ethnically diverse population, but women were also assuming new social and economic responsibilities, which threatened their traditional role as moral guardians.

Throughout the first decade of the twentieth century, candy advertisements increased in quantity and frequency and remained heavily gendered. White women endured as the ideal ambassadors for a product that claimed to be "perfectly pure" yet appropriately sensual. Huyler's continued placing advertisements in magazines and newspapers using the same images, and Lowney's introduced the Lowney Twins.[56] Pictured on the left side of advertisements was a woman offering the public a bonbon, and on the right her twin delicately sipped a cup of cocoa.[57] Walter Baker also began to distinguish between cocoa and chocolate candy and offered to send consumers an eighty-page recipe book that contained instructions on how to make "Wellesley College, Vassar College and Smith College Fudge." Pictured above this written offer were a little girl and woman peacefully sipping cocoa.[58]

Other companies followed Lowney's and Huyler's gendered advertising strategy. Wilbur's Chocolate Buds portrayed a lace-lined candy box and encouraged the reader to "get it to the dearest woman in the world."[59] Whitman's featured a woman standing in front of a glass-encased candy counter purchasing a "fussy package" of selected chocolates, honey white nougats, and Maraschino cherries from a druggist.[60] Johnston's promised that its Swiss style chocolate creams were the "favorite candy of your favorite girl" and "daintily packed . . . in gold boxes, tied with crimson satin ribbons." Another marketing campaign for Johnston's offered to send consumers a free sample box of chocolate creams and a "dainty" postcard titled "The Girl and the Candy." Ads described the women on these cards as "rarely beautiful with ideal heads."[61] Presenting images of women cheerfully opening boxes of candies, Taylor-Made Honey Comb Chocolate Chips also guaranteed to send "any lady . . . a fancy box of our famous confection" free of charge.[62] So irresistible was candy to women that poisoned chocolates seemed to be an effective method of murder. Mrs. John Andrews, after consuming tainted chocolates which had been sent to her through the mail, asserted that "certain persons who . . . desire to put [me] out of the way" were responsible for her near death.[63]

Advertisers did express uneasiness about employing the sexuality of women to sell products, but candy escaped this censure. During the summer of 1909, the use of "women as means of securing advertising attention" led to a lively debate among readers of *Printers' Ink*. Conceding the "universal interest in a pretty woman," the author of one article also observed "that the use of the woman in advertising is popular because timid and incompetent advertisers figure it out that the one safe bet for copy is a pretty woman."[64] Readers continued to write to the editors with one advocating the use of women because "sex appeal . . . is a true appeal" while acknowledging: "There have been many advertisements in bad form because they displayed too much of what might be called very good form." B. D. Walthouser condemned the "positively disrespectful flaunting of womankind on advertising pages."[65] With the final word on the subject, Joseph J. Bukey authoritatively established the proper place of women in candy ads and drew the debate on the pages of the *Printers' Ink* to a screeching halt:

There is such a thing as too much of a good thing and too much of the other kind. If we will trust to our infinite judgement, universal knowledge and good taste, we will use feminine loveliness only where it is usable; for instance, in advertising candy it would be somewhat rumbumptious to picture a stag party or the like. Woman is in her realm here and her smiling countenance will at once give the impression of a sweet, delicate, pure, dainty, luscious and winning bonbon.[66]

Candy had become so strongly gendered that the association between women and candy appeared "natural" to Bukey. Women were expected to be sweet, delicate, pure, and perhaps even luscious, just like a winning bonbon.

By 1908, candy eating had acquired the full-fledged status of a leisure time activity for some American women. In August, the *Ladies' Home Journal* displayed a print titled "A Fudge Party." Five white women were gathered around an elegantly adorned table where a double boiler filled with fudge was the center of attention. As one woman stirred the candy, another was pictured playing a guitar. Beneath this scene appeared the caption: "This is the last of a series of studies of the American College Girl at Her Sports and Pastimes, in Her Leisure, and at Her Work" (fig. 1.5). Two months later, this same print occupied the front cover of the *Ladies' Home Journal*. A Karo corn syrup ad also featured women cooking fudge with the typescript reading: "One thing the wise college girl knows. Karo makes dandy fudge."[67] Magazine articles offered fudge and other candy recipes submitted by college women who,

Harrison Fisher's College Girls

A Fudge Party
By Harrison Fisher

This is the last of a series of studies of the American College Girl at Her Sports and Pastimes, in Her Leisure, and at Her Work, which Mr. Harrison Fisher has drawn for THE JOURNAL.

Fig. 1.5. "A Fudge Party." *Ladies' Home Journal*, August 1908, 7.

weary from their studies, "gently [turned] to the chafing dish for rest, relief and recreation."[68] The *Woman's Home Companion* published a "rhymed receipt" for divinity that began:

> Throughout the land in ev'ry school and College
> Where girls do gather, there you'll find this knowledge,
> Lectures and lessons may all forgotten be,
> But never how to make "Divinity."[69]

Such portrayals offered powerful evidence of an ongoing cultural struggle surrounding "New Women."

In the late nineteenth and early twentieth centuries, college-educated women, many single and self-supporting, constituted a new social force. These "new women" embodied a complex tension between middle-class values of self-fulfillment and improvement through education and new roles for women. As women began to marry at later ages, their entrance into institutions of higher learning was understood by many turn-of-the-century Americans as an appropriate transition from adolescence to womanhood. However, the accompanying social and political changes created new anxieties and were not always valued. Contesting accepted notions of femininity, many college-educated women remained unmarried after graduating and lived on their own.[70] During a period when the number of females entering institutions of higher education rose dramatically, the thought of college women peacefully occupying their free time with single-sex fudge-making parties must have offered their mothers and fathers, as well as the entire nation, some sense of comfort.[71]

While women were the commanding and principal messengers of candy during the first decade of the twentieth century, ads that included images of men and children were slowly creeping into the iconography. Even these extremely rare appearances signaled that women's exclusive role as candy consumer was beginning to be contested. While Huyler's ads urged men to buy candy for women with such slogans as "A Man Is Known by the Candy He Sends — Of Course It's Huyler's She Wants," they also began advertising their own brand of Washington taffy. With a picture of George Washington on the front of their package, Huyler's offered taffy in the square shape of quarter-pound "cakes."[72] Revere ads featured a man on a galloping horse with hat in hand and arm raised proclaiming, "An unsurpassed delight."[73] Gunther's, foreshadowing an intense association between romantic love and candy, presented an impish man and woman kissing with the typescript "How

Good" below the image.[74] Peter's displayed a man on the peak of a mountain range with a bar of chocolate positioned under the caption, "High as the Alps in Quality" (fig. 1.6). Another ad from this same manufacturer featured a woman framed by a heavily laced heart, clutching a box of chocolates.[75] Rather than supplanting women, manufacturers were beginning to advertise candy as a commodity to be enjoyed by both sexes.

Men, Temperance, and War

Between 1910 and 1920, candy consumption by men became fully legitimatized. In a culture where consumption increasingly represented a fundamental principle, candy eating was transformed into an activity that expressed both femininity and masculinity. As historian William Leach has argued, "desire was democratized" and the right to possess goods and acquire a new sense of self became a measure of individual freedom.[76] Economic growth depended on men also expressing desire for commodities that had previously been considered frivolous and overly indulgent. All Americans were encouraged "to look with a little less suspicion upon [their] feelings and desires. . . . The universality of the taste for sweets cannot but be regarded as an indication of their probable dietetic value except to the mind which still looks with suspicion upon all pleasurable sensations."[77] The recasting of candy eating as a suitable male activity reflected the growing importance of men's role as consumers in a rapidly expanding market economy. However, the regendering of candy would not be accomplished without a great deal of apprehension, and this ambivalence was clearly expressed on the pages of the popular press.

The *New York Times* ushered in the second decade of the century with a revealing feature story on candy. Self-consciously describing America's love of candy, the author calculated that the amount of money Americans expended in one year on this commodity "would pay for all the subways and river tubes in New York. It would come close to building two Panama Canals. It would have constructed all the very tall skyscrapers of Manhattan Island." Expressing anxiety over this rate of consumption, the author was hesitant "to name the figure, it seems so absurdly large." With candy purchases devouring such mammoth sums of capital, one factor was impossible to ignore: "Everybody buys candy. It is the first treat in a child's life. . . . It is only when a man has passed the days of his strength that he loses his taste for it. As to women, none has yet lived long enough to demonstrate the final and absolute cessation of the taste for sweets."[78] While consternation over male candy eaters was evi-

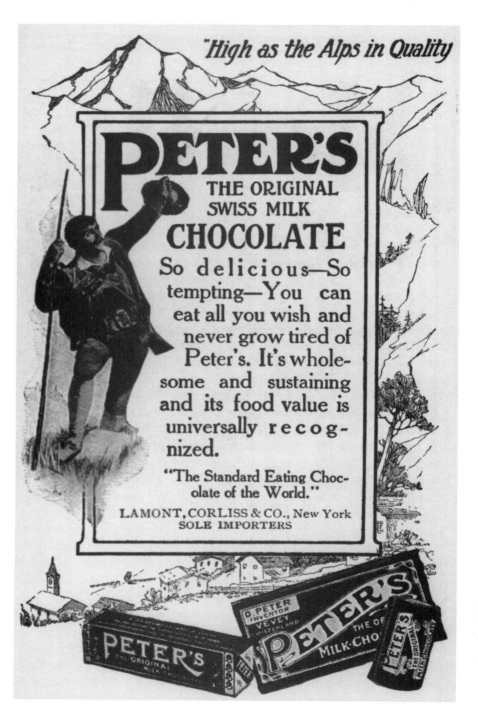

Fig. 1.6. During the first decade of the twentieth century, candy ads began including images of men. Peter's advertisements always included a bar of chocolate and a man pointing to the mountain peaks. *Harper's Magazine Advertiser*, August 1906.

dent, a new dialogue was being constructed. Skyscrapers, river tubes, and the Panama Canal (all examples of man controlling nature) represented virility in its purest form. Candy consumption was clearly being compared to images that men could relate to and talk about without risking their masculinity.

Another article noted that candy stores were often located in areas frequented by men and that men had been secretly eating candy for decades.[79] Although Mrs. Snyder, the owner of four candy shops, still held to the idea that women ate most of the candy, she insisted on opening two of her retail outlets "in streets with men's shops and the other two in a street convenient to a number of men's clubs."[80] Just one year later, Snyder acknowledged that "men are the great candy buyers. They buy it not only for their wives . . . , but also for themselves." Predictably, candy remained gendered in her view. "Men do not care so much for the rich, creamy candies which women prefer. They like something with more body to it, something they can really chew on."[81] Public candy eating among men was becoming more common, and it was no longer unheard of for a businessman to offer "a piece of candy . . . rather than a cigar" or to revive "his [own] flagging energies with a cake of chocolate."[82] As candy consumption continued to increase, it was no longer easy to attribute the success of this industry solely to the appetites of spoiled, white, rich women. For men, candy consumption was depicted as a practical activity that enhanced strength and improved endurance with little attention given to the pleasurable aspects.

Adding to this male discourse was the suggestion that candy acted as a substitute for alcohol, with many arguing that increased rates of candy consumption were directly tied to the temperance movement. As early as 1907, public health officials supported these claims when they patiently explained to the public that candy and alcohol possessed similar chemical structures. According to Dr. A. C. Abbott, health commissioner of Pennsylvania, "The appetite for alcohol and the appetite for candy are fundamentally the same." An individual's sex determined who would have a penchant for bonbons and who would display a craving for whiskey. An editorial in the *Independent* argued: "Women as a rule take to candy and men to alcohol."[83] Male resistance to candy as a substitute for drinking was expressed when the *Atlantic Monthly* reported that candy as a healthy alternative to drinking was still under debate and that Americans might be rushing to replace the "demon rum" with the "demon candy." "Some, indeed, go so far as to deduce the existence of a Demon Candy, and predict that eventually it will be necessary to make the mystic letters W.C.T.U. stand for the Women's Confectionery Temperance Union."[84] Portraying men who ate candy as "slaves" to a feminine indulgence remained a popular notion in 1910. As women continued to express political power through the call for temperance, the thought of men replacing a shot of whiskey with a dainty bonbon was more than some Americans could bear.

While many men were not totally convinced that lemon drops adequately replaced rum, candy was increasingly viewed as a requirement for individuals no longer imbibing. A reporter for the *New York Times* characterized candy as "a substitute which removes the insistent desire for whiskey."[85] A manufacturer, concerned with whether the domestic consumption of candy was a patriotic act during wartime, traveled to Washington, D.C., and consulted with the assistant secretary of agriculture. Upon her return to New York, Mary Elizabeth reported: "Human beings need sweets — must have them; while those who are omitting wines and liquors from their daily menus will find additional sweets almost a necessity."[86] Even during World War I and the resulting sugar shortages, loyal and patriotic citizens were urged to replace alcohol with candy made from honey, molasses, maple sugar, fruits, nuts, raisins, and chocolate. Only when Americans consumed beet and cane sugar were their political and national loyalties questioned. Astonishingly, the association between candy and alcohol had become so entrenched by 1920 that candy manufacturers were being implored to "make special efforts to present their wares in attractive and easily available forms" so that their use would be more widely utilized in preventing alcohol consumption.[87]

Advertisers who portrayed candy eating solely as a feminine activity only a decade earlier began to reconstruct their product. Gone was the long identifying name Johnston's Swiss Style Chocolate Creams and the slogan "Favorite candy of your favorite girl." Proudly emblazoned on candy boxes was simply Johnston's and just below in smaller print the city of origin, Milwaukee. While advertisers still addressed women and featured feminine images, Johnston's added such slogans as "chocolates to suit every taste" or "chocolate for every taste." In another ad, a tray full of chocolates was offered to both men and women seated around a table, and consumers were assured that a boxful of Lenox chocolates furnished "a wide variety of tasty centers — some hard, some soft — and a flavor to please every taste."[88] Necco announced that all five hundred varieties of their product were "good for everybody," and an ad pictured a man, woman, and child leaning eagerly over a box of candy.[89] A full-page ad in the *Western Druggist* instructing retailers on how to increase their candy sales asserted: "Almost every person — man, woman or child — entering your store is a possible candy customer. Fully 95% of them eat candy and will buy, every day, if you give them the right candy."[90] Employees of advertising agencies must have been working overtime in an effort to convince everyone that candy they had been eating for decades was now a sanctioned commodity.

Mint manufacturers marketed their product as after-dinner treats that families could consume together. Ads for U-All-No After Dinner Mints depicted a family gathered around the dinner table and urged Americans to serve mints after meals. In addition, these mints were "the ideal sweet for kiddies or grown-ups and their tempting goodness is enjoyed by everyone."[91] Malliard's of New York ran a series of ads claiming "the success of the dinner depends" on serving after-dinner mints. One ad pictured a mustached man, decked out in a driving coat and cap, standing next to his sporty convertible with his hand firmly grasping the steering wheel. While the man's body fully faced the reader, a woman was positioned in the passenger seat as she peered back over her shoulder. Above this purely masculine scene of a man, his car, and his woman were the words "Malliard Chocolate After Dinner Mints."[92] While urging consumers to "try Life Savers after dinner," the Mint Products Company also notified readers that their candy mints were "on everybody's tongue." In a special appeal, men were encouraged to eat mints after smoking cigars, with one man exclaiming, "Even the hole tastes good to *me*."[93]

In a full-page spread, Peter's ads detailed the scorn and humiliation Daniel Peter suffered during his early crusade to create a "new kind of chocolate." Not thought of as a manly pursuit at the end of the nineteenth century, Peter's daughters had been "pitied" for having a father who "wasted all his time" in the kitchen mixing creamy milk with chocolate. While Peter's daughters remained loyal to their father, others believed his work as a confectioner to be a "crazy idea." By 1920, however, Daniel Peter emerged as an all-American male, having invented "one of the foods of which the world is universally fond, a new and remarkably nutritious form."[94] Also illustrating that chocolate consumption was not incongruous with masculinity, a Patterson's tuxedo pipe and cigarette tobacco advertisement read, "Mellow-aged till perfect plus a dash of chocolate."[95] Patterson's, whose iconography featured strictly male images, broadened the notion of candy consumption to include the masculine act of smoking tobacco laced with chocolate. Absent from ads directed at men were references to candy as dainty, pure, and elegant. Candy was now conceived of as a food that fueled the world and a practical commodity that enhanced manly activities. Taffy and chocolates were characterized not as commodities that provided men with pleasure or satisfaction but as sources of energy and strength.

While candy was beginning to be marketed as a masculine product, it is important to note that women continued to be heavily targeted by advertisers.

Nut Tootsie Roll ads featured Candy Jim, a male candy producer. Pointing to a smiling woman who was eating a Tootsie Roll, he proclaimed: "I am for Women's Votes and Nut Tootsie Rolls. They are both right."[96] In 1916 and 1917, Johnston's conducted a blitz that no other candy company had yet attempted and rarely missed placing advertisements in the weekly published *Saturday Evening Post*. Every image featured a white woman holding a box of candy in her hands.[97] The American Candy Company even named their "refined" product Milady chocolates, and Nunnally's ad for its "candy of the south" pictured an antebellum scene with a man offering candy to a woman.[98] Women were portrayed as candy experts when Necco presented a blindfolded woman eating their brand of bonbons as she exclaimed; "Oh, you can't fool me they're Lenox chocolates."[99] Examples of the feminization of candy are endless. Men were a new audience for candy advertisers, but women were not to be ignored.

As candy eating became culturally sanctioned for men, a new shape emerged. Patents issued before 1910 consisted of ornamental designs for small, circular chocolate comfits and candy drops with trademarks featuring such names as Love and Queen (fig. 1.7). When William J. Burns of Georgetown, Kentucky, applied for a candy patent in 1872, he insisted that candy should be "pure, simple and beautiful."[100] In 1899, even a patent for licorice sticks included "rounded, bulging [and] curved portions," with the inventor explaining that his design was suitable to all forms of confectionery sticks. An illustration that accompanied this patent depicted a stick made from several rounded pieces of licorice stacked on top of one another.[101] However, by October 1909, companies began claiming rights to such brand names as Acme, Maxima, and Phoenix.[102] Exhibiting robust, virile iconography, Acme's application for trademark rights displayed what appeared to be a mammoth and phallic beehive positioned on top of a sturdy platform. Phoenix presented the stark, bold iconography of a powerful bird rising from the flames of a fire. In a September issue of *Printers' Ink*, Samoset Chocolates' trademark was exhibited, and it featured a bare-chested Native American skillfully maneuvering a canoe through river rapids with the epigram reading "Chief of Them All."[103]

Patent applications filed during the second decade of the twentieth century signaled that the era of the dainty breast-shaped bonbon was giving way to the decade of manly candy bars. On October 28, 1911, Robert Boeckel was granted a design patent for a "Bar of Candy."[104] William B. Laskey submitted to the U.S. Patent Office three pages of written text and exacting illustrations describing his invention of a "new and useful improvement in candy and the process of making the same." Laskey commented that he "preferred polygo-

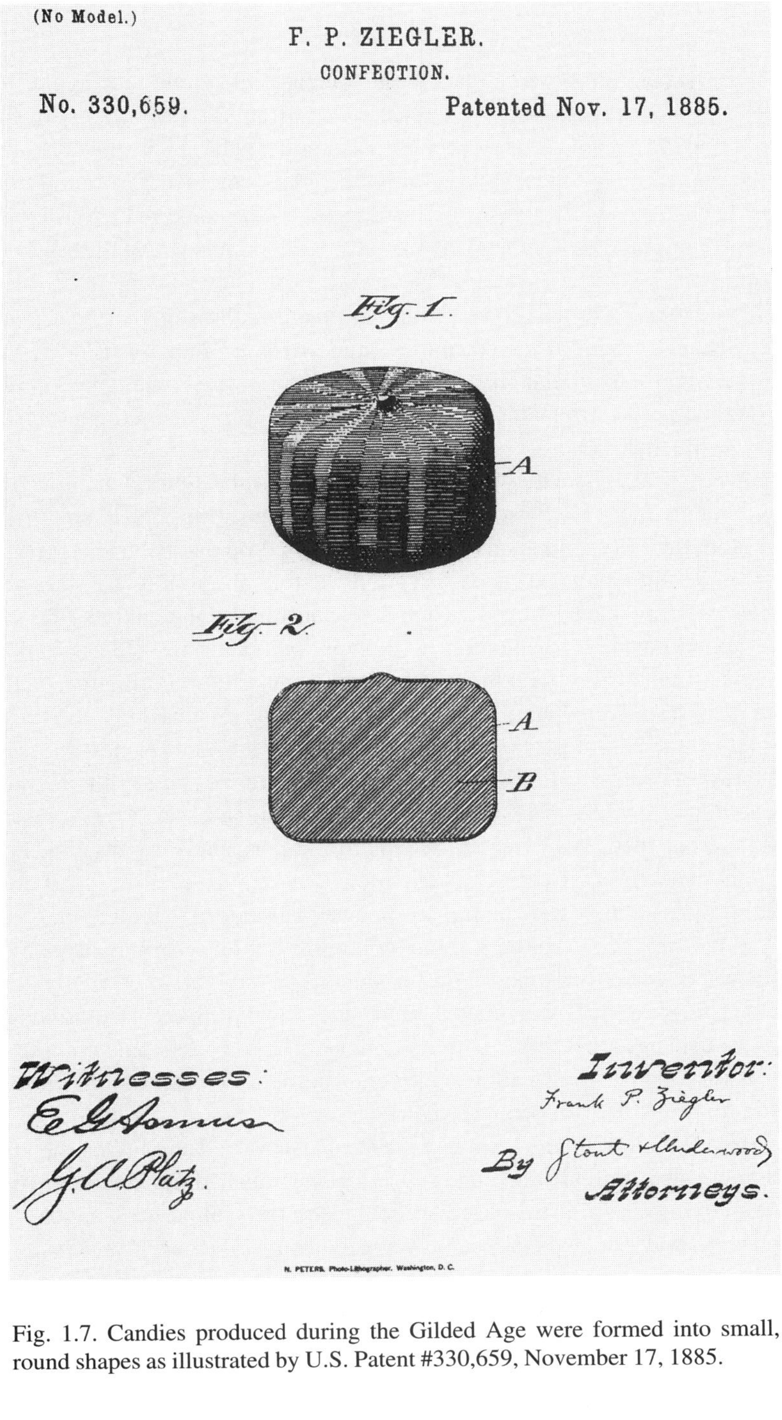
(No Model.)
F. P. ZIEGLER.
CONFECTION.
No. 330,659.
Patented Nov. 17, 1885.
Fig. 1.
A
Fig. 2.
A
B
Witnesses:
Inventor:
Frank P. Ziegler
By Stout & Underwood
Attorneys.
N. PETERS, Photo-Lithographer, Washington, D. C.

Fig. 1.7. Candies produced during the Gilded Age were formed into small, round shapes as illustrated by U.S. Patent #330,659, November 17, 1885.

nal" candies and proposed a machine that created elaborate rectangular bars so that the "candy may then be stretched out or pulled down to any desired size."[105] A 1915 patent request proposed a change in the shape of a chocolate-coated malted milk candy. Having previously been molded in a round tablet form, Livingston A. Thompson secured rights to the same malted milk confection configured in "cubical blocks."[106] Perhaps most revealing was the patent application of a Brooklyn, New York, resident that depicted a raised, rounded candy form positioned within a square tablet (fig. 1.8).[107] Candies were being squeezed, pressed, pulled, and stretched into forms with right angles rather than circular shapes. While inventors were creating new molds, it would take a full frontal assault by the U.S. War Department to place candy firmly in the male sphere.

American soldiers may not have made the world safe for democracy, but they certainly made candy consumption safe for men. Although the public did not readily identify soldiers as bonbon or lemon drop eaters, this association between fighting men and candy had a long history. Beginning in 1899, while women were being portrayed as the sole consumers of bonbons, the U.S. government began experimenting with including candy in soldiers' rations. *Scientific American* reported that American troops in the Philippines, Cuba, and Puerto Rico were being supplied with chocolate creams and lemon drops "in sealed one pound cans of a special oval shape, designed to fit the pockets of a uniform coat."[108] Hoping to improve the endurance and health of American soldiers, the U.S. War Department commissioned one New York firm alone to ship fifty tons of candy to Spanish-American War battlefields. By 1907 another author wrote: "The early prejudices against candy, . . . that it was an effeminate luxury, [were being] swept away or reduced to their residuum of reason. It is now fed to soldiers before going into battle."[109] Ironically, American soldiers consumed one of the products they fought to secure. As the century progressed, Cuba, Puerto Rico, and the Philippines would supply much of the sugar that fed America's enthusiastic and passionate craving for candy. Real men eating candy on foreign battlefields was too powerful a notion for the American people to ignore.

Bernard Shaw's play *Arms and the Man* also helped strengthen the association between soldiers and candy. Originally published in London in 1894, the play did not gain broad-based acceptance in the United States until 1909 when the satiric comedy appeared on Broadway billed as *The Chocolate Soldier*. Centered around Captain Bluntschli, a Swiss professional soldier who "has found by experience that it is more important to have a few bits of chocolate to eat in the field than cartridges in his revolver," Shaw's play

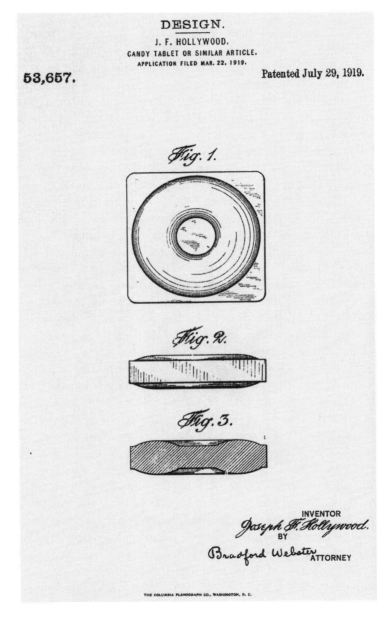

Fig. 1.8. By the 1910s, candies were being formed into manly shapes with right angles. This 1919 patent shows a raised, rounded candy form positioned within a square tablet. U.S. Design Patent #53,657, July 29, 1919.

attacks the notion of military heroism. Never eager to engage in the valor of war, the Captain abhors gallant calvary charges and concerns himself with practical soldiering. As Bluntschli retreats from an attacking enemy, he creeps into a woman's bedroom, pleading his case. Confessing that he would not harm her, the Captain discloses: "I've no ammunition. What use are cartridges in battle? I always carry chocolate instead; and I finished the last cake of that hours ago. . . . I wish I had some now." Immediately the female occupant of Bluntschli's new hideaway "sails away scornfully to the chest of drawers, and returns with the box of confectionery in her hand." Our mercenary responds, "You're an angel! Creams! Delicious!" and upon "ravenously" consuming the contents "he can only scrape the box with his fingers and suck them."[110] Although Shaw received criticism for creating the "chocolate cream soldier" and was accused of maligning a courageous and honorable vocation, American audiences received the play with laughter.[111]

At a time when social and sexual relations were in transition, *The Chocolate Soldier* allowed Americans to examine changing conceptions of masculinity and femininity in a humorous, nonthreatening setting.[112] Bluntschli was anything but the ideal officer, yet he was characterized as a seasoned soldier of fortune. A woman offering a thoroughly feminized box of chocolate creams to any fighting man challenged the popularly held notions of indulgent females and men as practical, restrained consumers. As he ate the chocolates, the Captain lost any trace of composure by sucking on his fingers, presumably demonstrating that eating bonbons not only was an effeminate activity but also caused this veteran fighter to display childlike behavior. Because the play was set in the Balkans and featured a Swiss soldier and a Bulgarian woman, Americans were able to comfortably view *The Chocolate Soldier* with the assurance that they were not laughing at themselves.

By 1917, soldiers and candy also became linked in advertisements. A Life Savers advertisement illustrated this association between war and candy by picturing cannons made from roles of Pep-O-Mint candies. As these candy cannons continuously fired Life Savers at aircraft passing overhead, it was not clear whether the candy was being offered as sustenance to friendly airmen or aimed at destroying the enemy.[113] Another ad campaign was simultaneously introduced with sailors stationed on a battleship shouting, "Yo-ho-ho!" upon receiving a box of Life Savers, and it urged readers to send their "sailor boy a *box* today — don't wait for him to write and ask" (fig. 1.9).[114] Lowney's named a sampler box of "delicious orange and pineapple cordials, luscious fruit nuggets, cluster nuts, Brazil nuts and nuts glace" the Medal of Honor.[115] Boxes of Whitman's Service Chocolates included a book and one pound of

Fig. 1.9. American soldiers may not have made the world safe for democracy, but they certainly made candy consumption safe for men. In 1917, the Mint Products Company featured sailors stationed on a battleship in Pep-O-Mint Life Savers advertisements. *Literary Digest*, November 3, 1917.

candy specially packed for the "boys at the front or in training camp." Described as "munitions of happiness," the lids of these samplers were covered with military insignias of the Navy and Army.[116] Candy had become a widely used weapon in the hands and stomachs of America's fighting men.

Soldiers and sailors based in the United States also received an allotment of candy. A top priority for the Red Cross was providing "every man with the colors," a Christmas package that included tobacco, pipes, pipe cleaner, knives, playing cards, licorice, chocolates, and hard candy.[117] Instructing readers on how to make patriotic Christmas candies without using white sugar, Mary Lewis suggested including soldiers and sailors based on American soil in on the fun since they found candy making a favorite form of entertainment.[118] Bonbons and lemon drops were being eaten in great quantities by men in uniform at the close of the war. One source reported that extra sour lemon drops were the favorite candy among soldiers and that twenty thousand pounds were shipped by the Quartermaster Corps each month to American soldiers alone. Astonishingly, this amount equaled only 15 percent of the total amount of candy furnished by the Army.[119] Candy companies found a powerful spokesman in a Marine Corps general who enthusiastically declared: "Men fight like the devil on chocolate."[120] While candy consumption by women had been surrounded with images of purity and indulgence, male candy eating was characterized by endurance and power. The contents of Whitman's samplers produced angelic women and devilish men.

Men Like Candy, Too!

Within twenty-five years, candy and the meanings attached to this commodity underwent a revealing metamorphosis. Candy's growing popularity between 1895 and 1920 signaled a nation coming to terms with values central to an expanding market economy. Changing notions of masculinity and femininity proved to be critical components in the transformation from an economic system based on production to one driven by consumption. Contrasted with Victorian values of restraint and temperance, candy eating celebrated self-gratification. These tensions between moderation and indulgence would remain constant in advertisements and other popular portrayals of candy throughout the Progressive Era. Late nineteenth-century advertisements transformed candy into a product that offered women freedom, self-fulfillment, and rejuvenation. Images of white middle-class women seductively eating rich, chewy chocolates provided powerful symbolism for a nation undergoing dramatic social, political, and economic change. Clearly, more than candy was being marketed in early bonbon ads where romantic love, sexuality, and consumption became associated with women.

Although candy eating was initially viewed as a feminine indulgence, candy consumption was never limited to one sex. Men were enjoying chocolate drops and lemon taffy but were hesitant to publicly acknowledge their acceptance of these commodities. Candy eating had become explicitly linked with the sexual appeal of women, and Americans approached both with a mixture of dread and desire. Only with images of soldiers eating lemon drops on World War I battlefields would candy consumption by men become fully legitimized. By the end of the second decade of the twentieth century, men were openly expressing a craving for an assortment of candy. An *Illustrated World* article described the experience of C. T. Monahan, whose longing for sweets led him to "experiment in [his] kitchen one night." As Monahan reported: "I did it just to satisfy my own desire for good candy."[121] In 1919, another periodical stressed the utilitarian quality of candy for men: "Candy is no longer tabued. . . . A man may walk a mile or more on the energy furnished by a single caramel."[122] Further evidence of the regendering of candy was provided when soldiers and sailors returning to the United States from World War I battlefields found candies dedicated to their wartime experiences and were offered the Legion's Buddy, a candy bar devoted exclusively to fighting men.[123]

In the decade following the close of World War I, a new form of candy — the candy bar — would experience unprecedented popularity with thirty thousand bars being developed and marketed to the American public.[124] By 1919, candy companies found it necessary to register trademarks that distinguished one candy bar from another. E. J. Brach and Sons of Chicago named their chocolate-covered marshmallow bars Rastus 711 with the iconography including two dice cubes bearing the numbers 7 and 11.[125] Grape-Ola and Sweet-Plus were the names assigned to the chocolate bars of two Indiana candy companies, while the Peter Paul Candy Manufacturing Company introduced the enduring Mounds bar.[126] Clark (1919), Nestle (1919), Baby Ruth (1920), Oh Henry! (1920), Milky Way (1923), and Snickers (1927) bars were also introduced in this post–World War I boom.[127]

While often viewed as frivolous and insignificant, artifacts can inform scholars about the culture in which these material objects emerged and endured. Candy consumption in the late nineteenth and early twentieth centuries revealed the uneasiness with which Americans approached a world in flux, and more important, it illustrates how these changes were negotiated. America's working class was not only absorbing new waves of immigrants from southern and eastern Europe, but women, and most troubling, married women made up a greater percentage of the labor force.[128] Women also exerted themselves politically, demanding the right to vote and hold elected office. In addition, some scholars argue that as the shipping and food industries underwent dramatic change, America's eating habits were also revolutionized. Food processing conglomerates applied technological advancements to mass food production and introduced cooking oil, vegetables, and candy stamped with brand names.[129] Americans were grappling with new cultural values and a politicized economy where gender was constructed and manipulated to serve economic interests. Many of the resulting anxieties surrounding these same notions of purity, indulgence, and gender remain with us today. Men who subscribe to rigid gender roles are likely comforted by eating mammoth Snickers and Hershey bars labeled "King size" and covered with dark brown wrappers. On the other hand, 3Musketeers and Hershey "miniatures" are directly marketed to women and promise romantic fulfillment.[130] Employing artifacts (like candy) as primary documents allows scholars to view the imprint gender leaves on the material world and partially explains the dependence Americans express for an endless array of factory-produced commodities. Clearly there is much to learn from studying material objects.

Notes

I would like to thank Warren Belasco, Miriam Formanek-Brunell, Jeff Longhofer, Alice Nash, Tobie Matava, and Priscilla Murolo for reading drafts of this chapter and Sherrie A. Inness for very helpful editing. Much of my early research was funded by a grant from the Women's Council at the University of Missouri — Kansas City.

A special note of thanks to Terry Anderson and David Cox in the delivery department at Kansas City, Missouri, Public Library, who made accessible many of the visual images included in this work, and to Jack Denzer, who photographed all of the illustrations in this chapter.
1. Marcia Mogelonsky, "Candy: Still Dandy," *American Demographics*, September 1995, 10.
2. Carol Kaesuk Yoon, "Chocoholics Take Note: Beloved Bean in Peril," *New York Times*, May 4, 1998, sec. 1, p. 1.
3. Eric Asimov, "Brave New Post-Chocolate World," *New York Times*, May 10, 1998, sec. 4, p. 1.
4. Dodi Schultz, "Candy: How Sweet It Is!" *FDA Consumer*, July–August 1994, 22.

5. Carole Sugarman, "Premenstrual Chocolate Syndrome," *Washington Post*, January 21, 1997, health sec., 20, and "Ten Reasons to Enjoy Chocolate and Not Feel Guilty," *Glamour*, February 1997, 52.

6. "Ten Ways to Break That Bad Habit," *Mademoiselle*, September 1996, 244.

7. Stacey Freed, "A Love of Licorice: One Woman's Dark Obsession," *Washington Post*, August 20, 1997, E1.

8. Schultz, "Candy: How Sweet It Is!"

9. Jules David Prown, "Mind in Matter: An Introduction to Material Culture Theory and Method," in *Material Life in America, 1600–1800*, ed. Robert Blair St. George (Boston: Northeastern University Press, 1988), 17–37.

10. Reay Tannahill, *Food in History* (New York: Stein and Day, 1973); Richard J. Hooker, *Food and Drink in America: A History* (New York: Bobbs-Merrill, 1981).

11. Waverley Root and Richard de Rochemont, *Eating in America: A History* (New York: William Morrow, 1976).

12. My research has been guided by the work of Miriam Formanek-Brunell, *Made to Play House: Dolls and the Commercialization of American Girlhood, 1830–1930* (New Haven: Yale University Press, 1993). I have profited from conversations with her about the meaning of this artifact. My thinking on the connections among advertising, consumer culture, and candy has also been influenced by the work of T. J. Jackson Lears, "From Salvation to Self-Realization: Advertising and the Therapeutic Roots of the Consumer Culture, 1880–1930," in *The Culture of Consumption: Critical Essays in American History, 1880–1980*, ed. Richard Wightman Fox and T. J. Jackson Lears (New York: Pantheon Books, 1983), 3–38, and T. J. Jackson Lears, *Fables of Abundance: A Cultural History of Advertising in America* (New York: Basic Books, 1994).

13. Eliza Acton, *Modern Cookery in All Its Branches* (Philadelphia: Lea and Blanchard, 1845), 368–70, and *The American Housewife: Containing the Most Valuable and Original Receipts in All the Various Branches of Cookery* (New York: Collins, Keese, 1839), 75–77, 89, 101; Catharine E. Beecher and Harriet Beecher Stowe, *The American Woman's Home; or, Principles of Domestic Science* (New York: J. B. Ford, 1869; reprint, Hartford, Conn.: Stowe-Day Foundation, 1975), 189; Mrs. J. Chadwick, *Mrs. Chadwick's Cookbook: A Collection of Tried Receipts, Both Foreign and Domestic* (Boston: Crosby, Nichols, 1853); Lydia Maria Child, *The Frugal Housewife* (Boston: Carter, Hendee and Babcock, 1831); and Sarah Josepha Hale, *The Good Housekeeper* (Boston: Otis, Broaders, 1841).

14. Mrs. Julia McNair Wright, *The Complete Home: An Encyclopaedia of Domestic Life and Affairs* (Philadelphia: J. C. McCurdy, 1879), 555–56; Senior Circle of King's Daughters of the Glen Ridge Congregational Church, *Glen Ridge Receipt Book* (Glen Ridge, N.J.: New York Press of Styles and Cash, 1895), 60–61; *The Successful Housekeeper: A Manual of Universal Application* (Harrisburg: Pennsylvania Publication Company, 1882), 92–99.

15. Henry Weatherley, *A Treatise on the Art of Boiling Sugar, Crystallizing, Lozenge-Making, Comfits, Gum Goods, and Other Processes for Confectionery, Etc. in Which Are Explained, in an Easy and Familiar Manner, the Various Methods of Manufacturing Every Description of Raw and Refined Sugar Goods, as Sold by the Trade, Confectioners, and Others* (Philadelphia: Henry Carey Baird, 1875), 19.

16. George V. Frye, *How to Make Candy: Comprising Receipts for the Finest Home-Made Candies, Especially Adapted for Manufacture in the American Kitchen* (Chicago: Morrill, Higgins, 1892), 3.

17. Perfecto, *Notes on American Confectionery: With Methods of Working Different Branches of Candy Making, Ice Cream, and Soda Water* (Philadelphia: Author, 1891), 7.

18. *Hood's Book of Homemade Candies* (Lowell, Mass.: C. I. Hood, 1888), 1.

19. "Candy Trade's Growth: Advance from Nothing in Less Than Twenty-Five Years," *New York Times*, December 20, 1903, 18.

20. "Candy," *New York Times*, January 1, 1874, 4–5.

21. John Lewis, New York, N.Y., to Mother and Brother, Este, January 10, 1876, John Lewis Letters, Division of Rare and Manuscript Collections, Carl A. Kroch Library, Cornell University, Ithaca, N.Y.

22. American Memory Project, Library of Congress, The American Variety Stage: Vaudeville and Popular Entertainment, 1870–1920, *The Lilliputians in Their Latest and Greatest Success, Candy, Great American Spectacular Musical Comedy with Chorus and Ballet in Four Acts and Six Tableaux*, Union Square Theatre Programe, New York, October 31, 1892, 11.

23. Robert Breitenbach, *Synopsis and Libretto of the Grand Spectacular Musical Comedy, Candy, 1892*, Harris Collection, Brown University Library, Providence, R.I., 3.

24. American Memory Project, *Candy*, 9.

25. "New York's Sweet Tooth," *New York Times*, February 26, 1899, 16.

26. "Candy Makers' Label," *Bakers' Journal: Official Organ of the Journeymen Bakers' and Confectioners' International Union of America*, October 28, 1899, 1.

27. Theodore Dreiser, *Sister Carrie* (New York: Harper and Brothers, 1900; reprint, New York: Bennett A. Cerf and Donald S. Klopper, Modern Library, 1932), 345.

28. "Hindoo Confectionery," *Bakers' Journal: Official Organ of the Journeymen Bakers' and Confectioners' International Union of America*, February 10, 1900, 2.

29. Philadelphia Crown Caramels advertisement, *Ladies' Home Journal*, September 1892, 18; Plow's Candy advertisement, *Ladies' Home Journal*, December 1893, 22; Acker's Candies Advertisement, *Ladies' Home Journal*, December 1894, 21.

30. Mrs. Sadie Reed's Restaurant and Confectionery advertisement, *American Citizen*, October 18, 1889, 3, and January 17, 1890, 4.

31. Miss Rosa Johnson advertisement, *Detroit Plaindealer*, July 22, 1892, 3.

32. Lowney's advertisement, *Ladies' Home Journal*, May 1895, 22; June 1895, 17; July 1895, 23; August 1895, 18; September 1895, 31.

33. Lowney's advertisement, *Ladies' Home Journal*, September 1895, 31.

34. Lowney's advertisement, *Ladies' Home Journal*, June 1895, 17.

35. Joan Jacobs Brumberg, *Fasting Girls: The Emergence of Anorexia Nervosa as a Modern Disease* (Cambridge: Harvard University Press, 1988), 175–76.

36. Huyler's advertisement, *Ladies' Home Journal*, January 1896, 21; *Saturday Evening Post*, May 20, 1899, 753; July 15, 1899, 48; March 18, 1899, 606; December 24, 1898, 416.

37. Lowney's advertisement, *Ladies' Home Journal*, February 1896, 30.

38. Lowney's advertisement, *Ladies' Home Journal*, April 1896, 24. A similar

ad appeared in a full-page format in the *Saturday Evening Post*, December 1, 1900, inside back cover and April 13, 1901, inside front cover.

39. John F. Kasson, "Rituals of Dining: Table Manners in Victorian America," in *Dining in America, 1850–1900*, ed. Kathryn Grover (Amherst: University of Massachusetts Press, 1987), 130.

40. Louise Fiske Bryson, *Everyday Etiquette: A Manual of Good Manners* (New York: W. D. Kerr, 1890), 97.

41. Kathy Peiss, *Cheap Amusements: Working Women and Leisure in Turn-of-the-Century New York* (Philadelphia: Temple University Press, 1986), 6–8.

42. Brumberg, *Fasting Girls*, 174–75, 178.

43. Lowney's advertisement, *Ladies' Home Journal*, December 1896, 45.

44. "The Nation's Annual Candy Bill and What the Money Would Do If Expended in Other Directions," *New York Times*, January 2, 1910, sec. 5, p. 8.

45. Taylor-Made Honey Comb Chocolate Chips advertisement, *Saturday Evening Post*, March 3, 1906, 16.

46. Park and Tilford Candies advertisement, *New York Times*, December 4, 1909, 5.

47. Whitman's advertisement, *Harper's Magazine Advertiser*, March, 1904, back advertisement section.

48. Peter's Chocolates advertisement, *Ladies' Home Journal*, December, 1905, 51; *Saturday Evening Post*, October 28, 1905, 23; Clark and Harris Butter Cups advertisement, *Western Drug Record*, 1904–5, 54.

49. National Licorice Company advertisement, *National Druggist*, November 1904, x.

50. U-All-No After Dinner Mints advertisement, *Ladies' Home Journal*, April 1920, 114.

51. "How Loft, Candy Advertiser, Was Converted to Car Advertising," *Printers' Ink*, September 22, 1909, 51; Necco advertisements, *Saturday Evening Post*, February 23, 1907, 28; April 6, 1907, 27.

52. Bell's Forkdipt Chocolates advertisement, *Saturday Evening Post*, May 5, 1906, 27.

53. Stacy's Forkdipd Chocolates advertisement, *Ladies' Home Journal*, April 1906, 57.

54. Remington's Pharmacy advertisement, *Printers' Ink*, January 23, 1907, 47.

55. "Selling Country Kitchen Candy," *Illustrated World*, September 1916, 239.

56. Lowney's advertisements, *Saturday Evening Post*, December 1, 1900, back cover; November 19, 1904, 22; *New York Times*, April 1904, 3; *Literary Digest*, November 19, 1910, 961; *Ladies' Home Journal*, December 1907, inside front cover; *Harper's Magazine Advertiser*, April 1906, front ad section. Huyler's advertisements, *Ladies' Home Journal*, December 1907, 50; *Saturday Evening Post*, May 11, 1901, 15; July 18, 1905, 24; December 15, 1906, 2.

57. Lowney's advertisement, *Saturday Evening Post*, October 14, 1905, 27.

58. Baker's Cocoa and Chocolate advertisement, *Harper's Bazaar*, April 1903, advertising supplement.

59. Wilbur's Chocolate Buds, *Colliers*, December 11, 1909, 35.

60. Whitman's advertisement, *Druggist Circular*, September 1909, 57.

61. Johnston's Swiss Style Chocolate Creams advertisements, *Woman's Home Companion*, April 1908, 32; *Ladies' Home Journal*, May 1908, 58.

62. Taylor-Made Honey Comb Chocolate Chips advertisement, *Saturday Evening Post*, December 9, 1905, 19; September 15, 1906, 22; June 1, 1907, 30.

63. "Mrs. Andrews Recovering," *New York Times*, July 5, 1904, 6.

64. Frank H. Holman, "The Sex Appeal in Advertising," *Printers' Ink*, July 21, 1909, 10–12.

65. "Are Pretty Women Pictures Good Advertising?" *Printers' Ink*, August 11, 1909, 8.

66. Joseph J. Bukey, "Is All Feminine Advertising Bad?" *Printers' Ink*, August 25, 1909, 34.

67. Karo Corn Syrup advertisement, *Ladies' Home Journal*, May 1910, 76.

68. Harriet A. Blogg, "Sweets College Girls Make for Their Frolics," *Ladies' Home Journal*, October 1913, 112 (quote from 1913 source); Alice Long Fuller, "The Goody 'Eats' I Made and Ate at College," *Ladies' Home Journal*, October 1911, 16.

69. Kimberly Strickland, "Rhymes Receipts for Toothsome Sweets," *Woman's Home Companion*, April 1911, 38.

70. Carroll Smith-Rosenberg, "The New Woman as Androgyne: Social Disorder and Gender Crisis, 1870–1936," in *Disorderly Conduct: Visions of Gender in Victorian America* (New York: Oxford University Press, 1985), 245–96.

71. Alice Kessler-Harris, *Out to Work: A History of Wage-Earning Women in the United States* (New York: Oxford University Press, 1982), 115–16.

72. Huyler's advertisements, *Saturday Evening Post*, September 1906, 2; July 8, 1905, 24; *Ladies' Home Journal*, April 1906, 28.

73. Revere chocolates, *Druggist Circular*, September 1909, 48.

74. Gunther's Bon Bons advertisement, *Western Drug Record*, 1905–6, 185.

75. Peter's advertisement, *Printers' Ink*, March 3, 1909, 44; *Munsey's Magazine*, March 1906, 45; *Harper's Magazine Advertiser*, April 1906, rear ad section; *Saturday Evening Post*, April 1906, 29.

76. William Leach, *Land of Desire: Merchants, Power, and the Rise of a New American Culture* (New York: Vintage Books, 1993), 5–7. Democratization of desire is taken directly from Leach's monograph.

77. "Here's Good News for the Children: Candy One of the Best Things They Can Eat, Doctors Tell Their Elders," *New York Times*, May 31, 1912, 13.

78. "The Nation's Annual Candy Bill," *New York Times*, January 2, 1910, sec. 5, p. 8.

79. "The Demon Candy," *Atlantic Monthly*, September 1910, 431, 432.

80. Florence May Swan, "Mrs. Snyder," *System: The Magazine of Business*, February 1919, 229.

81. Mary B. Mullett, "What a Big Candy Maker Has Found Out About Us Humans," *American Magazine*, August 1920, 45, 44.

82. First quote, "The Nation's Annual Candy Bill," *New York Times*, January 2, 1910, sec. 5, p. 8. Second quote, "Candy and Alcohol," *Independent*, August 22, 1907, 463.

83. "Candy and Alcohol," *Independent*, August 22, 1907, 463.

84. "The Demon Candy," *Atlantic Monthly*, September 1910, 431.

85. "The Nation's Annual Candy Bill," *New York Times*, January 2, 1910, sec. 5, p. 8.

86. Virginia Hunt, "Mary Elizabeth's Wartime Candies," *Ladies' Home Journal*, December 1917, 64.

87. "Alcohol and Candy," *Literary Digest*, November 6, 1920, 26; "Candy as a Food," *Literary Digest*, May 31, 1919, 31.

88. Lenox Chocolate advertisement, *Ladies' Home Journal*, December 1915, 70.

89. Necco advertisement, *Ladies' Home Journal*, July 1910, 44.

90. Fuller-Morrisson Company advertisement, *Western Druggist*, February 1916, 15.

91. U-All-No After Dinner Mint advertisements, *Ladies' Home Journal*, March 1910, 87; April 1920, 114; February 1920, 156.

92. Malliard's advertisements, *Ladies' Home Journal*, May 1916, 64; February 1917, 74; *Outlook*, January 31, 1917, 175.

93. Lifesavers advertisements, *Saturday Evening Post*, November 18, 1916, 38; February 24, 1917, 46; April 28, 1917, 80; May 26, 1917, 64.

94. Peter's Milk Chocolate advertisement, *New York Times*, November 21, 1920, picture sec., p. 5.

95. Patterson's Tuxedo Tobacco advertisement, *Outlook*, July 23, 1919, inside front cover.

96. Nut Tootsie Rolls advertisement, *Saturday Evening Post*, October 14, 1916, 49; March 24, 1917, 38; August 12, 1916, 39.

97. Johnston's advertisements, *Saturday Evening Post*, April 19, 1916, 38; July 15, 1916, 38; August 5, 1916, 38; September 9, 1916, 42; September 23, 1916, 47; October 14, 1916, 106; October 28, 1916, 69; November 25, 1916, 48; December 2, 1916, 78; December 16, 1916, 58; January 15, 1917, 30; January 27, 1917, 30.

98. Milady advertisements, *Saturday Evening Post*, April 28, 1917, 70; Nunnally's advertisements, *American Magazine*, July 1920, 104; *Atlantic Monthly*, December 1920, 140–41; November 1920, 136–37.

99. Lenox advertisement, *Delineator*, November 1912, 389.

100. U.S. Patent #123,149, *Improvement in the Manufacture of Candy*, William J. Burns, Georgetown, Ky., January 30, 1872; U.S. Design Patent #9,574, *Caramels or Candy Drops*, Walter A. Bryant, Hartford, Conn., August 29, 1876; U.S. Patent #315,559, *Confectionery*, August Schwarzschild and Nelson Greenfield, New York, N.Y., April 14, 1885; U.S. Patent #330,659, *Confection*, George Ziegler, Milwaukee, Wisc., November 17, 1885; U.S. Trademark Serial No. 72,572, *Love*, F. S. Love Manufacturing Company, Johnston, Penn., August 28, 1913, Claims Use since March 1890; U.S. Trademark Serial No. 29,312, *Queen*, Greek American Confectionery Company, New York, N.Y., August 9, 1907; U.S. Design Patents #40,268 and 40,269, *Chocolate Comfit*, Sylvester S. Marvin, Pittsburgh, June 5, 1909.

101. U.S. Design Patent #31,389, *Design for a Licorice Stick*, Charles A. Smylie, New York, N.Y., August 15, 1899.

102. U.S. Trademark Serial No. 45,162, *Acme*, National Candy Company, Jersey City, N.J., October 6, 1909; U.S. Trademark Serial No. 47,130, *Maxima*, Palmer and Company, Sioux City, Iowa, January 15, 1910; U.S. Trademark Serial No. 47,954, *Phoenix Brand*, Reinhart and Newton Company, Cincinnati, Ohio, February 23, 1910.

103. Samoset Chocolates Company trademark advertisement, *Printers' Ink*, September 1, 1909, 63; U.S. Trademark Serial No. 7,750, *Samoset Chocolates and Bonbons*, R. L. Perry Co., Boston, Mass., June 9, 1905.

104. U.S. Design Patent #42,162, *Bar of Candy*, Robert C. Boeckel, York, Pa., October 28, 1911.

105. U.S. Patent #1,107,325, *Candy and Process of Making the Same*, William B. Laskey, Marblehead, Mass., August 18, 1914. Other patents that depicted candy in rectangular shapes include: U.S. Design Patents #54,212 and 54,213, *Design for a Molded Candy, Chocolate, or Confection*, Charles F. Haug, Brooklyn, N.Y., November 18, 1919; U.S. Design Patent #53,422, *Design for a Bar or Cake of Candy or Confectionery*, Robert S. Manus, Cleveland, Ohio, June 10, 1919.

106. U.S. Patent #1,127,114, *Malted-Milk Confection*, Livingston A. Thompson, Waukesha, Wisc., February 2, 1915.

107. U.S. Design Patent #53657, *Design for a Candy Tablet or Similar Article*, Joseph F. Hollywood, Brooklyn, N.Y., July 29, 1919.

108. "Confectionery in Army Rations," *Scientific American*, January 6, 1900, 6.

109. "Candy and Alcohol," *Independent*, August 22, 1907, 463.

110. Bernard Shaw, *Seven Plays* (New York: Dodd, Mead, 1951), 119, 135.

111. Charles A. Carpenter, *Bernard Shaw and the Art of Destroying Ideals: The Early Plays* (Madison: University of Wisconsin Press, 1969), 89–98; Shaw, *Seven Plays*, 119–20.

112. John D'Emilio and Estelle B. Freedman, *Intimate Matters: A History of Sexuality in America* (New York: Harper and Row, 1989), 171–221; Kathy Peiss and Christina Simmons, eds., *Passion and Power: Sexuality in History* (Philadelphia: Temple University Press, 1989), 3–13.

113. Life Saver advertisement, *Western Druggist*, October 1917, follows 262.

114. Life Savers advertisement, *Literary Digest*, November 3, 1917, 1.

115. Lowney's Chocolates advertisement, *Literary Digest*, November 4, 1916, 1203.

116. Whitman's advertisement, *Literary Digest*, October 13, 1917, 50; December 15, 1917, 51.

117. "For the American Soldier's Happy Christmas: Gift-Laden Trees in All the Cantonments, Parties of Every Conceivable Sort in the Camps and Neighboring Cities," *New York Times Magazine*, December 2, 1917, 8.

118. Mary Lewis, "Patriotic Christmas Candies: Using No White Sugar, but Plenty of Nuts," *Ladies' Home Journal*, December 1918, 41.

119. "Candy in the Army," *Literary Digest*, April 15, 1919, 28.

120. "The Nation's Sweet Tooth," *Saturday Evening Post*, March 6, 1920, 38.

121. W. F. French, "A Corner in Sweets," *Illustrated World*, June 1917, 593.

122. "Eating Between Meals," *Literary Digest*, December 27, 1919, 94.

123. U.S. Trademark Serial Number 106,426, *Sammie*, Imperial Candy Company, Seattle, Wash., September 25, 1917; U.S. Trademark Serial Number 115,601, *Our Heroes*, Richmond Candy Company, Boston, Mass., February 3, 1919; U.S. Trademark Serial Number 135,858, *Liberty Dough Boy*, Liberty Candy Company, Grand Rapids, Mich., August 6, 1920; U.S. Trademark Serial Number 115,996; Ray Brockel, "Land of the Candy Bar," *American Heritage*, October/November 1986, 75.

124. Philip P. Gott, L. F. Van Houten, et al., *All About Candy and Chocolate* (Chicago: National Confectioners' Association of the United States, 1958), 24–25; Ray Brockel, "Land of the Candy Bar," *American Heritage*, October/November 1986, 75; "Behind Nickel Bars," *World's Work*, April 1932, 48–52.

125. U.S. Trademark Serial Number 115,367, *Rastus 711*, E. J. Brach and Sons, Chicago, Ill., January 22, 1919.

126. U.S. Trademark Serial Number 141,488, *Grape-Ola*, Dilling and Company, Indianapolis, Ind., December 24, 1920; U.S. Trademark Serial Number 143,736, *Sweet-Plus*, Cook-Welker-Hire Company, Fort Wayne, Ind., February 18, 1921; U.S. Trademark Serial Number 141,801, *Mounds*, Peter Paul Candy Manufacturing Company, Inc., New Haven, Conn., January 3, 1921.

127. Ray Brockel, *The Great American Candy Bar Book* (Boston: Houghton Mifflin, 1982), 11, 22, 44, 63, 99; "Behind Nickel Bars," *World's Work*, April 1932, 48–52.

128. Kessler-Harris, *Out to Work*, 109.

129. Harvey Levenstein, *Revolution at the Table: The Transformation of the American Diet* (New York: Oxford University Press, 1988), 32, 43; Susan Strasser, *Satisfaction Guaranteed: The Making of the American Mass Market* (Washington, D.C.: Smithsonian Institution Press, 1989), 7, 22.

130. 3Musketeers advertisement, *Prevention*, April 1996, 9; Hershey's advertisement, *People Weekly*, February 19, 1996, advertising insert following p. 58.

Campbell's Soup and the Long Shelf Life of Traditional Gender Roles

KATHERINE PARKIN

An October 1921 advertisement in the *Ladies' Home Journal* extolled the virtues of Campbell's soup with a headline describing it as the "modern way of 'making' soup." By qualifying the word *making* with quotation marks, the advertisers acknowledged that heating up a can of soup was not the same as making one's own. Convenience food advertising such as this helped perpetuate traditional gender roles in the face of modernity. Ads targeted women with gendered messages and sowed guilt and insecurity about their abilities as hostesses and homemakers. They told women that these roles were of the utmost importance and that cooking with their products guaranteed success. Food advertisers sought to quell women's doubts about cooking with their store-bought goods and went so far as to warn that failure to serve their products would doom women as wives and mothers.[1]

This chapter analyzes Campbell's magazine advertisements between their debut in 1905 and World War II. It focuses on those placed in the *Ladies' Home Journal* because of the magazine's influence during the first half of the twentieth century. Advertisers knew by the early 1900s that women were the major consumers of household goods, and so they placed gendered advertisements in magazines designed specifically for female consumers. Thereafter, food ads appeared on an increasingly consistent basis in popular magazines throughout the country.[2]

The Joseph Campbell Company began making condensed soups in the 1890s and was one of the earliest believers in the powers of advertising, especially in reaching a national market. The company, eventually known as the Campbell Soup Company, was a consistent, influential advertiser that spent extraordinary amounts of money to reach women nationwide and in so doing carved out a strong identity in the *Ladies' Home Journal* and other women's magazines. Early on, food manufacturers like the Campbell Soup Company and magazine editors realized that they needed the same female consumers and that their partnership, in the form of advertising, would be lucrative. To encourage food manufacturers to advertise on their pages, periodicals featured menus suggesting advertised products and included articles to foster women's interest in cooking.[3]

American culture in the twentieth century bound women, food, and love together. American society, and advertising in particular, saw the preparation and consumption of food in distinctly gendered terms. While everyone ate food, society held women responsible for its purchase and preparation. Cooking for their families was an activity emblematic of women's love. Women generated feelings of love even from foods they did not cook, exemplified by the response wives and mothers got from heating up convenience foods. For many Americans, the enduring associations between women, food, and love formed early in life. By commodifying these attitudes and beliefs, food advertisers promoted the belief that food preparation was a gender-specific activity and that women should cook for others to express their love. This emphasis on giving was so complete that ads rarely portray women finding gratification in eating.

Campbell's ads featured women who presumably spent their days caring for the home and their children, while men generally had no evident role in the home. In spite of the record number of women working outside the home and the growing number of men spending leisure time at home, Campbell's advertisements did not advertise their soups to young women living in apartments or to fathers who cooked for their families while wives worked. Campbell's ads did not try to fit the product into consumers' realities; instead, they invited consumers into an idealized setting.

Industrialization, immigration, war, and economic depressions marked the early twentieth century. It is conceivable that upheavals in the American workforce brought on by these changes might have created a different gender paradigm in the kitchen. However, the division of labor continued to exist relatively intact for the entire period examined. In her examination of production and consumption patterns, Susan Porter Benson found that working-class gender roles were probably more fluid than those of the middle class by necessity. She surveyed 391 married working-class women and learned that 61 of their husbands did some housework. Still, food ads generally did not acknowledge any diversity in consumers' lifestyles and instead featured only women grocery shopping, cooking, and serving meals. Food advertising is one of the reasons traditional ideals about food preparation and consumption generally prevailed in the society.[4]

Cooking has historically been the focus of cultural analysts who seek to define women's role in the home and in society. Domestic reformer Catharine Beecher, feminist theorist Charlotte Perkins Gilman, and a host of their contemporaries in the nineteenth century advocated changes in cooking practices, including increasing its efficiency and moving it out of the home altogether.[5] With minimal fanfare, food advertising co-opted these once radical ideas and helped deradicalize them into normal aspects of daily life in the twentieth century. Yet the transformation of cooking and eating patterns was not the result of an organized movement to liberate women from kitchen drudgery. While it may have lessened their work, canned foods did not challenge women's exclusive responsibility for the homemaking role.

Food manufacturers suggested that their products would transform women's lives and appealed to women's desires to be modern and progressive. A 1926 ad sang the praises of "ambitious" women who used Campbell's soups: "These women do not neglect their housekeeping. Far from it. They do it more efficiently every day. But they accomplish better results with less drudgery. They serve better food with less time in the kitchen. They raise the standard of their family's health and their own — with less expense and effort. All praiseworthy steps in the onward march of their social ambition."[6] Modernity's blessings had limits, evidently, because the advertisements never once suggested that a man or child could heat up a can of soup. Advertisers tried to convince women that only they possessed the skill to cook in the modern world.

Insecurity is a prevalent theme throughout Campbell's advertisements. The advertising business, according to historian James D. Norris, "tapped a very deep American insecurity and deadly pressure to conform by equating consumption of an article with social status and approval."[7] Regardless of an ad's tone, cajoling or foreboding, it always carried the same implied threat: not using Campbell's soups would result in some type of failure. Their ads sought to exploit women's doubts and anxieties. They attempted to make women feel vulnerable and uncertain about providing for their families, so that they would pay attention to Campbell's admonitions.

In conjunction with insecurity, Campbell's ads employed a variety of strategies to win women's brand loyalty; many ads used several approaches at once. The most consistent appeal was to mothers and their desires for their children to be smart, strong, and healthy. Additionally, the ads catered to women's sense of themselves as homemakers and their efforts to satisfy their families. Ads also consistently relied on male authority to persuade women to believe Campbell's claims about their soup and gender roles. Finally, advertisers recognized the potency of feminism and its threat to the authority of men and co-opted it to sell more soup.

"Do Not Disappoint Your Own Children"

An important goal for the Campbell Soup Company was to entice women, especially mothers, who needed to cook for a large number of people. One way they tried to attract these women was through an early ad campaign that showcased the Campbell Kids, created by Grace Gebbie Drayton in 1904. The Kids were drawings of plump children, and their appearance was meant to convey that mothers who served Campbell's soup would make their children robust and healthy. Some of the ads were explicit. One showed a Campbell Kid looking at his shadow created by his candle: "Gracious me! What can it be, That shadow round and fat? This soup I know, Makes youngsters grow, But do I look like that?" Ads used the Kids to create a playful atmosphere. They did endearing "kid" things, such as performing a piano recital or playing outside. Their appeal, therefore, extended to both women and their children. Advertisers hoped that children's attraction to the Kids would enlist their influence over their mothers' shopping lists.[8]

The Campbell Kids embodied archetypal gender roles. Ads showed girls doing domestic chores and other presumably female activities, such as talking on the phone, looking at themselves in a mirror, and taking care of baby dolls. Conversely, ads showed boys performing a wide variety of jobs, such as bricklayer, architect, astronomer, chef, coal miner, and hunter. There were exceptions for the girls, occasionally showing them outside the home working as nurses or marching in parades (in support of Campbell's soup), but ads never showed boys caring for children or cooking.[9]

Most of the Campbell Kid scenarios were fairly staid, but a few went to unusual lengths to attract women's attention and demonstrate how much children liked the soup. A 1911 ad depicted a Campbell Kid sitting and eating a bowl of soup while smoke and flames shot from the window behind him. Next to him appeared the doggerel: " 'O boy why wait; This fiery fate; When all but you have fled'; 'Tis not too late; For one more plate; Of Campbell's Soup,' he said." In 1912 another ad depicted a Campbell Kid wearing a disguise breaking into a can of Campbell soup, asserting, "I'm Burglar Bill. All primed to kill. You know my awful fame. This is the break — I like to make — And the treasure I'm bound to claim." The Kids appearing in such daring, action-packed scenarios are always male; the females never participate in any adventures outside of the kitchen.[10]

The Kids were a constant feature of the magazine ads, although they changed in appearance from ad to ad. Generally, they did not have names or personalities, and they could be upper class in one ad and working class in the next. This amorphous quality enabled them to participate in a wide variety of activities and assume many roles. For example, the Kids appeared in a 1916 ad, with a girl in a fur coat and a boy in a tuxedo, while other ads portrayed them as grocers or housewives. Giving the Campbell Kids a loose identity gave the company a great deal of maneuverability in their advertising campaigns. By embracing both male and female characters that could potentially be any class or any age, the Campbell company created enduring advertising icons. The Kids served as a flexible tool to persuade women and children to consume their product.[11]

The company made other appeals to maternalism, promising that their soups would make children smart, strong, and healthy. Campbell's ads encouraged mothers to take responsibility for their children's educational performance. Most of these ads appeared at the start of the school year. These ads suggested to mothers that Campbell's soup would help children "in both body and mind." One ad, appearing in October 1919, showed a female elementary school teacher pointing to Europe and the Soviet Union on a world map and stating that children "must grapple with new tasks, with harder problems. They have fresh worlds to conquer." This ad sent two messages to mothers. First, their children were starting a new school year that would have new and more difficult lessons. Second, their children lived in a changed world following the First World War, and if they wanted them to excel in the competition with communism, they had best give them Campbell's soup. Other ads with educational references suggested that Campbell's soup would help make children alert and thereby better able to study. In the latter half of the 1930s, there were many ads encouraging women to feed their children soup when they came home from school for lunch. Ads placed responsibility for children's gratification and well-being on their mothers, warning them, "Do not disappoint your own children." [12]

Campbell's ads assured mothers that Campbell's soups would help their children withstand disease. The ads claimed that Campbell's soup was a healthy food, highlighting the overall energy and health that the soups offered children. However, while ads did show girls and boys playing together, many ads suggested that Campbell's Soup would affect them differently. Take for example the contrast between two typical ads, both featuring Campbell Kids. The first, an ad for ox tail soup, depicts a boy wrestling an ox to the ground. The second shows a girl with the doggerel, "My rosy cheeks, And winning looks, Are really due, To Campbell's cooks!" Campbell's ads consistently alluded to different outcomes for males and females. One 1933 ad featured a painting of an adoring, cute girl standing next to a strong, tough boy after a football game in which he has just played. The caption, "It's health that makes him a hero!" focuses attention on his strength, ignoring the girl in the picture. The boy looks out confidently at the viewer, while the girl looks at the boy, content in her supporting role. [13]

The Campbell Soup Company was not content merely to offer promises of better health. It also relied on scare tactics to persuade women to cook with Campbell's soups. In the midst of the Depression, the company ran an ad with the headline "Play is just health out for a good time!" At first glance, it is an upbeat ad, with boys playing in the snow, building snowmen and forts, and making snowballs. However, the text of the ad served to exacerbate mothers' fears for their children's future: "You want your child to be right out there in the thick of it, mingling with the rest of the children in normal, wholesome, healthful fun. It's the alert and able-bodied children who are the natural leaders in their little world, just as the strong prevail in later life." [14] Campbell's ads capitalized on mothers who wanted their children to have the health and potential to succeed in a cruelly competitive economic environment and prescribed their duties in preparing their children for an uncertain future.

"What Will People Say?"

Convenience food ads also focused on women's desire to be good homemakers and their fears of inadequacy. In addition to being a good mother, homemaking included household efficiency, economic acuity, and being a popular hostess. Campbell's advertising presented countless social scenarios that might expose a woman's failings. A 1927 ad explicitly asked the all-important question: "What will people say?" The ad went on to give the answer, declaring, "Of course women are sensitive to every criticism or comment, however slight and trivial, about their homes. Why shouldn't they be? The home is their special responsibility and delight. It is the sign and proof of the kind of people who live there."[15]

Advertisements counseled women that to avoid humiliating themselves and their family, they ought to have a supply of Campbell's soup on hand. In 1912, the company began urging customers to order cans of soup either by the half dozen or an even dozen, and by 1915 it had escalated to recommending buying it by the case, always reminding women of the possibility of an emergency. An April 1914 ad has a woman open the door to three unexpected guests, exclaiming, "This is a delightful surprise! Come right in. We'll have luncheon in a jiffy." The next paragraph assured the reader that "a neat little row of red-and-white labels on the pantry shelf" meant that she was ready for this "emergency." Campbell's ads wanted women to live in fear of social embarrassment in order to get them to overstock soup.[16]

Campbell's ads tried to alleviate women's fears that cooking with convenience foods could be evidence of selfishness or callousness. They assured women that cooking their soup was a sign of love and highlighted several factors, including the soups' variety, quality, value, and health benefits. Campbell's ads reminded women they could choose from their "21 Kinds" to please their families. Historically, changing seasons affected people's eating patterns. This was true not only because of peoples' preferences, such as wanting to eat cold meals in the summer and hot ones in the winter, but also because many types of produce were not available in the winter. The Campbell Soup Company proclaimed that their soups made it possible for women to please their families by serving a varied diet year round. Ads for some of the more exotic soups stated, without reservation, that these were soups "no home kitchen could produce." To produce variety, women needed Campbell's soups. The pressure for variety in cooking created more work for women. It was no longer enough simply to cook for a family; to demonstrate their love, women had to provide a varied menu.[17]

Campbell's advertising suggested different meals women could make with their soups. While the range of meals they suggested expanded over time, their message remained the same: If women are going to cook, Campbell's soup can help. Besides serving it as a course in a larger meal or as a meal in itself, ads positioned the soup for use in other meals as a sauce or the base of other dishes. The ads served as a constant reminder that women who varied their cooking with Campbell's soups were good homemakers.

From the turn of the century to the eve of World War II, Campbell's advertising contended that the best homemakers relied on the quality of Campbell's soups. In many ways and forms, the ads asserted, "No matter how particular you are nor how much you pay, you cannot make nor buy better soups than Campbell's." Ads warned that while some people had tried bargain soups, they would not do. These types of ads put a premium on loyalty to the Campbell Soup Company and tried to make women feel guilty if they used a different brand. Women would have only themselves to blame if competitors' inferior products ruined their luncheon or dinner party.[18]

Campbell's campaigns tried to subvert the idea that women's kitchens were better than factories. By claiming the best quality produce and a clean, antiseptic kitchen, ads asserted that Campbell's soup was a superior product to what women could hope to achieve. Throughout the early twentieth century, ads repeatedly stressed that their food contained no adulterants or chemicals. One ad went so far as to assert that the soup contained not a particle of impurity. Others emphasized the health and wholesomeness of the natural, unprocessed ingredients. A 1917 ad explained that "selected large fresh ox-tails are sent to us carefully dressed and packed in paper-lined boxes specially for this soup. There could be nothing more dainty and attractive." The ad described the ox-tails as though they were a dozen roses, trying to make women visualize the soup ingredients as fresh and inviting. Moreover, to further undermine women's confidence in their own kitchens, ads focused on sterilized cooking utensils and stressed that cleanliness extended to the employees, who received regular manicures and wore uniforms.[19]

Efficiency and cost-saving measures were critical components of success in the workplace, and many homes also embraced these ideals in the twentieth century. An important selling point for the soups was their economical value. The Campbell Soup Company sold its products on the premise that condensed soups were two soups for the price of one. Ads also claimed that canned soup cost less than homemade. The company based this claim on the amount of time that homemade soup took to prepare, the lack of waste, and cooking costs. For many women, this sales pitch had the advantage of being true. For women who worked outside the home, it took much less time to purchase, cook, and clean up a can of Campbell's soup than to make meals from scratch.[20]

Fundamental to their discussion of efficiency and cooking ease was the advertisers' understanding of women. Often advertisements suggested that women were delicate. Sometimes, even in the same ad, however, the company sold its soup based on the idea of women being overworked. Advertisements simultaneously suggested that women needed help because they were frail and that they needed deliverance from their strenuous work. A 1912 ad had three women lunching in their finery, with one exclaiming, "And only one maid! How do you manage so nicely?" The text of the ad asks, "How does any woman with only one maid — or sometimes with no help at all — manage dainty little luncheons and other company affairs with perfect smoothness and ease?" Advertisers used the difficulty women had completing their own housework and the problem of finding good household help to sell the products' ease of preparation. Campbell's ads reminded women that their soups were available if they were busy washing clothes, ironing, washing dishes, sewing, and cooking. Ads assured them that Campbell's soup was "sure reliance" in the midst of " 'nervous' tiring work." Regardless of a woman's role in the home, whether she primarily supervised the work being done or did it alone, ads promised that their soup was used by the "modern house-wife."[21]

Campbell's ads also explicitly promised that using its products would demonstrate women's love for their families. Advertisements took special care to assure women that buying Campbell's soup did not mean they were putting any less love into their cooking than if they had made the soup themselves. A 1918 ad proclaimed, "The most affectionate mother could not exercise a greater care in preparing food." Using a different tactic, other ads threatened women that making soup at home is "now distinctly passé" and challenged those who belonged to the "fast diminishing list of women who go to all the trouble of making their own soup" to try Campbell's soups.[22]

By the 1930s, the company had gained enough confidence to shift from polite invitations to stern demands that women cease making their own soups. The ads pitted the holdouts and the Campbell Soup Company as rivals in competition to make the best soup, and of course the recalcitrant home cooks were the losers. The advertisements complimented women and feigned praise for their skills, but their ultimate goal was to show the futility of making one's own when Campbell's soup was clearly the best.

The campaign acknowledged that while women might take pride in their cooking skills, their wisdom should make them acquiesce to convenience foods. These more assertive ads of the 1930s challenged women's authority in their kitchens: "Occasionally — we admit it — there is a woman who will tell you that all her soup is home-made and that she would never buy canned soups at the grocery store. Sometimes — and may it rest very lightly on her conscience indeed — she is indulging in one of those forgivable little deceptions dear to every woman jealous of her reputation as cook and manager." This ad condescends to women who claim they would never buy canned soups. A 1936 ad grabbed women's attention with the title "Wife Beaters." It showed a picture of a woman serving soup to her husband and another man, presumably his boss. The shocking headline not only drew attention but implied that women could be in physical danger if men are dissatisfied with their food. The text of the ad explained, "Women everywhere are cheerfully admitting that Campbell's beat them at soup making. The better the cooks, the more ready they are to admit it." With this clever phrasing, Campbell's advertisers classified those women who maintained that their homemade soups were better than Campbell's as poor cooks.[23]

"When a Man Says It's Good . . . It's Good!"

Campbell's soup advertisements relied heavily on male authority. The ads used male images and pronouncements to convince women of the validity of their claims. From religious figures to scientists, chefs to husbands, they drew on male authority in a variety of fields and capacities to influence women's attitudes about convenience foods and gender roles.

Campbell's ads used professional authority to legitimize its soups in the early 1900s, which was possible because it did so at a time when the mass media was replacing "family wisdom as the major source of culinary advice for American housewives." Campbell's ads used references to and pictures of doctors and nurses to suggest that medically trained professionals endorsed their soups. One ad showed a nurse bringing soup to a woman resting, with the text below reading, "Every physician knows that such tomatoes are full of elements that promote digestion and purify and enrich the blood." Campbell's ads took full advantage of the influence of medical practitioners and their dietary admonitions.[24]

One of the most common assurances was that eating Campbell's soups worked as a "wholesome, healthful tonic to appetite and digestion." Campbell's ads from the late 1910s through the early 1930s, particularly in summer months, promised that their soup would make food digest better and yield more nutrition. Many of these ads based their appeals on a scientific understanding of food. In keeping with an overall effort to convince consumers of their quality and purity, the ads used science to assert that Campbell's soups were good for people's health. Even without official representatives mentioned or pictured, ads used scientific jargon like "fortified" and "energy-value" to affirm that Campbell's soup was good for the body.

The company also used chefs, the ultimate food authorities, to affirm that Campbell's soups were of the highest quality. A 1930 ad highlighted Campbell's "Head Chef Emeritus," a Frenchman who had supposedly cooked for Campbell's kitchens for twenty-seven years. The French government gave him an award "for having contributed in distinguished degree to the appreciation of the artistry of French cooking throughout the entire civilized world." Campbell's ads drew on the authority of French cooking and chefs and suggested that women who bought Campbell's soups could serve "the genius and art of the world's most famous chefs!" Women, however, never appeared as chefs, even though the ads dictated that women should be solely responsible for cooking.[25]

Ads also drew on the U.S. government and its representatives for expertise. A 1912 ad pictured a man carrying a piece of meat out of a meat locker and claimed the company made its beef soup with "whole quarters of fresh, high-grade beef, certified by the Government inspection stamp." This certification was important because of the negative exposure meat processing received in the early twentieth century, most infamously in Upton Sinclair's 1906 sensational novel, *The Jungle*. Ads had to pacify the fears and disgust raised about the health dangers posed by processed meat. During World War I, the Campbell Soup Company again found itself touting the approval of the U.S. government. For those women eager to do their part at home, ads asserted that by eating Campbell's soup, "You are in line with the urgent food requirements of our Government, and at the same time you meet an essential health requirement of your family in a most practical way."[26]

Ads also offered Campbell's soups as the perfect helpmate to pious women. They promoted a line of vegetarian soups to adherents of the religious tenet prohibiting consumption of meat on Fridays. In addition to promoting them as a Friday staple, the ads appealed to women to cook Campbell's vegetarian soups for Lent. More than merely presenting an option, they intimated that without Campbell's soups women would have difficulty providing delicious, nourishing meals because of the exclusion of meat. A 1930 ad presented Campbell's soups as women's savior, when it reassured them, "At such times when your choice seems more than ever limited and when your daily problem of serving fresh and attractive meals is intensified, how comforting and helpful to have these splendid soups at your command." No more subtle was a 1910 ad, titled "A Lenten Delicacy," which suggested, with a picture of a woman having lunch with a priest, that Campbell's tomato soup was of the highest order.[27]

The Campbell Soup Company occasionally relied on this deference to the male leadership of the Catholic faith to appeal across class lines. In the 1910s, the Curtis Publishing Company, which published the *Ladies' Home Journal* and the *Saturday Evening Post,* wanted to convince the Campbell company and other food manufacturers of the importance of advertising in their magazines. The study, conducted by researcher Charles Coolidge Parlin, found that "Campbell's soups knew no class. Everyone regardless of income ate one or more of the twenty-one varieties." In the first decade of the century, Campbell executives had thought, because of the prices they charged, that primarily the middle and upper classes bought their soups. Parlin's study demonstrated the company's broad appeal to the working class. The Campbell company realized, as Richard Ohmann observed, that "consumption is class specific, and advertising had to be so, too." Appealing to Catholic women by way of their priests and their piety began to make good economic sense. Therefore, while many ads continued to portray Campbell's soups being served in elegant settings, some ads reflected an open recognition that women of *all* classes were buying their product.[28]

Ads credit men with a great deal of authority for "knowing" good soup and good economic practices. A 1935 ad put it bluntly, "When a man says it's good . . . it's good!" The advertisers assumed that in normal American practice, women were constantly trying to gratify men with their cooking, while men sat in judgment. A 1911 ad quoted the adage "the way to a man's heart is through his stomach" and then added their twist, "And many a dainty young housewife has discovered that one of the easiest 'short cuts' is Campbell's Tomato Soup." In a 1912 ad, a husband and wife sit discussing homemade soup, with the headline "Don't tie yourself down to needless drudgery." The husband admonishes his wife, "I don't want you to live in the kitchen. Do as I do in business. Take advantage of modern ideas. Don't bother with homemade soup. Use Campbell's Soups." In these types of ads, men brought their outside business world authority to challenge women to be more modern and efficient. They gave approval to the store-bought product. So while in the modern world soup changed from homemade to store-bought, gender roles did not change.[29]

For married women, ads promised that Campbell's soups would please difficult-to-please husbands. Phyllis Palmer notes, "By the 1920s, women's magazines purveyed a picture of sexy, well-educated partners in companionate marriages." This trend was not reflected in Campbell's advertisements during the 1920s or 1930s, which had an altogether different view of marriage roles. Most ads featuring female-male relationships did not suggest a shared partnership, but instead featured discerning men being served by women. The ads portrayed men as emotionally immature, needing to be appeased or pampered. Ads promised that Campbell's soup would "stamp out grouchiness" or make him " 'snap out of it' . . . [until] he becomes an affable companion instead of just somebody at the other end of the table."[30]

"The Campbell Label Stands for Women's Rights"

To showcase the value of Campbell's soups, ads created the sense that homemakers were experts by empowering them, flattering them, and drawing attention to their expertise and experience in the kitchen. As early as 1906 the company asserted in an ad, "Housewives of America insist on these soups." Another early ad considered women part of the litany of experts, when they claimed, "A thousand judges — particular housewives, critical diners-out, expert chefs and others — all agree in favor of Campbell's Soups." An ad appearing in 1919 bore the headline "Common Sense Enlightening the World" and had a female Campbell Kid atop a Campbell's soup box posed as the Statue of Liberty, cleverly suggesting: "You probably know a great deal more about diet and food-values than your grandmother knew. Every intelligent housewife studies these questions now-a-days. But the most advanced ideas of today are after all plain common sense." The company created a type of expertise wherein an "experienced 'strategist' in meal-planning uses soup." Employing feminist principles, they suggested that women's judgment and experience were best applied when determining which Campbell's soup to cook.[31]

Ads appropriated feminist themes and deftly turned them into marketing tools. The Campbell Soup Company's manipulation of themes such as freedom, judgment, and skill enabled them to appeal to women's sense of themselves as independent actors. Throughout the period, their ads subverted women's assertiveness and freedom. Some ads, such as one in 1911, suggested that women demonstrate their autonomy by choosing which Campbell's soup to have. The ad assured women who were housecleaning and had no time to prepare a hearty meal: "Just think how independent you are when provided with Campbell's Soups. You can pick out exactly the 'kind' that appeals to you at the moment — the Tomato Soup, . . . the 'Ox Tail', . . . the Beef Soup, hearty and substantial, almost a meal in itself; or whatever you choose from the whole varied list." Many ads focused on the idea of escaping housework, like the 1939 ad that declared, "Wise ladies are closing up their kitchens, and faring forth to freedom. There's worlds of good in a half-day off; you'll find it's so, if you try it. And it's easy — far easier than you may think."[32]

Ads appearing in the late 1910s and the early 1920s occasionally combined the changing public role of women and suffrage themes. They reduced these political aims into support for Campbell's soup. A 1922 ad used a female Campbell Kid marching in a parade holding a placard with the header "Our Candidate." The candidate was a can of tomato soup and below the picture of the can it read: "Stands for health and happy homes." Into the 1930s ads appeared with reminders that "The Campbell label stands for women's rights to carefree summers." These types of ads often appeared in the summer months when the heat of the kitchen made it especially uncomfortable to cook. Advertisements suggested that the goal of the women's rights movement was to achieve the right to leisure, rather than political equality. Using words like *independence* and *freedom*, advertisements co-opted meaningful political ideology and used it to sell Campbell's soup. They hoped to diffuse the threat of women's aspirations into more traditional pursuits.[33]

Using these varied approaches, ads appealed to women to embrace their traditional duties as wife, mother, homemaker, and hostess. The ads assured women that Campbell's soups would enable them to achieve success in each role. Campbell's creation of a market niche and its subsequent endurance in the American marketplace owes a great deal to its successful manipulation of women's imaginations. Advertising could not dictate the behavior of the prewar American woman, but Campbell's ads encouraged women's actions in ways they hoped would benefit the company. Not only did advertising messages have to be palatable to prevailing attitudes but, more important, they had to protect profits actively by making women's aspirations and fears as predictable as possible. Despite shifting social conditions, the Campbell Soup Company marketed their soups to women and enforced the notion that women should be solely responsible for shopping and cooking. While the company did not create this division of labor that made women consumers and cooks, it did capitalize on it. Campbell's soup ads exploited traditional gender ideals to persuade girls and women not only to buy their products but also to buy their vision of how women ought to live and work.

Notes

Special thanks to Chris DeRosa, Margaret Marsh, Herbert Ershkowitz, Allen Davis, Julie Berebitsky, Nancy Banks, and Frank Hoeber for their thoughtful comments and suggestions.

1. *Ladies' Home Journal* (*LHJ*), October 1921, 27.

2. In addition to the *LHJ*, Campbell's advertisements also appeared in magazines such as *American Magazine, Collier's, Delineator, Good Housekeeping, Harper's Bazaar, McCall's, Pictorial Review, Saturday Evening Post*, and *Woman's Home Companion*. There were no significant differences between the content of food ads placed in various magazines during this period.

3. In 1921, the Joseph Campbell Company was dissolved. It was bought and renamed the Campbell Soup Company. Between 1913 and 1928 the Campbell Soup Company spent $17,892,455 on magazine advertising, making it the top-ranking food advertiser in the nation. *Crowell Magazine's National Advertising Department: National Markets and National Advertising, 1928* (New York: Crowell, 1928), 15.

4. Alice Kessler-Harris, *Out to Work: A History of Wage-Earning Women in the United States* (New York: Oxford University Press, 1982); Susan Porter Benson, "Living on the Margin: Working-Class Marriages and Family Survival Strategies in the United States, 1919–1941," in *The Sex of Things: Gender and Consumption in Historical Perspective*, ed. Victoria de Grazia with Ellen Furlough (Berkeley: University of California Press, 1996), 212–43. See also Jennifer Scanlon, *Inarticulate Longings* (New York: Routledge, 1995), for her discussion of women's housework and paid work.

5. Catharine E. Beecher, *A Treatise on Domestic Economy for the Use of Young Ladies at Home, and at School* (New York: Harper, 1845); Charlotte Perkins Gilman, *Women and Economics* (New York: Harper and Row, 1966); Dolores Hayden, *The Grand Domestic Revolution: A History of Feminist Designs for American Homes, Neighborhoods, and Cities* (Cambridge: MIT Press, 1981); Kathryn Kish Sklar, *Catharine Beecher: A Study in American Domesticity* (New Haven: Yale University Press, 1973).

6. Ruth Schwartz Cowan, *More Work for Mother: The Ironies of Household Technology from the Open Hearth to the Microwave* (New York: Basic Books, 1993); Roland Marchand, *Advertising the American Dream: Making Way for Modernity, 1920–1940* (Berkeley: University of California Press, 1985); *LHJ*, December 1926.

7. James D. Norris, *Advertising and the Transformation of American Society, 1865–1920* (Westport, Conn.: Greenwood Press, 1990), 92.

8. Douglas Collins, *America's Favorite Food: The Story of Campbell Soup Company* (New York: Harry N. Abrams, 1994), 47–53; *LHJ*, November 1909, 39; *LHJ*, February 1914, 53; *LHJ*, April 1921, 27.

9. *LHJ*, February 1906, 28; *LHJ*, August 1913, 24; *LHJ*, August 1915, 47; *LHJ*, June 1917, 31; *LHJ*, January 1935, 29.

10. *LHJ*, May 1, 1911, 33; *LHJ*, July 1912, 21.

11. *LHJ*, December 1916, 35; *LHJ*, July 1935, 31. While the Campbell Kids

changed from ad to ad, their race remained constant. The Kids were always white. In the late nineteenth and early twentieth centuries, several food manufacturers used either black adults or black children as symbols of their products and found success with characters based on racist stereotypes. The ads for Knox Gelatin and Konelia's Kinks Flakes are just two examples of the tendency for food manufacturers to use African Americans as symbols of their companies. The only soups Campbell's illustrated with an African American woman cooking them are pepper pot (colonial Philadelphia) and chicken gumbo ("old" New Orleans), and even these rarely appeared. For nearly forty years, the Campbell Soup Company had virtually no black people in their ads. Those who did appear were always servants, and they were realistic drawings of people, never Campbell Kids. See also Marilyn Kern-Foxworth, *Aunt Jemima, Uncle Ben, and Rastus: Blacks in Advertising, Yesterday, Today, and Tomorrow* (Westport, Conn.: Greenwood Press, 1994).

12. *LHJ*, May 15, 1911, 1; *LHJ*, September 1916, 33; *LHJ*, October 1919, 35; *LHJ*, February 1920, 33; *LHJ*, October 1920, 33; *Saturday Evening Post*, September 19, 1937, 126; *LHJ*, July 1938, 31; Marchand, *Advertising*, 228–32.

13. *LHJ*, June 1917, 31; *LHJ*, April 1917, 29; *LHJ*, November 1933, 33; *LHJ*, April 1935, 39.

14. *LHJ*, February 1932, 25.

15. *LHJ*, May 1927, 41.

16. *Saturday Evening Post*, December 7, 1912, 49; *LHJ*, March 1913, 95; *LHJ*, April 1914, 71; *LHJ*, March 1915, 57. Ostensibly to help women be good homemakers, the company created menu books that contained recipes, meal planners, and guidance on how to present their meals. These gimmicks offered women lessons on homemaking etiquette and technique, replete with reminders to always use Campbell's soups. The home economics movement complemented Campbell's efforts by encouraging women to cook by the book and placing a great deal of importance on being good homemakers. Many women sent for manufacturers' compilations of recipes, the most popular form of promotional material. One early menu book promised, "A refined, well appointed home table gives a recognized social standing which money alone will not achieve, among people who are worthwhile." To help women achieve an elegant, cultured home, menu books prescribed the correct room temperature, the appropriate styles of serving meals, and the importance of serving soup every day. Susan Strasser, *Satisfaction Guaranteed: The Making of the American Mass Market* (New York: Pantheon Books, 1989), 131; *Campbell's Menu Book* (Camden, N.J.: Joseph Campbell Company, 1910), 3; Collins, *America's Favorite Book*, 90.

17. Richard Hooker, *Food and Drink in America: A History* (Indianapolis: Bobbs-Merrill, 1981), 214; *LHJ*, March 1923, 35.

18. Collins, 110; *LHJ*, September 11, 1909, 41.

19. "The Story of Campbell's Soup," *The Optimist* (Camden, N.J.: Joseph Campbell Company, 1922); *LHJ*, September 1913, 42; *LHJ*, August 1917, 37; *LHJ*, June 1920, 33. These claims were especially important because of the scrutiny placed on food after the passage of the Pure Food Act in 1906.

20. Warshaw Collection #60, Food, box 3, folder 36, National Museum of American History, Washington, D.C.; *LHJ*, August 1915, 47; *LHJ*, February 1919, 33.

21. *LHJ*, May 1, 1911, 33; *LHJ*, 1919, 31; *LHJ*, 1920, 33.

22. *LHJ*, February 1918, 29; *LHJ*, May 1927, 41; *LHJ*, November 1931, 31; *LHJ*, July 1935, 31.

23. *Saturday Evening Post*, January 14, 1933; *American Magazine*, February 1936; *American Magazine*, March 1936; *Woman's Home Companion*, October 1936; *Pictorial Review*, October 1936.

24. *Collier's*, November, 1925, 33; *LHJ*, July 1910, 27; *LHJ*, May 1, 1911, 33; *LHJ*, April 1915, 69; *LHJ*, February 1917, 29; *LHJ*, April 1917, 29; *LHJ*, March 1918, 25; *LHJ*, June 1918, 31; *LHJ*, May 1919, 29; *LHJ*, August 1919, 31; *LHJ*, October 1919, 35; *LHJ*, March 1920, 33; *LHJ*, May 1927, 41; *LHJ*, May 1930, 39; *LHJ*, November 1931, 31; T. J. Jackson Lears, *Fables of Abundance: A Cultural History of Advertising in America* (New York: Basic Books, 1994), 157–58; Harvey Levenstein, *Paradox of Plenty: A Social History of Eating in Modern America* (New York: Oxford University Press, 1993), 31; Norris, 108.

25. *LHJ*, December 1913, 59; *LHJ*, May 1920, 33; *LHJ*, May 1930, 39.

26. *Saturday Evening Post*, July 1918, 21; *LHJ*, December 1912, 30; *LHJ*, December 1917, 31; *LHJ*, January 1919, 27; *LHJ*, February 1919, 33; *LHJ*, June 1919, 31; Upton Sinclair, *The Jungle* (New York: New American Library, c. 1906, 1960); Juliann Sivulka, *Soap, Sex, and Cigarettes: A Cultural History of Advertising* (Belmont, Calif.: Wadsworth, 1998).

27. *LHJ*, March 1910, 33; *LHJ*, March 1929, 39; *LHJ*, April 1930, 39; *LHJ*, March 1931, 33.

28. Collins, 89–90; Charles Coolidge Parlin, "Garbage Dump Marks Long Ago Beginnings of Market Research," *Advertising Age*, April 1980, 68; Charles Coolidge Parlin, "Dry Waste Survey Presentation" (post-1911), Curtis Publishing Company, Special Collections, Van Pelt Library, University of Pennsylvania, Philadelphia; Richard Ohmann, *Selling Culture* (London: Verso, 1996), 114.

29. *LHJ*, April 15, 1911; Campbell's Archives, List "B" Ad, February 17, 1912; *Saturday Evening Post*, September 21, 1921; *American Magazine*, May 1935.

30. Levenstein, 36; Phyllis Palmer, *Domesticity and Dirt: Housewives and Domestic Servants in the United States, 1920–1945* (Philadelphia: Temple University Press, 1989), 7; *LHJ*, March 1910, 33; *LHJ*, April 15, 1911, 1; *LHJ*, July 1911, 38; *LHJ*, June 1913, 36; *LHJ*, January 1916, 48; *LHJ*, January 1918, 25; *LHJ*, April 1935, 39.

31. *Country Life in America*, February 1906, 462; F. Wallis Armstrong Co., Advertising Agents, North American Building, Philadelphia, Ad Sheet no. 569X, Campbell Soup Company Archives; *LHJ*, July 1919, 31; *LHJ*, November 1926, 33.

32. Norris, 94; Stuart Ewen, *Captains of Consciousness: Advertising and the Social Roots of the Consumer Culture* (New York: McGraw-Hill, 1976), 160; *LHJ*, April 1, 1911, 48; *LHJ*, July 1939, 35.

33. *LHJ*, November 1920, 31; *American Magazine*, 1922; *Saturday Evening Post*, April 14, 1937.

"Now Then—Who Said Biscuits?"

The Black Woman Cook as Fetish in American Advertising, 1905–1953

ALICE A. DECK

One of the prevailing images of black women in American culture that has persisted since the early days of slavery is that of the quintessential cook and housekeeper. In novels,[1] films,[2] television sitcoms, and print ads for cooking products, the black domestic is portrayed as a very large, dark earth mother who represents fecundity, self-sufficiency, and endless succor. This black cook/domestic, often referred to as Mammy,[3] exists to do nothing but prepare and serve food, along with a hearty helping of her homespun wisdom about life, to her own black family and to the white families for whom she works. Mammy's legendary creativity with preparing food is attributed to her "magical" powers with blending just the right foods and spices to delight those whom she feeds. The black cook, according to both popular imagery and culinary historians, works best not from printed recipes but from a memory that links her to previous generations of slave women and black earth mothers.[4] Given her propensity for improvisation, to "add a little of this and a little of that" as the spirit may move her on a given day, the same dish never tastes exactly the same no matter how many times she may prepare it.[5] Though she is sometimes portrayed in the popular media with a black male companion, Mammy's large breasts, muscular arms, and wide hips signify a unifying of male and female sexualities. She usually needs no other to complete her, yet many others in her orbit can be completed by her. All of this renders the black Mammy, as we see her depicted in American popular culture, as a fetish — an idealized representation of an autonomous black woman.

By examining what William O'Barr refers to as the secondary discourse in several advertisements for flour, pancake flour, and baking powder published between 1905 and 1953 in American newspapers and magazines,[6] we can read the idealized representations of the black cook as fetishism that is overdetermined by the class, gender, and race politics in American social discourse. In two of the ads, the fetish works in the nineteenth-century sense of anything that is irrationally worshiped, as was the mythic Mammy figure in postbellum southern white literature. In most of the ads, the black cook also serves as a cross-cultural fetish; she is the idealized postbellum bridge across the great Civil War divide between the plantation South and the industrialized North. Related to this fostering of cultural nondifference is the sexual nondifference of Mammy fetishism in these ads. The black cook in four of the ads exudes a masculine energy that attracts the white housewife who, left alone while her husband works outside of the home, feels safe in her Mammy's care and culinary tutelage. As most white American households could not actually afford a live-in cook, advertisers of certain processed foods engaged in commodity fetishism whereby the black cook's face appeared on the box of pancake flour to suggest that she would be going home with the consumer as a spiritual guide during the cooking process. The Aunt Jemima pancake flour box thus represents a symbolic social relationship between a white housewife and a black cook, which exists apart from that between the box and the manufacturer. In three of the ads discussed in this chapter, the white housewife gradually becomes as capable a cook as her Mammy; after this transformation, the black woman's physical presence in the ad shrinks into a tangible symbol (a face on the box of pancake flour, a Mammy doll, and various Mammy-imaged kitchenware items, for example), a concrete "idea" that the white woman can fondle in private but not have to compete with for culinary dominance of her own kitchen.

During the first decade of the twentieth century, the Washburn-Crosby milling company ran a series of black-and-white ads for its Gold Medal flour that featured a black woman dressed as a Mammy, standing next to either a large sack of flour or a table laden with breads, cakes, and pies that she

Fig. 3.1. "Now then — Who said Biscuits?" Advertisement for Gold Medal flour, 1906 copyright. Published by St. Nicholas Advertisements, 1910. Collection of Alice Deck.

presumably baked. In all of its primary and secondary details, a 1910 publication of the ad (fig. 3.1) exemplifies the idealized representation of the black woman cook as a cross-cultural fetish. Primarily, the ad attempts to convey the idea that no matter which of the particular American regional recipes used, one can make superior biscuits with Gold Medal flour. It appeals to the potential buyer's sense of belonging to a nation unified by a particular type of baked bread. Yet the secondary discourse emerging from the specific details of this particular picture relies on the viewer's familiarity with the nineteenth-century idealization of the southern black Mammy — wearing a white bandanna and a checkered apron — as the sole authority on baking biscuits. The black woman stands alone in this ad with only the large sack of flour and a tabletop. The isolation from other people signifies her autonomy, yet she is tied to the white sack of flour by the visual similarities between its tied ends and the tips of her white bandanna. Hence she is as much defined as a cook by her relationship to the flour sack as she exemplifies the image of reflexivity — her Mammy costume is the signifier of itself as autonomous agency.

An integral part of the Mammy's attire is the broad smile displaying clean, even, white teeth because it suggests not only a cheerful personality but also pleasure in what she does. This cheerful aspect actually works to counterbalance the potentially aggressive signals contained in the pointed ends of her bandanna and the sharp angles of her elbows and hands. Her right index finger points toward the viewer but, like her gaze, is at an angle as though to soften the implied command/reprimand. Her left hand is balled into a fist placed on her left hip, which, in other contexts, could suggest anger, defiance, or a sassy retort. In the context of the caption at the top of the frame ("Now then — Who said Biscuits?"), the woman's body language suggests a friendly command to use the product or even a friendly challenge to a biscuit bake-off using Gold Medal flour. Not only is the black woman the only person pictured in the ad, she dominates the right side of the ad's frame such that her left elbow can barely be contained within the black border. All of this says that the black woman is a powerful, uncontested authority on baking biscuits and we had better trust her endorsement of the product.

In a 1905 ad for Gold Medal flour that appeared in the July issue of *McClure's Magazine* (fig. 3.2), the same woman is photographed in the same costume on the left side of the frame and cropped at an angle that draws our attention to Mammy's broad shoulders and the width of her hips. In contrast to the taller, more angular image of figure 3.1, in this one the Mammy's spherical shape emphasizes her womanly fecundity and nurturing skills. Her large arms are posed to suggest that she could cradle the potential consumer and viewer of the ad next to her ample bosom. In contrast to the sharp points on the bandanna in figure 3.1, the ends of Mammy's bandanna in figure 3.2 are short, small, and suggestive of a soft bow on the top of her head. It is the mark of a female being who, in the context of the message written below the picture, personifies the natural forces of the physical body. The language in this ad commingles scientific, dietary, and psychological vocabularies, and it plays upon this multilayered variability. Specifically, the ambiguity of the word *nature*, as it was understood at this time, allows the advertisers to easily "slip"

Fig. 3.2. "Good Bread—Good Nature." Advertisement for Gold Medal flour. *McClure's Magazine,* July 1905, 1.

from one meaning system to another, a characteristic of the fetish. *Nature* in this ad references bodily functions, physical strength, vitality, and humor, and implies its sexual connotations. "Good food, good digestion, and good nature go hand in hand. Nearly all good natured people use Gold Medal Flour." Reference to good waste elimination is the absent presence in the former sentence. Any food that is good for one's digestion also aids the body with waste elimnation and this in turn, the ad implies, fortifies one's physical strength and the power of one's other bodily fluids.[7] The words *hand in hand* refer to a coupling of the benefits of good food, good digestion, and good nature, but they imply as well the coupling of people. In light of this and the caption above Mammy's bandanna-covered head that links good bread with good nature, her wide smile in this instance suggests that she is in on the joke about sexual potency. She is good-natured herself, according to the prevailing stereotype of black women's fecundity and joviality, and baking bread with an ingredient she endorses assures the consumer of maintaining this aspect of one's constitution.

The two representations of the black woman cook in these particular ads for Gold Medal flour show us a full breasted, wide-hipped female whose large, muscular, and potentially aggressive arms generate a male energy and strength. The white bandannas in both ads hide her hair, decreasing any hint of femininity and increasing her sexual nondifference. Devoid of any other people and set not in a kitchen but against a gray backdrop signifying an ethereal supremacy, these ads suggest that this black woman is above laboring to prepare and serve food. Instead, the two captions pictured over her bandanna-covered head read as the commanding voice of omniscience. Her confidence, self-sufficiency, physical strength, and infectious gaiety are all apparently as abundant as the flour in the large sack. She is appealing in that she promises the satisfaction of hunger for warm bread and for sexual hungers not yet felt.

The overall appearance of the black woman in the two ads for Gold Medal flour draws on another one first used to sell pancake flour at the World's Columbian Exposition of May–November 1893 in Chicago. There, a woman named Nancy Green was hired by the Davis Milling Company to mix a processed pancake flour and cook pancakes on an open griddle. Nancy Green was padded to fill out her physique and then attired in a full-skirted dress and a white apron, with a bandanna tied around her head. She answered to the name of Aunt Jemima, and while cooking pancakes, she greeted guests, sang songs, and told stories of life ("her past life") on a Louisiana plantation. The Aunt Jemima exhibit attracted large crowds, and many merchants who attended placed orders for the pancake flour. After the exposition, Nancy Green, as

Aunt Jemima, began participating in sales promotions across the country.[8] An image of her face was placed on the outside of the box containing the pancake flour that to this day bears the name of Aunt Jemima.

Of particular relevance to this chapter is the contextualizing "life story" of Aunt Jemima that was created as early as 1895 and printed in the thousands of ads and pamphlets that were distributed nationally. Aunt Jemima, according to her "biographers," was a slave before the Civil War on a Louisiana plantation owned by Colonel Higbee. After the war, she chose to remain on the plantation as Colonel Higbee's cook, and she took pleasure in serving her famous pancakes to the many guests who came to visit. Missing from this "biography" of Aunt Jemima is any mention of a wife for Colonel Higbee. One study suggests that the creators of the Aunt Jemima legend wanted the white woman consumer to insert herself into the story as Colonel Higbee's wife and the mistress of his plantation, to imagine herself being waited on by contented black servants and a doting husband.[9] My own reading of this omission is based on the historical accounts of the relationship between the southern white master and black women slaves who were assigned to work in his house. It was sometimes a relationship based on sexual coercion due in part to a tacit agreement among white southern men that a gentleman, no matter his wife's protests against it, was entitled to have a paramour.[10] Other reasons include the death or infertility of the white mistress or, if she had given birth to children, her subsequent disinterest in sex.[11] The absence of any references to Colonel Higbee's wife in the legend merely foregrounds a historical reality that some southern white women relinquished many of their conjugal and domestic duties to a female slave, including feeding their infants, children, and husbands. This white-wife gap in the legend allows Aunt Jemima to serve alone as Colonel Higbee's mistress. She, as his uncontested female subordinate, satisfied his desire to be fed on her limitless supply of warm food, personal devotion, and loyalty. The effect all of this may have had on white women who read the legend of Aunt Jemima in the turn-of-the-century ads for the processed pancake flour was a desire not just to hire a black cook but to replace Aunt Jemima altogether as the primary source of Colonel Higbee's nourishment.

Aunt Jemima's loyalty to Colonel Higbee was without bounds. According to the version of the legend printed on a 1926 ad appearing in the *Pictorial Review*, she never revealed her secret recipe for her famous pancakes until after Colonel Higbee died. She then sold it to the representative of a northern milling company, which developed it into a product that people all over the United States could use to make pancakes as good as those made originally by

Aunt Jemima. Aunt Jemima agreed to attend the Columbian Exposition in 1893, and to travel the country selling the pancake flour for the milling company afterwards, out of the goodness of her heart and an earnest desire to help Americans enjoy their breakfasts.

In his *Slave in a Box: The Strange Career of Aunt Jemima*, M. M. Manring explains that this legend encompassed an idea about the Old South and its usefulness to the new post–Civil War United States. The Old South, as imagined by postbellum white southerners in their diaries and letters, was a place of white leisure, an abundance of well-prepared food, and a host of contented black people who did all of the work.[12] The imaginary Old South did not disappear after the Civil War, primarily because of ad campaigns that featured people like Aunt Jemima and Rastus, the black man on the Cream of Wheat cereal box, who were so dedicated to domesticity in the service of white people; hence the Old South was a New South only in its desire to share its culture with northern white entrepreneurs and to forget any cultural and political differences that may have led to the Civil War. Unlike the millions of blacks who migrated north beginning in the late nineteenth century through the first three decades of the twentieth century, Aunt Jemima never tried to forget her southern culture and assimilate into the northern urban lifestyle. She sold her pancake flour out of a belief that southern "down home" cooking could be adapted to a northern, faster paced lifestyle and retain its high standards of nourishment.

The 1920 ad for Aunt Jemima pancake flour (fig. 3.3) directs our attention to the social discourse on the role of women during the modern era in America. The home economics movement during the Victorian era and the first two decades of the twentieth century emphasized the "science" of taking care of a home.[13] Each decade introduced more and more labor-saving appliances and processed food products so that by the 1920s, women were expected to devote all of their creative energies to cooking (from a recipe), cleaning, and taking care of the children, while the American man worked outside of the home. The ad for Aunt Jemima pancake flour appearing in the *Pictorial Review* for March 1920 presents an interesting commingling of messages about labor, economics, and domesticity as related to black and white Americans. The caption at the top of the ad laments: "Poor Aunt Jemima Had to Mix Everything Herself!" We see an elderly Aunt Jemima concentrating on pouring and stirring some milk into a bowl. The counter in front of her is cluttered with a number of flour sacks and bags of all sizes, a large pitcher, and a smaller bowl. An elderly black man dressed as a butler is carrying a tray loaded with a steaming beverage, cups, and saucers. He is standing

Fig. 3.3. "Poor Aunt Jemima Had to Mix Everything Herself!" Advertisement, *Pictorial Review*, March 1920, 63.

before a door suggesting that he is about to carry the tray into the next room to serve whomever is there. Though advanced in age, Aunt Jemima and the butler are both still physically strong and smiling, but not at one another. They seem to be focused on the bowl of pancake batter either in anticipation of its end product or out of a sheer joy of preparing and serving food. In the lower half of the ad we see a young white couple also standing in a kitchen. The

Alice A. Deck

young husband holds a newspaper and wears a vested suit suggesting a white-collar job in an office. His gaze on his wife suggests admiration, a genuine interest in her, and satisfaction that she is preparing his breakfast. The young wife wears a soft-colored dress, and stands before an uncluttered counter mixing batter in a bowl. The box of pancake flour bearing Aunt Jemima's picture sits near a plate of pancakes the young wife has presumably just prepared. As a labor-saving device, the processed pancake flour allows the white housewife the "luxury" of engaging her husband in a conversation or at least in an exchange of smiles and eye contact while she mixes the batter, whereas Aunt Jemima has to stay focused on her mixing with her back to the butler because she is working from the original, memorized recipe she created.

The variability of the word *poor* in the ad's caption both succeeds and fails to stabilize the economic and social differences between the black and white cooks. It is intended to evoke pity for the humble Aunt Jemima who had to work so hard at mixing her original recipe for pancakes and to emphasize the low economic status of the old black couple. The potential consumer of the Aunt Jemima pancake flour, like the young white housewife in the lower half of the ad, is supposed to feel grateful for the modern conveniences in her kitchen, such as the processed pancake flour, that free her from having to work so long and hard at preparing breakfast. Yet the older black couple pictured in the ad genuinely enjoy what they are doing and do not ask for pity. In fact, they have an abundance of energy, and Aunt Jemima is able to provide nourishment to those whom she feeds with her pancakes. This comes across in the interesting juxtaposition of the pitcher of milk she is holding and her large breasts; it is as if this key ingredient in her pancake batter is flowing from her.[14] In fact, an earlier 1918 ad appearing in the *Ladies' Home Journal* suggests this very thing about the milk already in Aunt Jemima pancake mix: Everything is already mixed in the flour. You are spared even the trouble and expense "of adding milk, for the Aunt Jemima people have gone to a great deal of expense, a great deal of trouble to evaporate all the moisture from sweet milk, so that it can be 'ready-mixed' in powdered form with the flour" (70). Apparently Aunt Jemima did more for the representatives from the northern milling company than just sell them her secret recipe for pancake mix. She gave of herself and at a great deal of expense, which adds another connotation to the words "Poor Aunt Jemima . . ." at the top of the ad. The idea that it is Aunt Jemima's own milk in the pancake mix is also suggested by the rest of the narrative in the 1920 ad, which proclaims: "The flour is so rich it needs no eggs, the milk is already in it." The young, modern housewife pictured in the lower half of the ad is standing in front of an uncluttered counter, with a kettle of boiling water on the stove behind her. "A little of the flour — a little water — a moment's mixing — and your golden-brown pancakes are done almost as soon as you start!" If she is to satisfy her husband's hungers, the ad suggests that the young wife can (and must) access Aunt Jemima's sweet liquid "magic," which is already in the mix, because she herself is not as succulent. Which of the two women pictured in this particular ad, then, is truly "poor"?

Literally, "the Aunt Jemima people" in the 1918 caption refers to the Aunt Jemima Mills Company, which produced the pancake flour from 1914 until 1926, when it was then sold to the Quaker Oats Company. By using the phrase "the Aunt Jemima people," a slippage occurs between the literal milling company (whose assembly-line workers were mostly white women immigrants)[15] and Aunt Jemima's people, implying the contented blacks who labored with Aunt Jemima on the fictional Higbee plantation. Moreover, by referring to itself as "the Aunt Jemima people," the company lays claim to the black woman as an idealized and displaced image of itself — a fetish. The company desires that others desire Aunt Jemima, thus rendering its product into a commodity fetish, one that consumers such as the white couple in the 1920 ad can carry home. Like most Americans of the time, the young couple cannot afford to hire a cook and butler, so the picture of Aunt Jemima on the box of processed pancake flour serves a psychological need both to believe they have access to a black cook and to reassure themselves of their higher economic status. In rendering itself into a commodity fetish, the Aunt Jemima Mills Company capitalizes on the white American desire for class distinctions from black servants and for a sense of itself as modernized in contrast to old-fashioned cooking methods.

Aunt Jemima, as fetish, serves as a spiritual guide for the American cook in ads from the 1920s. The box of Aunt Jemima pancake flour also serves as a cross-cultural fetish. It is a material object believed to bridge the span of time between the old plantation South and the modern North. Commodity fetishism comes out in these ads in that Aunt Jemima's southern magic for making pancakes is packaged in a container bearing her image. The northern white housewife then carries home the material box of pancake flour and the magic it contains to help her in the kitchen because she cannot afford, or manage to hire and keep, a good cook and servant. The social meaning of the fetish is useful in understanding the implied message about class and race relations in America as portrayed in 1920 ads for Aunt Jemima pancake flour. As Marcia Ian explains, using William Pietz's theory, the fetish depends for its meaning and value on a particular order of social relations, which it, in turn, reinforces.[16] The fetishization of the black cook in American advertising for cooking and baking products reinforced the social position of white middle-class America as higher than that of black people, because it conveyed the idea that the black woman as the superior cook was actually a labor-saving device for whites. As she did during slavery, the black cook pictured in ads for baking products continued to serve white society's needs. During the 1920s, it was a combined need for the white woman to emerge as a good cook who remained at home and a determination to keep the black woman in a lower social status symbolized by her reduced size on material objects such as the packages containing pancake flour.

The Great Depression of the 1930s put millions of American men out of work. This challenge to the American man's image of himself as the primary provider for his family meant that even if the American woman was able to find work outside of the home, she was rarely hired. Society insisted even more than in the previous decade that the woman's true place was in the home, making do with her husband's meager salary. Many college-educated women rebelled against this by pursuing a career and not getting married at all or, if they were married, insisting on finding work to help feed the family. In the latter case, the working wife and mother had to contend with the condemnation of other women who argued that she was unfairly competing with men who had families to support: "Panicked by economic disaster, both men and women once again made woman a scapegoat. It was almost an automatic reflex, propelled by economic self-interest and sexual stereotype, against which rational argument cried like a small voice inside a mob."[17] Although women almost never displaced men from jobs during the Depression and the female unemployment rate increased during the 1930s as the male rate fell, society wanted to blame the job-seeking woman for the crisis of high unemployment.

American advertisers supported the prevailing social ideology of the 1930s that woman belonged at home. American families could not afford domestic servants during the Depression, so Aunt Jemima continued to appear in American newspapers and magazines providing succor and nourishment to a nation under economic stress, the ever-happy cook willing to assist the American housewife with feeding the family a meal that was inexpensive and easy to prepare. In a 1936 ad for Aunt Jemima buckwheat pancake flour, we see a large, brown-skinned black woman standing in a field of buckwheat. Reminiscent of the late nineteenth- and early twentieth-century gestures of actors in American minstrel shows, Aunt Jemima shows us the whites of her eyes and teeth as she smiles up at the box of buckwheat pancake mix that she is holding in her right hand. Her left open palm rests on her left hip. The caption above her head, intended to represent a southern folksy black dialect, invites America to celebrate national buckwheat week. This clarion call for a national celebration is emphasized with a representation of the Capitol in Washington, D.C., in the background over Aunt Jemima's left shoulder. To facilitate the celebration of national buckwheat week, the ad includes three menus in the right-hand corner that feature buckwheat pancakes. "I'se fixed you up some very special celebratin' menus, too. They's Magic Menus, guaranteed to be very aggravatin' to the appetite." A three-frame inset placed on the left side of the ad shows Aunt Jemima sharing some of her magic by teaching a young white actress how to make buckwheat pancakes with the ready mix. It is an idealized representation of black and white women in 1930s America. While both women are smiling to indicate their pleasure in teaching and learning food preparation, Aunt Jemima's authority in the situation is emphasized by the fact that she is the only one whose "voice" we hear in the ad extolling the great taste of buckwheat pancakes. She is also the only one holding a cooking utensil as she teaches the young actress how easy it is to prepare pancakes. The fact that she occupies more physical space in the frames than does the "sweet little lady from the Broadway Show 'Boy Meets Girl,' " facilitates our noticing the vast physical differences between the two women. The voiceless white actress, dressed in a suit and hat, represents a woman who works outside of the home, while Aunt Jemima's costume represents a servant who has been working in white homes since slavery days. The white woman actually has a career on stage, hence her presence in the ad learning to make pancakes shows society's opinion of where this woman should be spending most of her time — at home in the kitchen. To encourage this entertainer to stay at home, this ad plays on a desire for emotional fulfillment and human connections that domesticity was purported to provide. Aunt Jemima assures her that the pancakes are as easy to prepare as "One! Two! Three!" Yet there is an undertone of condescension toward the "sweet little" white female as though she were just another "dumb blonde" incapable of understanding anything that requires her to count above the number three. The white woman is "sweet" and therefore malleable and not likely to resist being domesticated. Her smaller physique suggests the ideal size for a "feminine" woman who nonetheless needs the black cook's nourishment.

In the lower right-hand corner of the same ad we see a small picture of another well-dressed white woman standing before a display case of Aunt Jemima pancake mix. Aunt Jemima's large, smiling face on the display case is strategically situated lower than that of the smaller head of the white woman. This assures the potential consumer that regardless of Aunt Jemima's culinary superiority, she is still a servant who occupies a lower social class than that of the well-dressed white woman. Yet the white woman's bent neck as she stands before the display can be read either of two ways. She is indeed condescending to Aunt Jemima from her higher social position as she reads the pancake box, or she is bowing her head as a gesture of respect and reverence — if not for the lower-class black woman, then for the black woman's magic believed to be contained in the processed pancake flour she clutches in her hands. To the left of the display is a quote from Aunt Jemima intended to assure potential buyers of her support in their cooking endeavors: "You'll see my smilin' picture next time you goes to the grocery store. Look for me, 'cause I'll have right next to me all the fixin's you need for my swell Magic Menus." Hence, like the message contained in the 1920 ad, we see the fetishization of a black cook for purposes of using her magic in the service of domesticating the white middle-class woman. The 1936 ad goes one step further to show Aunt Jemima's compliance in this sociopolitical scheme. By identifying with the idealized and displaced image of herself on the grocery story display, Aunt Jemima in this ad shows that she desires to be the object of the white woman's desire.

At the top of the six-frame narrative cartoon advertising Calumet baking powder (fig. 3.4), we see an artist's rendition of a smiling Kate Smith holding a small Mammy doll that is dressed in a checkered bandanna, an apron, and a full skirt. It is yet another example of the objectification of a black woman cook for purposes of sustaining the higher social status of white women. This 1939 ad entitled "Kate Smith's Mammy Doll" ran in *Needlecraft*. Kate Smith, the popular singer and radio personality, appeared in three Hollywood films: *The Big Broadcast* in 1932, *Hello Everybody*, and *Hollywood on Parade*, both in 1933. She also starred in three stage musicals: *Honeymoon Lane* in 1928, *Hit the Deck* in 1928, and *Flying High* in 1930. Her live radio shows, which began airing in 1931, were sponsored by A&P Coffee from 1934 through 1936. Then in 1937 the General Foods Corporation began sponsoring the *Kate Smith Hour*, a variety show also broadcast live on radio, during which Kate would sing, interview celebrities, and do commercials for Swans Down cake flour and Calumet baking powder. Popularly known as the Songbird of the South, the buxom singer never married. She always had a cook and a maid to take care of her own chores so that she could meet the demands of her career.[18] Nevertheless, her long association with General Foods baking products contributed to her very popular image as a "bluesy" singer whose passion for cooking and serving well-prepared full-course meals to relatives and friends emanated from her very large physique. On one level we could read this 1939 ad for Calumet baking powder as an early example of the type of celebrity

Fig. 3.4. "Kate Smith's Mammy doll."
Advertisement for Calumet baking powder. *Needlecraft*, 1939.

endorsement of a product that American advertisers continue to use as a way
to sell anything from milk, to Jell-O, to Coca-Cola, to whiskey, to Hertz rental
cars and sport attire. In the context of this discussion of the fetishization of the
black Mammy, however, this ad clearly shows how the General Foods Corporation assisted in perpetuating the dominant social ideology of white female

domesticity by appealing to the desires of the white American housewife to learn to cook as well as, if not better than, a black domestic servant.

The narrative in the 1939 ad for Calumet baking powder reads as the female version of the Oedipal desire to slay the father in order to take his place in the mother's affections. Only here it is the desire of the white "daughter" to slay the black "mother" in order to take her place in the white husband's affections for a good cook. In the first of this six-frame vignette, we see a young woman sitting at a table in a kitchen lamenting to her Mammy that ever since she left home (and left Mammy's care) to get married, she has not been able to make caramel cake using Mammy's recipe. Mammy, standing over the young woman holding a teapot as though she has just finished serving tea, tells her: "You jes ain't got a way wid an oven, honey chile!" The power dynamic in this frame clearly favors the black Mammy, which is why she is so forthright with her opinion about the white woman's lack of baking skills. Her reference to the young woman as "honey chile" doubles as a term of endearment and Mammy's way of asserting her own superiority as an experienced adult as opposed to the novice. The black Mammy is larger than the svelte white woman, and the conversation takes place in the kitchen where Mammy has been in control since before the young white woman left home. Second, the Mammy's memorized recipe works only for her because she has a mystical "way" with an oven and the white woman does not. Taken figuratively, the Mammy in this particular ad resembles Hestia, the Greek keeper of the flame and goddess of the hearth. In this white home it is an honored position relinquished only after a successor proves her mettle. The young white female determines to do this by using another recipe than Mammy's for caramel cake. She must find a written one that will enable her to construct a different social order in her own household with the white woman in a class by herself as a good cook superior to the black domestic servant.

We learn in the second frame that the young housewife must develop cooking skills not only to surpass her old Mammy but also to be an economic asset rather than a liability to her husband if she is to keep his affections. Frame three, set "a week later," shows the white newlyweds at their dining table exclaiming over the caramel cake the wife baked using a recipe she ordered after listening to *The Kate Smith Hour*. The young wife is thrilled that her "luck's changed" as a baker. Realizing the culinary victory in his wife's success in baking a better caramel cake, the husband urges her to take Mammy a piece and make her "green with envy." The husband, clearly enthralled by the cake, here aligns with his wife in her efforts to dethrone her Mammy from her position as the best baker. In frame four we see the young white woman back in Mammy's kitchen. Mammy is eating the piece of caramel cake the woman has baked, and she proclaims, "Baby, Dat cake o' yours is grand!" Again, Mammy's term of affection for her former charge — "baby" — signals a reluctance to acknowledge the younger woman as her equal, even if the caramel cake is delicious. Yet the sensual connotations of "baby" as it is used in African American dialect factor into this scene. Mammy's relish for the caramel cake prompts her call for a copy of Kate Smith's recipe book. She thus acknowledges having been surpassed by a white woman's cooking skills. The younger woman, clearly jubilant over her victory, busies herself with a small hairless black doll she holds in one hand and a piece of cloth spread before her on Mammy's table. She asks Mammy, "How do you tie your turban anyway?" In frame five, we see likenesses of Kate Smith and her manager, Ted Collins, opening fan mail and admiring the "Mammy Doll" that arrived. Kate Smith declares it "cunning," and in frame six we are allowed to read the note that accompanied the Mammy doll sent in by a "grateful listener" who, had always "wanted to be as good at baking as my old Mammy — and now I am. All on account of your recipe book and that . . . sure-fire Calumet!" Kate Smith is then urged to keep the doll in her dressing room as a reminder of a grateful fan.[19]

The doll, a shrunken version of the newlywed's Mammy, is passed from an aspiring white woman cook to an accomplished, older white woman cook as though it were a trophy won at the end of their race against the black woman for control of the oven. My reading suggests that the only way Mammy could be defeated was by using "white" witchcraft. The husband assures his wife that the caramel cake she baked using (the white) Calumet baking powder would "make Mammy green with envy." Later, Mammy is so mesmerized by the taste of the newlywed's caramel cake that she seems not to notice the small replica of herself that the white woman is holding in her hands. The white woman does not tell Mammy what she is going to do with the doll, but Kate Smith's referring to the doll as "cunning" reads in two ways. It refers to the pleasing appearance of the doll, and it acknowledges the younger white woman as shrewd, crafty, and skillful in overpowering her old Mammy. Finally, the young woman's note to Kate Smith extolling the Calumet baking powder as economical and "sure-fire" speaks to its reliability as well as to its metaphoric association with gunpowder — or at least a type of incendiary device that enabled her to defeat Mammy's mystical "way wid an oven." Granted, this ad acknowledges that since most Americans could not afford to have a live-in cook during the Depression, white women needed to learn to cook well and inexpensively to take care of a family. But, unlike the Mammy fetishes we have seen in the ads for Aunt Jemima pancake flour, the Mammy doll in this ad for Calumet baking powder does not serve as a spiritual guide for the white women. The black woman's image is not used as the trademark for Calumet baking powder, so she is not quite the same type of a commodity fetish as Aunt Jemima's face on the box of processed pancake flour. One could argue that it is a commodity fetish in that the doll was made by the young white newlywed who established a relationship with it as a replica of her old Mammy. More important here is its use as a sign of her culinary victory over the old Mammy, not as a sign of culinary dependence on her. Once Kate Smith received the doll and put it in her dressing room, she was supposed to think of her "grateful" white fan, not the original black Mammy, as so many of the other commodity fetishes I discussed seem to represent. The fetish in this ad establishes a link between the two white women cooks as victors over the black Mammy.

Kate Smith proves to be the answer to the young white woman's prayers not only because of her recipe for caramel cake and the magic ingredient, Calumet baking powder, but also by virtue of her large size. White Kate Smith has the mettle necessary to compete with the large black Mammy. On the cover of the 1940 anniversary edition of *Kate Smith's Favorite Recipes* (fig. 3.5), the phallic symbolism of the upheld wooden spoon combines with Smith's very wide face, broad shoulders, large breasts, and very muscular arms to evoke her masculine energy. Similar to the mixed feminine/masculine energies emanating from the black woman in the ads for Gold Medal flour, Kate's smile tries to soften the potentially aggressive gesture of the wooden spoon. Her "dainty" apron, her flower-shaped brooch pinned at the center of her bosom, and her coifed hair all attempt to emphasize her femininity, but they fail to completely erase her masculinity given that her overall shape parallels that of the refrigerator standing in the background. She, like the black woman in the Gold Medal ads, stands alone in this picture to signify her uncontested authority as a baker. This media-created image of a popular white singer and radio personality who knew her way around a kitchen appealed to millions of American housewives who ordered copies of her cookbook in 1939 and again in 1940.

At the end of World War II, when American men returned to the work-force, women were expected to relinquish the construction and other indus-trial jobs they held during the war years. From the mid-1940s through the mid-1960s, Americans were bombarded with idealized images of the two-parent suburban household in television programs, movies, and all forms of advertising. The postwar economic growth had only a residual effect on the

Fig. 3.5. Cover of the anniversary edition of *Kate Smith's Favorite Recipes*. General Foods Corporation, 1940.

lives of African Americans who were involved in demonstrating against the segregationist laws and practices found throughout the country. Domestic service in white households continued as a main source of income for thousands of black women in both the South and the North. White women were expected to remain at home supervising their domestic help, if they could afford to hire

Alice A. Deck

maids, or to follow the most efficient domestic methods made available to them in home economics classes, guidebooks, and women's magazines.

A 1953 ad for Aunt Jemima pancake flour that ran in the *Saturday Evening Post* perpetuates the pattern of racial stratification that we have seen in the ads for baking products discussed earlier in this chapter. We see Aunt Jemima, this time wearing makeup in addition to her usual bandanna, apron, and red-checkered dress, posed next to a slender white woman identified as Mrs. America (bride-of-a-year Evelyn Joyce Schenk). The two women represent, once again, the idealized domestic images of black and white American women. Their smiles meet in mutual recognition of their respective roles as the black cook and the white middle-class housewife. Both are wearing aprons as signs of their domesticity; however, Mrs. America's thin apron is lace-trimmed to emphasize her beauty, grace, and delicate femininity, whereas Aunt Jemima's thicker white apron not only accentuates her broader hips but suggests that she does the heavier, messier work in the kitchen. Mrs. America is holding a plate of pancakes in one hand and a fork with a slice of pancake in the other. Aunt Jemima's left open palm is on her hip, and she holds a pancake on a spatula in her right hand as though she is insisting that Mrs. America eat more than she already has on her plate. A closer examination of the way the two women are holding the spatula and the fork augments my reading of the black masculinity of Aunt Jemima and the white femininity of Mrs. America. Aunt Jemima's large hand grips the spatula, whereas Mrs. America's smaller fingers curl out and away from the fork. We see this same dainty hand gesture later in the ad where Mrs. America is shown holding a cup of batter as she makes some pancakes herself. At one point in this ad, Mrs. America is shown serving her husband a pancake supper. In response to his exclamation, "Gee, pancakes!" Mrs. America, in the only speaking part assigned to her in this ad, corrects her husband: "Don't say pancakes, say Aunt Jemimas." The plural "Aunt Jemimas" refers to the numerous pancakes stacked on the husband's plate. However, it also works as an interesting deflection of his hunger-driven enthusiasm for the food away from Mrs. America and onto the real source of the pancakes, the black woman Aunt Jemima. This makes Aunt Jemima the absent presence in the frame showing the white housewife serving her husband, which is an intriguing revision of the "absent white plantation mistress" pattern in the original legend of Aunt Jemima. The white housewife in this ad from 1953 appreciates the black cook's experience and guidance through the preparation and serving of pancakes, but it is Aunt Jemima, not Mrs. America, who supplies the plate of food that satisfies the white male's gastronomic and sensual cravings.

The final image we see in this ad is of a plate of pancakes, a fork, and a matched set of a sugar bowl and creamer. Neither Aunt Jemima nor Mrs. America is pictured in this particular frame. The caption reads in part: "Picture of perfection . . . only one thing is missing. The camera can't picture that richer Old South flavor. That's for you to discover!" Intriguing to me is the presence of the sugar and creamer, the handles of which are replicas of two black servants: a butler holding his hat and a Mammy holding a white plate. These two fetishes of black servants comprise the "flavor" of the old South that the ad claims to be missing from the picture. The millions of middle-class Americans who could not afford a butler and a maid could use these replicas to enhance their psychic well-being and social standing. Each time the creamer and sugar bowl are handled, the two black figures are put into the service of adding flavor to foods. So it is the flavor of old black servitude, an American craving that is permanently fixed in these two figures — another example of the fetishization of black people in American material culture and advertising.[20]

My discussion of the above ads shows an effort on the part of the advertisers (which includes the products' manufacturers and the advertising agencies) to idealize the cooking skills of a black woman as so highly desirable as to evoke the envy and jealousy of white middle-class women — the potential consumers. In all but the two ads from 1905 and 1910, the svelte young white women who clearly represent the American standards of feminine beauty are depicted as eager to learn how to cook as well as, and even better than, the Mammy so as to keep their white husbands' affections and their higher social status. Physically lacking the Mammy's earthly amplitude, which makes her a natural source of nourishment, the white women are being led in these ads on a circuitous route to satisfy the white male desire for attention and aesthetic sensations by learning to cook tempting foods.

Between 1905 and 1953, black women were idealized in advertisements for baking products as quite content in their roles as cooks for the American white middle class. Their large breasts, muscular arms, and wide hips signal an abundance of natural energy and nourishment that they are more than willing to share even as elderly women. This idealization drew on the historical reality of the position of the female slave on antebellum southern plantations and the romanticized depictions of her that filled the pages of white-authored late nineteenth-century diaries and sentimental novels. The ads discussed in this chapter show how the product manufacturers and the advertising agencies — all white males — gave form to white middle-class America's deep-laying desires for black domestic servants and being catered to by contented black women concerned only with satisfying their sensorial cravings. It is an ostensibly venerable depiction, but beneath its surface lies the political determination to keep the black woman forever in that class as a happy servant. Even when she is not physically present in the ad, representations of her image on boxes of pancake flour, small dolls, and kitchen utensils render the idea of her subordination palpable.

Notes

I wish to thank Kal Alston, Cathy Johnson Adams, Juliana Chang, Maurice Manring, and Rychetta Watkins for a series of stimulating conversations about this topic while I was developing this chapter.

1. In novels such as Harriet Beecher Stowe's *Uncle Tom's Cabin* (1852), William Faulkner's *The Sound and the Fury* (1929), Fannie Hurst's *Imitation of Life* (1933), Margaret Mitchell's *Gone with the Wind* (1934), Margaret Walker's *Jubilee* (1966), and Toni Morrison's *Song of Solomon* (1977) and *Tar Baby* (1982), a black woman known for her associations with food preparation, with feeding other characters, and with emotional nurturing plays a central role.

2. See *Hallelujah*, 1929; *Imitation of Life*, 1934; *Gone with the Wind*, 1939; *Clara's Heart*, 1988; *Ghost*, 1990; and *Soul Food*, 1997.

3. Mammy was a name given to black women who worked in any number of capacities in white homes on antebellum southern plantations. There is considerable scholarly debate as to the accuracy of popular representations of Mammy. See Deborah Gray White's *Aren't I a Woman? Female Slaves in the Plantation South*, Trudier Harris's *From Mammies to Militants: Domestics in Black American Literature*, and Patricia Turner's *Ceramic Uncles and Celluloid Mammies: Black Images and Their Influence on Culture*. In this chapter, I will be referring to Mammy as a cook and examining how she is portrayed in ads for American cooking products.

4. By black earth mothers I am referring specifically to Mary McLeod Bethune (1875–1955), founder of Bethune Cookman College and in 1935 the National Council of Negro Women, and Dorothy Height (b. 1912), president since 1957 of the National Council of Negro Women. Their recipes for traditional African American dishes are routinely included in cookbooks such as *Celebrating Our Mothers' Kitchens* published by the National Council of Negro Women (1994).

5. In her novel *Sula*, Toni Morrison's description of a once thriving, culturally rich black community includes a reference to Reba's Grill, a black-owned eatery whose owner "cooked in her hat because she couldn't remember the ingredients without it" (3). Wearing a hat while preparing food in this instance meets more than a sanitation requirement. The hat is endowed with magical properties. In *The Welcome Table: African American Heritage Cooking*, Jessica B. Harris discusses the fact that many black cooks, women and men, did not and do not cook from a printed recipe, nor do they use measuring cups and spoons. The best recipes are passed down orally from one generation to the next. See Harris, 83.

6. William O'Barr explains the secondary discourse of advertisements as "ideas about society and culture" emerging from the context of use of a particular commodity such as ideas about social relationships, inequality, and power. See "Analyzing Social Ideology in Advertisements," in *Culture and the Ad: Exploring Otherness in the World of Advertising*, 1–16.

7. According to the *Compact Edition of the Oxford English Dictionary* (1971), the word *nature* once referred to male semen and female menses.

8. Two excellent cultural and historical studies of the Aunt Jemima figure and its impact on American advertising are M. M. Manring's *Slave in a Box: The Strange Career of Aunt Jemima* (see esp. chap. 3, "From Minstrel Show to the World's Fair: The Birth of Aunt Jemima," 60–78); and Doris Witt's *Black Hunger* (see esp. chap. 1, "Look Ma, the Real Aunt Jemima . . . ," 21–53).

9. Maurice Manring makes this argument in his *Slave in a Box*, "The Absent Mistress," 139–42.

10. I refer specifically to the sexual harassment of slave women by white men as described in *The History of Mary Prince, A West Indian Slave, Related by Herself* (1830) and in Harriet Brent Jacobs's *Incidents in the Life of a Slave Girl* (1861). As a domestic servant living in close proximity to the white family, the slave woman/concubine was also the victim of the slave mistress's jealousy. See Minrose Gwin, "Green-Eyed Monsters of the Slaveocracy: Jealous Mistresses in Two Slave Narratives." See the following historical studies for discussions of the sexual plight of female slaves in the plantation South: Eugene Genovese, *Roll, Jordan, Roll: The World the Slaves Made*, 413–31; Herbert Gutman, *The Black Family in Slavery and Freedom, 1750–1925*, part 1; and Deborah Gray White, *Aren't I a Woman? Female Slaves in the Plantation South*, 27–118.

11. Two American novels, Margaret Mitchell's *Gone with the Wind* (1936) and Margaret Walker's *Jubilee* (1966), include a portrayal of a white wife who refused to have a sexual relationship with her husband after giving birth to his child or children. Walker includes it as an explanation for the birth of her central character, the mulatto slave Vyry, whose black slave mother, Hetty, died from having too many babies too soon by her white master. See *Jubilee*, 3–14.

12. See Manring, *Slave in a Box*, 95–109.

13. For a full discussion of this, see Laura Shapiro's *Perfection Salad: Women and Cooking at the Turn of the Century*, 6–7.

14. I am reminded here of a old woman character, Therese, in Toni Morrison's novel *Tar Baby*, who repeatedly extols the fact that she has "magic breasts" that continue to produce milk.

15. The role of immigration in the expansion of consumer capitalism at the turn of the century is discussed in Elizabeth Ewen, *Immigrant Women in the Land of Dollars: Life and Culture on the Lower East Side, 1890–1925*, 23.

16. See Marcia Ian, *Remembering the Phallic Mother: Psychoanalysis, Modernism, and the Fetish*, 61.

17. Peter Filene, *Him/Her/Self: Gender Identities in Modern America*, 160.

18. Richard K. Hayes, in his biography of Kate Smith, talks about how she liked to cook but had very little time to actually do it. See *Kate Smith: A Biography*, 21.

19. The fact that Kate Smith is going to keep the Mammy doll in her dressing

room rather than in her kitchen parallels an interesting fact about Smith. According to Richard Hayes, there were always four cakes (baked with Swans Down cake flour and Calumet baking powder) in the studio during Smith's radio shows. One cake was given away to a winning member of the audience during each of the two shows. One cake was for Kate Smith, which she ate in her dressing room, and the other one was reserved for the cast and crew. See Hayes, *Kate Smith: A Biography*, 101. For a discussion of Kate Smith's lifelong struggle to control her weight, see Hayes, 214–15.

20. For a full discussion of the social and political implications of material replicas of African Americans, see Kenneth W. Goings, *Mammy and Uncle Mose: Black Collectibles and American Stereotyping*, 1–18.

Works Cited

Aunt Jemima products. "Poor Aunt Jemima Had to Mix Everything Herself!" Advertisement. *Pictorial Review* March 1920: 63.

———. "Do You Make Your Husband Happy?" Advertisement. *Ladies' Home Journal*. Jan. 1918: 70.

———. "Never Before: A Recipe So Many Women Have Tried and Liked." Advertisement. *Pictorial Review* Oct. 1926: n.p.

———. "Glory Be, Folks! Aunt Jemima's Invitin' You, One and All, to Celebrate National Buckwheat Week." Advertisement. *St. Louis Post* [date?] 1936: n.p.

———. "Aunt Jemima Gives Mrs. America . . . a Taste of Her Newest Pancake Success." Advertisement. *Saturday Evening Post* 14 Feb. 1953: 99.

Ewen, Elizabeth. *Immigrant Women in the Land of Dollars: Life and Culture on the Lower East Side, 1890–1925*. New York: Monthly Review, 1985.

Faulkner, William. *The Sound and the Fury*. New York: Vintage Books, 1954.

Filene, Peter C. *Him/Her/Self: Gender Identities in Modern America*. 3d ed. Baltimore: Johns Hopkins University Press, 1998.

General Foods products. "Kate Smith's Mammy Doll." Advertisement for Calumet baking powder. *Needlecraft* 1939: n.p.

Genovese, Eugene. *Roll, Jordan, Roll: The World the Slaves Made*. New York: Pantheon Books, 1976.

Goings, Kenneth W. *Mammy and Uncle Mose: Black Collectibles and American Stereotyping*. Bloomington: Indiana University Press, 1994.

Gutman, Herbert. *The Black Family in Slavery and Freedom, 1750–1925*. New York: Pantheon Books, 1974.

Gwin, Minrose. "Green-Eyed Monsters of the Slaveocracy: Jealous Mistresses in Two Slave Narratives." *Conjuring: Black Women, Fiction, and Literary Tradition*. Ed. Marjorie Pryse and Hortense Spillers. Bloomington: Indiana University Press, 1985. 39–52.

Harris, Jessica B. *The Welcome Table: African American Heritage Cooking*. New York: Simon and Schuster, 1995.

Harris, Trudier. *From Mammies to Militants: Domestics in Black American Literature*. Philadelphia: Temple University Press, 1982.

Hayes, Richard K. *Kate Smith: A Biography, with a Discography, Filmography, and List of Stage Appearances*. Jefferson, N.C.: McFarland, 1995.

Ian, Marcia. *Remembering the Phallic Mother: Psychoanalysis, Modernism, and the Fetish*. Ithaca: Cornell University Press, 1993.

Kern-Foxworth, Marilyn. *Aunt Jemima, Uncle Ben, and Rastus: Blacks in Advertising, Yesterday, Today, and Tomorrow*. Westport: Praeger, 1994.

Manring, M. M. *Slave in a Box: The Strange Career of Aunt Jemima*. Charlottesville: University Press of Virginia, 1998.

Mitchell, Margaret. *Gone with the Wind*. New York: Avon Books, 1964.

Morrison, Toni. *Sula*. New York: Plume, 1982.

———. *Song of Solomon*. New York: Plume, 1982.

———. *Tar Baby*. New York: Plume, 1982.

National Council of Negro Women. *Celebrating Our Mothers' Kitchens*. Memphis: Wimmer, 1994.

O'Barr, William. "Analyzing Social Ideology in Advertisements." *Culture and the Ad: Exploring Otherness in the World of Advertising*. Boulder: Westview, 1994. 1–16.

Shapiro, Laura. *Perfection Salad: Women and Cooking at the Turn of the Century*. New York: Farrar, 1986.

Smith, Kate. *Kate Smith's Favorite Recipes: Anniversary Edition*. 2d ed. General Foods Corporation, 1940.

Stowe, Harriet B. *Uncle Tom's Cabin*. New York: Macmillan, 1994.

Walker, Margaret. *Jubilee*. New York: Bantam Books, 1966.

Washburn-Crosby products. "Now Then—Who Said Biscuits?" Advertisement for Gold Medal flour. 1906.

———. "Good Bread—Good Nature." Advertisement for Gold Medal flour. *McClure's Magazine*, July 1905: 1.

Witt, Doris. *Black Hunger: Food and the Politics of U.S. Identity*. New York: Oxford University Press, 1999.

The Joy of Sex Instruction

Women and Cooking in Marital Sex Manuals, 1920–1963

JESSAMYN NEUHAUS

Cookbooks published in the United States, beginning in the early twentieth century and continuing well into the 1960s, often instructed their readers in the fine art of catching and keeping a man. In 1923, for example, the author of *Recipe Book with Household Hints* began her cookbook by stating that the "way to the hearts of men" was through "a well-cooked dinner." In 1950, *Betty Crocker's Picture Cook Book* contained a chapter of cookie recipes entitled "Beau-Catchers and Husband Keepers." Mimi Sheraton's 1962 publication, *The Seducer's Cookbook*, urged women to employ a variety of culinary tricks to lure a man into the boudoir. *The How to Keep Him (After You've Caught Him) Cookbook* (1968) warned wives that a husband wouldn't notice whether or not a wife starches the tea towels, but "what he does care about is what goes into his stomach."[1] Cookbooks, as prescriptive literature, frequently and openly evoked sexuality and marriage in their directions to women. Conversely, marital sex manuals published during the same period frequently, but more subtly, evoked women's role in cooking and food preparation in their prescriptions for women's marital sexual behavior.

Historians, sociologists, and cultural critics have often looked to nineteenth- and twentieth-century marriage and sex manuals for information about normative gender ideology.[2] Such work has been criticized, however, by feminist scholars who argue that while historical investigations of prescriptive literature bring attention to how various authorities instructed women to behave, they fail to account for how women actually did behave. There is no simple way to assess the impact of marital sex manuals on individual lives.[3] Even sales figures are not necessarily a reliable way of determining actual impact.[4] Simply because a married couple purchased a copy of a certain manual does not mean that they read or were affected in any way by it, nor can historians presume to guess a couple's interpretation of or response to the material.

While not unsympathetic to these critiques, I believe that it is critical for historians to better understand the ways that popular discourse constructed and maintained gender norms.[5] We need to ask how texts defined the social roles of men and women. As feminist historian Joan Wallach Scott argues, we should attempt "to understand the operations of the complex and changing discursive processes by which identities are ascribed, resisted, or embraced, and which processes themselves are unremarked, indeed, achieve their effect because they are not noticed."[6] Marital sex manuals offer historians a set of those "discursive processes." They articulated the *ideal*, that is, how the "experts" (self-proclaimed or widely recognized) believed sexuality and gender identity should be expressed and understood.[7]

What is particularly striking about marital sex manuals published between 1920 and 1963 is how the advice and proscriptions in these texts expanded beyond dictating sexual behavior. I believe "marital sex manual" offers the most descriptive term for these books, given how they did not focus exclusively on sexual behavior, yet contained far more detailed information about sex technique than did "marriage manuals" (a more general kind of marriage advice literature). Marital sex manuals focused on sexual issues and technique, but often included a wide range of domestic and personal advice. That advice varied a great deal, from decorating a home to dealing with troublesome in-laws. But, significantly, almost all the manuals in my sample that offered such advice did explore one nonsexual issue: cooking. Marital sex manuals did not give extensive cooking instruction (although a few contained entire chapters on homemaking skills), but they regularly asserted that an important part of being a married woman was cooking and serving the daily

meals. In this chapter, I will argue that the advice given and pronouncements made by marital sex manuals concerning women's private role as
family cook revealed cultural anxieties about gender norms.[8] In particular,
manuals evoked women's cooking duties in their assertions that white middle-
class women's employment outside the home would adversely affect United
States society.

The marital sex manual emerged as a type of advice literature between
1890 and 1920, when the "modern sensibility" in sex began to shape American culture.[9] Consumerism, advertisements, pulp fiction, Hollywood films, a
growing youth subculture, and Margaret Sanger's active campaign for birth
control helped create an environment conducive to the publication of a new
kind of marriage manual. Previously, religious and secular popular literature
in the nineteenth century had characterized sex as an "unfortunate necessity"
that enabled procreation. Nineteenth-century advice depicted sex as a potentially dangerous activity, debilitating by its nature, an invitation to moral
slackness, and authors often advocated, in the strongest possible terms, moderation and restraint.[10] That changed at the turn of the century, when first
a trickle and then a flood of marital sex advice began to redefine sexual intercourse as a desirable, even necessary, act of pleasure in a marriage.[11] By
1920, manuals that actually promoted sexual expression, and aimed their
advice at married or soon to be married readers, emerged as a specific kind of
publication.[12]

In addition to their emphasis on sexual expression in marriage, on the
necessity for women to overcome their sexual inhibitions and for men to be
considerate lovers, tenderly "awakening" their wives' pleasure, the authors of
marital sex manuals in the 1920s and 1930s anxiously commented at length
upon what they saw as the precariousness of marriage as an institution and the
possible contribution of women's changing public roles to that precariousness. (Of course, other shared characteristics of these manuals — in particular,
the virtually unanimous support of birth control in secular manuals — are also
historically significant.)[13] The anxieties expressed by these authors were not
unfounded. By the 1920s, beset by internal conflict and widespread political
conservatism and apathy, the feminist movement that had brought about
women's suffrage had sharply declined and young "flappers" dismissed feminists as humorless man-haters rather than marching in the streets for equal
rights.[14] But popular unease about a "woman's place" indicated that the
effects of women's increasing public roles still caused extensive debate. Statistics that demonstrated a rising divorce rate helped fuel the debate.[15] And
throughout the 1920s, the number of women working for pay outside the

home increased steadily.[16] Women's employment came under increased fire during the economic hardships in the 1930s, and family life in general seemed dangerously threatened by the era's deprivations.[17]

As one historian notes, marital sex manuals articulated a direct response to such postwar anxieties: "A major reason for the appearance of these manuals was the widespread popular belief in Western society that traditional marriage was failing. One source of fuel for this belief was the changing status and influence of women, which led to demands for greater equality in marriage."[18] Most authors discussed concerns about the state of marriage in the context of changing gender mores, and by the early 1930s, marital sex manuals seemed especially concerned with women working outside the home. The 1934 manual *How to Stay Married* included a chapter called "Shall the Wife Keep Her Job?" in which the author asserted a common Depression-era argument against women working: "There are so many women competing with the men for the available jobs that the young man cannot make enough money to support a wife in the style to which she has so recently become accustomed. She stepped out and got a job that she did not actually need, in order to have pretty clothes and to be independent of her parents in a financial way; and she thereby lowered the earning power of her own future husband so much that is now takes the combined earnings of the man and his wife to support the family."[19]

Some authors were much less pessimistic, arguing that women sought employment out of economic and personal necessity. A few even asserted that female employment actually benefitted marriage by making it a more equitable institution. The author of *Marriage in the Modern Manner*, published in 1929, reassured the reader that although women's roles were changing, that did not necessarily mean marriages — and men — would be adversely affected. He wrote that men needed to assume new household duties, just as women were assuming new economic roles: "If a woman is going outside of the home to help the man in his job of financing the family, it is not unmanly for him to help the woman with her job of managing it inside the home. If he happens to be a better cook than she, why shouldn't he cook the dinner?"[20] But manuals that asked, "Why shouldn't the husband cook the dinner?" were far rarer than those that strongly argued against swapping gender roles in this way. In fact, authors mentioned cooking more regularly in these exhortations against swapped gender roles than any other household task.

Authors, again and again, insisted that if a woman assumed employment or other activities outside the home, the first thing to suffer would be her homemaking capabilities, and they nearly always mentioned cooking specifi-cally. The author of the revealingly titled *Recipe for a Happy Marriage* be-gan her injunction against the employed married woman by pointing out that such women would be rendered unable to properly prepare food: "A married woman who works outside of her home usually has to prepare a dinner at night with canned foods that are more expensive, and not as healthful as though she were able to buy at leisure and use a little care in selecting her foods for quality and price."[21] She went on to instruct women about the dangers of letting outside interests interfere with their cooking duties: "It is well for your husband to have to prepare his own meals once in a while, but don't let him come home too often from work and find you visiting with a neighbor, or still at a bridge party or movie and no dinner ready for him. This is often the beginning of a divorce action."[22] This typical passage illustrates how manuals absolutely equated cooking with the duties of a married woman. A woman who failed to have dinner on the table invited "a divorce action." As the title of this manual suggests, a woman's ability to follow a recipe seemed indis-pensable to a happy marriage. Similarly, in 1934, the author of *How to Stay Married* warned that a woman who chose to engage in outside employment after marriage ran the risk of pettishly refusing her husband that which he "dreamed of during the courtship," that is, home cooking: "If her working hours are long, there is little or none of that home-cooking of which he dreamed during the courtship. She has to leave too early to cook breakfast and she is too tired to cook dinner. What does he think she is made of? Iron?"[23]

The sexual double entendre here, the hint that home cooking may have encompassed more than a nice steak dinner, was borne out in a number of marital sex manuals after World War I. Authors utilized cooking to proscribe both women's social and sexual roles: they evoked food preparation not only as a domestic duty but as a metaphor for female sexual behavior. For instance, a 1936 manual aimed directly at female readers — *The Married Woman: A Practical Guide to Happy Marriage* — advised the bride that among her many new functions, she had a duty to inform herself about sexual intercourse. The authors drew a parallel between this kind of preparation and learning how to cook:

So one might for the first time in one's life enter the kitchen to prepare a meal, convinced that cooking is delightful and necessary, but unless one also knew something about the management of a cook-stove, refrigerator, egg-beater and can-opener, and the probable behavior of different substances when acted upon by varying degrees of heat, cold and friction, the first meal prepared would be likely to be a sorry mess. To be sure, one could take with one into the kitchen some ready-to-eat foods which would require a minimum of specialized skill in preparation, consisting only in the opening of boxes and bottles, and set forth in a few minutes a delectable cold meal. Likewise, one may come to one's wedding bed stocked with a few ready-made plans.[24]

Such advice emphasized the centrality of cooking to the definition of wifehood. Used here to illustrate the authors' points about sexual knowledge, it also revealed their assumption about the effectiveness of this particular metaphor. Food preparation in these manuals assumed layers of meaning, symbolizing everything from a wife's devotion to maintaining her sexual attractiveness to her homemaking abilities. It stood for a wide range of traditional female activities and duties — traditions that were changing as the century progressed.

   Twentieth-century anxieties about gender manifested themselves in marital sex manuals and coalesced around food preparation. Some historians point out that the emergence of cookbook rhetoric in the late 1920s and 1930s that emphasized both the creative potential in cooking and the importance of food preparation to a wife and mother's role in the family was part of a backlash against the political and social advances made by women in the two decades preceding the Depression. Moreover, this era saw the decline of servant labor in the United States; middle-class women were assuming new levels of household work and being urged to enjoy it.[25] Cookbooks in the 1920s and 1930s frequently commented on this shift, describing it as a fact with which middle-class women would simply have to contend. Like the prescriptions found in cookbooks, writing about cooking in marital sex manuals began to fulfill a specific cultural, social need for maintaining gender roles. For example, Mary Borden's 1933 *Technique of Marriage* drew on fears about modern living, political systems, race, and gender norms to paint a sinister picture of a disintegrating nation, torn asunder by the new woman's inability to prepare wholesome food. The title of one chapter — "Cookery Book or Communism" — made a direct link between women's acceptance of traditional gender roles (cooking in particular) and social stability.

Quick-lunch counters, cafeterias, and drug stores are multiplying like weeds, and they are phases of the new communal American state. If the women of America accept them and abandon their kitchens in favor of them, the rest will follow, and with it, eventually, the whole of our individualistic system. Is there an oven in any house in any state of the forty-nine that bakes bread for a family? Is there a wife or mother of Anglo-Saxon stock anywhere between the Pacific and Atlantic seaboard who knows how to knead the dough and takes time to make the bread? If there is, the young women of New York, Chicago, Cleveland, Buffalo, and San Francisco don't know of her existence.[26]

The choice outlined here by Borden was clear: the homemade bread of solid, dependable American homes or the "quick-lunch counters" of the socially degenerate cities. Feckless young women, warned Borden in a bitingly sarcastic tone, should consider the alternative to traditional gender roles, that is, communism of the vilest sort:

No one will have kitchens, all the cooking will be done in communal kitchens, and all the communal food you eat will be eaten very much as now in communal dining rooms. You will never have to order a meal or wonder what on earth to have for dinner by way of a change. You won't even have to pay for it. You and your husband will sally out three times a day with your food tickets and sit down in the communal dining hall of your district and be fed. I say you and your husband, but I should correct that and say, you and your comrade of the moment; for you will not be married in any sense worth considering; since the family as a social unit will be long since abandoned.[27]

When the communal kitchen took over, Borden prophesized, the abandonment of the "family as a social unit" could not be far behind. She ended her tirade with a clarion call for women to forget their silly notions about higher education and their overly romanticized ideas about marriage:

If you want your husband to love you romantically in the years to come, don't be romantic about yourself or about him. Think of his stomach, or better still, consider his stomach as a vital part of your married romance. . . . [D]ig your toes in and defy your neighbors and your school teachers who have taught you French, Latin, and music; buy a cookery book, take a course in domestic science, if necessary.[28]

Recall that this is a marital *sex* manual. In this text, sexuality, marriage, and gender became inextricably entangled with cooking, which, in turn, became freighted with political value. Borden's somewhat extreme passages illustrate how cooking always meant more than cooking in these texts. More than a way to ensure the romantic love of one's husband, cooking also stood for the "American way of life." Specifically, cooking by women in the home stood for the American way of life. "Cookery Book or Communism" dealt not simply with the importance of home-cooked meals but with the importance of women cooking at home.

Of course, manuals were not usually so blatant in articulating normative ideology. Still, as a site of "gender contestation," discussion of food in marital sex manuals illustrated how popular discourse after World War I revealed uncertainties about gender norms at the same time it sought to reinforce them.[29] For instance, in the 1925 manual *How to Hold Your Husband*, Simon Katzoff chastised a wife who would presume to dictate the tastes of her husband, stating, "Let him have the kind of food *he* likes — not the kind *she* thinks is good for him."[30] Manuals often offered injunctions against a wife being so "fussy" as to force her tastes on her husband, as did the male author of *How to Stay Married*:

A man has a right to have the kind of grub that he likes, provided he is willing to pay for it, even if his wife does not like that kind of grub. Not only that, but he has a right to have it cooked the way he likes. You may not like fish or pork or something that he dearly loves, but that is no reason for not serving it for the rest of the family. Get yourself something else, if you are going to be so fussy. And it is no good to tell him that he can eat the things you do not like when he eats downtown. He does not want to get them downtown. They do not know how to cook them right in restaurants. He wants them at home and he has a right to have them, so there.[31]

The author's tongue-in-cheek petulance about a man's "right" to have a home-cooked dinner revealed a deeper concern about who had charge of the home. Instructions directed at the woman to put her husband's culinary tastes before her own affirmed the husband as head of the household. For example, the author of *Live with a Man and Love It* cautioned that a woman's cooking duties also included humoring her husband if he should take it into his head to cook one day and raving about the results of his kitchen prowess even if wasn't to her taste: "Perhaps his meal is a queer combination, or maybe you don't like spaghetti cooked that way. Eat it and let him know how fine you think it is. Offer a quiet suggestion about something that *might* improve it next time. But whatever you do, don't make fun of him or the meal he cooked."[32]

Leaving aside the possible subtext of male sexual anxiety in this advice, I want to point out the way such passages about food and eating reinforced the "traditional" role of the husband. Unlike their prescriptions for sexual behavior — which usually emphasized the need for a husband to put aside his own selfish sexual urges and concentrate on awakening his wife's pleasure — discussions of food in marital sex manuals in the 1920s and 1930s instructed women that male pleasure/the male palate must come first. As Simon Katzoff summarized, "If she really loves him and has sufficient intelligence, the very least she can do, is to see to it that he gets food of the kind that he likes, as much as he likes, when he likes it. The key to happiness often lies in *food*" (original emphasis).[33] It would be almost impossible to prove whether or not passages like this one actually modified or reinforced any one individual's behavior. But what we can see in them is a persistent, urging voice of authority, which insisted that women remain positioned, figuratively and literally, in the kitchen.

If women pursued an education, if they sought employment outside the home, and if there were fewer and fewer servants, who would cook dinner? In *The Married Woman* (1936), Groves and Ross pointed out that feminist criticism of gender roles "prejudiced" young women against housework: "Some women, whether prejudiced by the complaints of an unhappy mother, or soaking up, sponge-like, the blatant querulousness of loud-speaking and sharp-writing women who have reason of their own for not being happy in homework or for whatever other cause having an emotional complex against home-labor, are afflicted with an antipathy toward all forms of activity that can be described as house duties."[34] For the authors of *The Married Woman*, a lack of interest in house duties constituted nothing short of pathology. How, many authors wondered, could the institution of marriage be maintained without women's presence in the kitchen? For example, the popular advice author Paul Popenoe, on the very first page of his 1925 manual *Modern Marriage*, emphasized the importance of cooking in catching a husband, and then went on to bemoan the ignorance of young women concerning this critical skill: "After a young man who has been eating his meals at a dairy lunch for a few years is invited to take Sunday dinner with the family once or twice, and is casually told that 'Katherine made these biscuits' or 'Katherine baked this cake,' he is in a frame of mind to become a 'prospect.' " He continued: "Many a graduate of a woman's college knows less about home-making than does a twelve-year-old child who has been well brought up. It is a disgrace to modern civilization that girls' education should be thus defective; and it results in a great deal of unhappiness."[35] These manuals fought for male authority and privilege, even as they acknowledged the eroding or, at least, the changing nature of that privilege. They attempted to limit the options open to the college-educated woman or the employed woman, ridiculing her lack of knowledge about cooking and cleaning as a "disgrace to modern civilization." Cooking remained the line that could not be crossed; it was the final straw. Women may have been entitled to full orgasmic pleasure in these texts, but usually they were not entitled to forego their cooking duties.

It should not be surprising that marital sex manuals published after World War II continued to suggest the importance of women's role in the kitchen. Like the 1920s and 1930s, the 1950s were a time of rapidly changing sexual mores. The publication of the Kinsey reports constituted a major turning point. The instant success of *Playboy* magazine, first published in 1953, and the best-selling *Peyton Place* by Grace Metalious, published in 1956, also bespoke a rise in popular, widely circulated "sexy" material. Teenagers — a new consumer category — were evoking much concern among their elders by indulging in the new, sexually charged trend of "going steady."[36] The rapidly growing numbers of "pop psychology" purveyors took up the issue of sexuality with a vengeance. During the 1950s, gender roles also became a source of much discussion and debate. Recently some historians have asserted that both popular and academic analysis of the war have overestimated the challenge wartime America presented to gender norms. But many feminist and cultural historians, while acknowledging the ways wartime propaganda sought to limit women's advances into the workplace, argue that the war was instrumental in advancing women's roles outside the home. Others take a middle approach, asserting that many gender norms remained unchanged or even strengthened during the war, but in a few important ways some women did challenge the status quo.[37]

Thus, despite the stereotype of June Cleaver, Americans after World War II actively debated the roles men and women played in society. On the one hand, many Americans strongly desired a "return to normality" — including traditional gender roles — after the upheaval of the war. Pop psychologists, such as Ferdinand Lundberg and Marynia Farnham in their widely cited *Modern Woman: The Lost Sex* (1947), asserted that unless a woman totally embraced her life's work as wife and mother she was doomed to a frigid, unfulfilled existence. Advertisements and sitcoms regularly depicted women as solely homemakers, wives, and mothers. But, at the same time, suburban white, middle-class women embraced civic life, volunteerism, and activism in political or religious organizations and community groups. Even as popular culture produced powerfully normative images of women, it also depicted uncertainties about domestic ideology and gender roles. And although it often meant part-time or low-paying "female" employment such as secretarial work, married women's employment outside the home steadily increased during the 1950s.[38] Again, the anxiety expressed in marital sex manuals does not necessarily reveal the *truth* of married life. Rather, it articulated resistance to changing norms or concern over how those changes would impact society.

Post–World War II manuals echoed some of the same fears that had shaped earlier manuals. Like those published in the 1920s and 1930s, they lamented the deteriorating state of marriage, frequently citing the rising divorce rate.[39] For instance, the authors of the 1958 manual *Why Marriages Go Wrong* pointed out, "At any one moment, certainly one out of every three, and possibly one out of every two, couples is chafing at the domestic bit," adding their own editorial comment on American priorities: "Apparently that American know-how that has given us priority in material achievement throughout the world does not extend to the area of family living."[40] Like earlier manuals, 1950s manuals often began by earnestly pointing out the necessity for marital sex advice in an era when the very institution of marriage seemed threatened.

Women's employment outside the home continued to be debated and discussed in the 1950s, and although many authors accepted the fact that women would desire to work outside the home, they almost invariably cautioned that the fragile male ego, and hence the marriage, would be imperiled. And, as in earlier manuals, a significant number of authors worried about the impact of a woman's outside employment on her ability to prepare meals. A 1958 manual by a Unitarian minister argued that a woman's employment actually ended up taxing the family's resources: "A greater problem is the cost of working. Have you considered yet the cost of a wife's working? Sometimes this entails two cars rather than one. It means that short-order cooking may have to replace well-balanced meals. This may entail buying more expensive cuts of meat. It may necessitate eating some of your meals out. This, of course, is costly."[41] Similarly, the author of *The Bride Looks Ahead* (1959) warned: "When a young woman works, and has very little time to spend in the kitchen, she necessarily spends more money on food. She hasn't the opportunity to shop for the featured sale items at the supermarket, nor the hours needed for preparation of most economical but nutritious meals."[42] Again, cooking was only briefly mentioned in chapters and sections on "shall the wife work?" in marital sex manuals. But cooking assumed an important symbolic meaning in such chapters. Cooking stood as a kind of domino theory: once a woman wasn't cooking the daily meals, the rest of her gender role was sure to fall apart. And once a woman assumed outside employment, her cooking became immediately imperiled.

Kate Constance, author of *How to Get and Keep a Husband: A Christian Businesswoman's Answer to One of the Most Perplexing Problems of Our Time* (1957), asserted that employment outside the home constituted a threat to the very essence of womanhood and, indeed, masculinity as well (despite the admission that she herself had been a businesswoman for many years and had received "over one hundred" marriage proposals before finally settling down with the man of her dreams):

If she is egotistical, puffed up with self-esteem and a feeling of superiority because she makes more or has a better job than her husband's and if she flaunts her earning capacity, this attitude will hurt his vanity. It is likely to crush his pride to such an extent he will lose ambition, and he might go so far as to want to get away from her who belittles him in his own eyes, even is she does it with the sweet venom of innuendo. It is likely to affect his virility if aggravated to a marked degree. . . . She should forever keep her husband assured of the fact that her work is only incidental to his earnings which represent the mainstay of their economic welfare. He should be made to feel that what he does is more important, hers only the side-kick.[43]

Again, the prescriptions here offered normative advice and, simultaneously, revealed anxieties and uncertainties about those norms. Constance described men as so sensitive that any threat to their masculinity could easily imperil their ambition and virility. Constance's advice, even as it sought to uphold the traditional role of the husband as breadwinner, also demonstrated how threatened that role could be. If a woman must assume outside employment, warned the author of *The Bride Looks Ahead*, she must also ensure that her husband's fragile ego is protected from the threat of gender roles turned upside down:

He feels less than a man because she is helping do his job. . . . In extreme cases he may become physically ill. Sometimes a man will turn to another woman, one who makes him feel nine feet tall because she wants him to take care of her. . . . One of the unfortunate results of a wife's working is that she may become less of a woman. . . . The gentle nature of her femininity may atrophy in the competitive atmosphere of the business world. Her mind becomes sharply honed, quick and facile. The so-called male characteristics can become dominant in her—aggressiveness, ambition, the competitive spirit.[44]

A woman's outside employment, warned authors in passages like this one, constituted a fundamental threat to the white, middle-class home: a woman would become "quick and facile" and so much less feminine, less needy, that her husband's ego would be shattered, he would be driven to infidelity, and, one assumes, the home would be broken.

In these texts, cooking neutralized the threat that women's outside employment presented in the home. Feed him, these authors advised, and you will feed his self-worth. Like earlier sex manuals, authors drew on the highly charged imagery of food and food preparation to reiterate traditional gender norms. And, like earlier manuals, authors often noted that while a good sexual "adjustment" was crucial to marriage, a woman's ability to excel at her traditional role was also essential. For instance, Clifford R. Adams, author of *Preparing for Marriage*, wrote: "A modern girl would be outraged if, in proposing, a man said, 'Do you love me?' and then went on to inquire, 'Can you cook? Do you like housework? Are you a thrifty shopper, a skilled needle-woman, a careful business manager?' Yet as wife, the average woman will be called upon to discharge all these duties and more. . . . She must provide good meals, in all probability prepared by herself, and she must see that they are served at the hours that suit her husband."[45] Similarly, in *The Art of Happy Marriage* (1947), James Magner stated authoritatively: "Among the first qualifications for the average wife is ability to cook. Good food is an important factor in marital bliss. It has often been said and with considerable truth that the surest way to a man's heart is still through his stomach. A wife who cannot cook and will not manage the kitchen may turn out to be a considerable liability."[46] And the author of *Sex and You* (1949) listed "ability to cook" as a number one priority for wives: "First, feed him well (that does not mean too much). Especially feed him when he comes home at night and then wait for thirty minutes before unloading upon him your troubles of the day."[47] Over and over, marital sex manuals paused in their detailed instructions for improved sexual technique and offered words of wisdom on the topic of cooking. Like earlier manuals, in the 1950s authors urged women to forget some of their overly romantic ideas of sex and marriage and settle down to regular servitude.

Marital sex manuals in the 1950s, however, expressed markedly more concern about women's sexual duties in marriage than in the 1920s and 1930s. If earlier advice on cooking had been in contrast to assumptions about the necessity for female sexual pleasure and orgasm, advice on cooking after 1945 was quite in keeping with a new emphasis on women's sexual dysfunction, women's hygiene, women's neuroses, and women's frigidity. Manuals in the 1950s constantly advised women to ceaselessly monitor themselves for poor grooming, mental problems, and sexual inadequacies that might drive a husband to infidelity. Authors routinely evoked food preparation to drive home their messages concerning women's new, expanded responsibilities. In this typical passage, the author of *How to Fish Your Man and Chain Your Husband* (1947) compared a woman's preparation of good food with a well-groomed wifely body: "If you see food well prepared, served on a sparkling table beautifully arranged, your appetite will be tickled and you will eat with great joy. On the other hand, if the food is badly prepared, served on a dirty and disorderly table, where a few roaches trot up and down as though the whole table and food belonged to them, unless you are starving, you would hardly touch that food. The same applies to the appearance of your body, in relation to sex desire. You can hardly inspire desire in your husband if you keep your body dirty and in bad shape."[48] Continuing with the food metaphor, she advised the wife to be sure to offer her most beautiful self up to her husband's appetites or "he will lose the appetite for your food and go restore himself in another restaurant."[49]

The author of *Sex Satisfaction and Happy Marriage* also drew on the metaphor of food and food preparation to demonstrate that a wife's careful preparation of a faultless dinner was akin to her careful attention to her appearance and to the comfort of her husband. After advising women to be meticulously groomed and to be as attractive as possible for their husbands, he offered a description of a woman cooking a meal to illustrate his point that such a wife would ensure her husband's fidelity:

Suppose a wife, expecting her husband's arrival from business, had prepared dinner for him. Marketing in the morning, she remembered his choice of meat and was careful to get an extra-fine cut, and she has cooked it to a turn. The vegetables are such as he likes. The soup and salad have been matters of concern to her, and she has been successful throughout. She has taken special care in the arrangement of the table — her best cutlery and dishes and finest linens are all in evidence. . . . Now I submit that it would be absurdly impossible to suppose that that man, hungry, seeing the attractiveness of everything, would ever turn his back on the exquisite meal provided for him and leave the house and by choice go off to some restaurant where he would not even be quite sure of the quality of the food that would be served. Such action would be simply unthinkable. But if the wife, though amply supplied with funds, is constantly setting him down to indigestible meals, cold and unappetizing, with nothing properly cooked, set out on the kitchen table with a dirty cloth, she need not be surprised if her husband frequently telephones from the office that business will prevent him from being home for dinner, and that he will just get a "snack" down town. As a matter of fact, he is probably staying down town so that he can get a bit of something decent to eat, for a change. And it is too often just the same with his sex life.[50]

Drawing on food metaphors, Théodore Bovet, in his 1958 *Love, Skill, and Mystery: A Handbook to Marriage*, criticized the way sex manuals emphasized a variety of sexual techniques and argued that a woman would do better to focus on her own attitude and appearance rather than on a smorgasbord of sexual tricks:

To illustrate what I mean let me say that it is a good thing for a housewife to make sure of plenty of variation in the diet but it would be a fundamental mistake for her to imagine that she can keep her husband faithful to her by changes of diet alone, for it is precisely the stay-at-home husband who gets the most pleasure from going to a little restaurant now and again. Whereas if the wife manages to create an atmosphere of ease and gaiety, humor and affection, at her table, then she can put potatoes and white coffee in front of him every day and he will never feel any need to go anywhere else for his food.[51]

Women's duty to their appearance — their own and the table they set — paralleled their sexual duty. In sharp contrast to 1920s manuals, much of the advice in 1950s manuals was not aimed at husbands, whose faulty sexual technique denied their wives pleasure. Rather, it was aimed at women's own deficiencies and made female orgasm secondary to the stability of the marriage. In the following passage from *Looking Ahead to Marriage* (1951), the author counseled the wife who had trouble attaining an orgasm to view sexual intercourse as a loving gesture on her part—similar to the daily meals she prepared for her husband: "Nor should she forget that her love induces her to cook for her husband and to see to his comfort—neither of which brings her to a climactic thrill. That same love may enable her to give sexual comfort to her husband even though she may have no climax. And, if her husband has any insight at all, he will recognize and praise her action just as he would her cooking."[52] This was not the only 1950s manual to assert that a woman's affections were both sexual and culinary and to urge men to recognize this fact. *Common Sense in Marriage*, for instance, noted, "Sex is only a small part of the matter. When she cooks, she cooks because she loves her man."[53] In such passages the husband had a duty to recognize the importance of cooking and the symbolic gesture of love it represented—but, of course, a woman had a duty to do the cooking in order to express her love for her husband.

The Marriage Guide (1950) took the husband to task for his impatience with his bride's cooking ability, but then went on to emphasize that a woman who wanted to keep her husband's affection should learn how to cook well as soon as possible:

One of the curious things about men is that they expect the marriage ceremony to transform a girl who couldn't boil water into a master cook. Where before marriage these men showed not the slightest concern about their fiancée's ability to roast a chicken or bake an apple pie, they are outraged when they find their wives lacking such skills. This, of course, is unreasonable.

But it is also unreasonable for a wife not to make a determined effort to cook to please her husband. . . . In this day of complete and instructive cook books, any woman can learn to cook to please her husband if she really wants to. And every good wife will want to, knowing that the way to a man's heart is through his stomach.[54]

Even given the attention to male responsibility here, the anxieties hovering around the stove were multifaceted: Were women less and less prepared for their role as wife and homemaker? Get a cookbook! Would outside employment and an expanded social role make women less eager to keep house? Remember that the way to a man's heart is through his stomach! Could the frail male ego withstand the assault of changing gender norms? Remember that when she cooks for you, she shows her affection! Dr. Rebecca Liswood, in her 1961 manual *A Marriage Doctor Speaks Her Mind About Sex*, cited a "case study" in which a husband longed for the "old days" when a wife's cooking could, clearly and easily, be read as a sign of male privilege and prestige in the household: "One man who came to me for counseling told me that he wished his wife would treat him the way his grandmother treated his grandfather. 'When she served the family at dinner,' he said, 'she always served my grandfather first and then the children.' This little act of consideration made the man of the family feel important and wanted. And this is the sort of thing any wife can do to make her husband feel that effort he puts into taking care of his family is appreciated."[55] Cooking for him could make a man feel "important and wanted" by his wife and reassure him that the norms which dictated that he was in charge of the family would be bolstered. Such passages revealed the concern that, for some baffling reason, men no longer could be assured of their own importance. The anxieties about male and female social roles that had been powerful in the 1920s and 1930s, in the wake of feminism and changing sexual norms, became even more pronounced in the 1950s, after the upheaval of World War II and in light of the increasing number of women employed outside the home.

I do not mean to suggest that this was the uniform, transparent message in all 1950s marital sex manuals, every time an author mentioned food or cooking. There were exceptions. The same authors of *The Marriage Guide* who urged women to learn to cook well also scoffed at a woman who would give up all her favorite foods just to please her husband: "Can you be too unselfish in marriage? Yes. While many married people aren't unselfish enough, there are some who go overboard in constantly putting their mate's tastes and preferences before their own. We know wives, for example, who cook only the foods their husbands like even though the women themselves loathe the dishes."[56] Marital sex manuals contained a good number of such contradictions. I also do not wish to suggest that postwar marital sex manuals offered extensive, detailed advice on cooking and food preparation. Authors usually limited their discussion of food to a few lines or a few paragraphs out of hundreds and hundreds of pages. Nonetheless, advice to women on food preparations appeared regularly and consistently. And *most* such references were part of a discourse that constructed women as domestic creatures, who belonged at home, attending to the comforts of their husbands.[57]

It is the way these statements about food preparation hung around the edges of these texts that I find significant. As historians and cultural critics, we must examine a multiplicity of sites where gender norms are questioned and affirmed; we must search for all the sneaky ways texts posit ideology — or subvert ideology. Marital sex manuals did not focus most of their prescriptions on food. Yet cooking stubbornly appeared as a persistent side note, creating moments where sexuality, gender, and gender norms converged around the issue of food preparation. Cooking was a small part of the way these texts constructed "women" but a notable one, given its tenacity and its constant citation in discussions of women's outside employment and interests. Authors of marital sex manuals positioned themselves as experts and authorities on the fundamentals of "male" and "female." Housekeeping in general and cooking specifically were part of their definitions. Again, we cannot conclude that women necessarily followed the dictates laid down in these manuals, nor can we dismiss the ways women may have gotten deep satisfaction from providing good food for their husbands and families. Cooking was probably indeed a joy for many women (and men for that matter). Yet published discussions of cooking like those found in marital sex manuals loaded the act of preparing food with gendered meaning that constructed women as essentially domestic creatures.

In many ways, the construction of cooking as an expression of the love and devotion of a woman to her family persists. The publisher of Alex Comfort's *Joy of Sex* (1972) advertised this sex manual as a "gourmet guide to love making."[58] Comfort gave his chapters culinary titles like "Main Courses" and "Sauces and Pickles." Despite the title of his manual, Comfort argued that sex should not be a formulaic undertaking; it should not follow a "recipe" for intercourse. Nonetheless, *The Joy of Sex* contained little that was new: its emphasis on variety, orgasmic pleasure, and the shedding of inhibitions echoed the advice of 1920s, 1930s, and 1950s manuals. But its lurid drawings, groovy language, and relentless insistence upon higher and higher peaks of sexual excitement pointed to an intensification of the way such literature constructed sexual intercourse as the cornerstone of romance and love. Similarly, to the present day, the meaning of cooking for the family has intensified: concerns about nutrition, pesticides, allergies, cholesterol, and so on have added a new layer of responsibility to meal preparation. In addition, the employment of white, middle-class women outside the home is a reality for the majority of married couples, but advertisements for fully cooked dinners available for take-out in supermarkets and other kinds of convenience foods continue to play on the theme that a good wife and mother provides a hot meal at the end of the day.[59] American culture has, today, a "gourmet" standard that shapes our meals, as it does our lovemaking. The privacy of our bedrooms and our kitchens is not always a refuge from the cultural messages that define gender. By tracing the continuities of a discourse — marital sex manuals in the postwar eras — where cooking and sexuality merged, we can begin to see that food preparation was more than "the way to a man's heart." It was at the heart of being a married woman.

Notes

I would like to thank Dr. John Neuhaus and A. Lori Neuhaus without whose help I could not have completed my research at the Kinsey Institute for Research in Sex, Gender and Reproduction. Also, I'm indebted to my friends and colleagues who offered numerous helpful suggestions concerning this essay: Kelly Austin, Kelly Douglass, Michelle Ladd, Peter Laipson, and Michelle Mancini. Finally, I wish to thank Sherrie A. Inness for her unfailing encouragement and support during the writing of this chapter.

1. Helmina Oie, *Recipe Book with Household Hints, Diet Suggestions for the Sick, and Other Useful Information* (Minneapolis: Augsburg, 1923), n.p.; *Betty Crocker's Picture Cookbook* (New York: McGraw-Hill, 1950), 174; Mimi Sheraton, *The Seducer's Cookbook* (New York: Random House, 1962), 1; Jinx Kragen and Judy Perry, *The How to Keep Him (After You've Caught Him) Cookbook* (Garden City, N.Y.: Doubleday, 1968), x.

2. Michael Gordon and Penelope J. Shankweiler, "Different Equals Less: Female Sexuality in Recent Marriage Manuals," *Journal of Marriage and the Family* 33, no. 3 (1971): 459–66; Ronald Walters, *Primers for Prudery* (New York: Prentice-Hall, 1974); Peter Laipson, "Kiss Without Shame, for She Desires It: Sexual Foreplay in American Marital Advice Literature, 1900–1925," *Journal of Social History* 29, no. 3 (1996): 507–25; Meryl Altman, "Everything They Always Wanted You to Know: The Ideology of Popular Sex Literature," in *Pleasure and Danger: Exploring Female Sexuality*, ed. Carole S. Vance (Boston: Routledge, 1984); Martin S. Weinberg, Rochelle Ganz Swensson, and Sue Keifer Hammersmith, "Sexual Autonomy and the Status of Women: Models of Female Sexuality in U.S. Sex Manuals from 1950 to 1980," *Social Problems* 30, no. 3 (1983): 312–24; Mary M. McComb, "Rate Your Date: Young Women and the Commodification of Depression Era Courtship," in *Delinquents and Debutantes: Twentieth-Century American Girls' Cultures*, ed. Sherrie A. Inness (New York: New York University Press, 1998).

3. A few psychologists and sexologists have speculated on the individual impact of marriage manuals, but such studies fail, I think, to take into account the complex ways consumers read and interpret popular literature. They also assume a "correct" method of engaging in sexual intercourse. For an example of such a study, see Viewpoint, *Medical Aspects of Human Sexuality* 4, no. 10 (1970): 50–63.

4. Available evidence does suggest that many marital sex manuals and sex manuals achieved substantial sales. See Regina Wolkoff, "The Ethics of Sex: Individuality and the Social Order in Early Twentieth-Century American Sexual Advice Literature," Ph.D. diss., University of Michigan (1974). See also Dennis Brisset and Lionel S. Lewis, "Guidelines for Marital Sex: An Analysis of Fifteen Popular Marriage Manuals," *Family Coordinator* 19, no. 1 (1970): 41–48.

5. See Sally Humphrey, "What Is Women's History?" *History Today* 35 (1985): 38–48. "Women's history has to define its subject matter as the history of conceptions of gender (i.e., of 'men' and 'women' as social, not natural beings) and of the social relationships and experiences to which gender ideologies are tied, rather than as the history of 'women' in isolation" (42).

6. Joan Wallach Scott, "Experience," in *Feminists Theorize the Political*, ed. Judith Butler and Joan W. Scott (New York: Routledge, 1992), 33. See also Joan Wallach Scott, *Gender and the Politics of History* (New York: Columbia University Press, 1988). In the latter, she writes: "The story is no longer about the things that have happened to women and men and how they reacted to them; instead it is about how categories of identity have been constructed" (6).

7. Michael Gordon and Charles M. Bernstein, "Mate Choice and Domestic Life in the Nineteenth-Century Marriage Manual," *Journal of Marriage and the Family* 4 (1970), 672.

8. My sample — drawn from the Library of Congress in Washington, D.C., and the Kinsey Institute for Research on Sex, Gender, and Reproduction at the University of Indiana, Bloomington — consisted of forty-six marital sex manuals published between 1920 and 1940 and forty-four published between 1945 and 1963. I categorized these texts by author's profession or qualifications and gathered information with a set of questions about how the author(s) defined male and female sexuality, sexual responsibility, and the role of sex in marriage. In my sample of books published between 1920 and 1940, fourteen of the authors were physicians, three were psychologists, nine were general "marriage guide" authors, either laymen or physicians, three were religious leaders, and the remaining seventeen were authored by a variety of professionals and laymen, ranging from the publisher of *Physical Culture* magazine to YMCA leaders to judges and reformers. In my sample of books published from 1941 to 1963, ten of the authors were psychologists, nine were physicians, four were religious leaders, one was a sexologist, and eight were general "marriage guide" authors, either laymen or physicians. The remaining twelve books were written by judges, sexual education instructors, and married women offering single women premarital advice. Each of these categories could be the subject of study, but I believe I obtained a reasonably representative sample, based on the Kinsey collection, which has deliberately set out to obtain a representative collection of this kind of material. I did not examine in depth the few "big names" in the field (e.g., Havelock Ellis), nor did I examine books that had not originally been written in English. The publication dates I chose were based on studies that mark 1920 as a turning point in the history of sex advice literature. I agree with those historians who argue that the post–World War II era may be understood to extend from 1945 to 1963, when the Kennedy assassination marked the end of both a political and cultural period in American history.

9. Ellen K. Trimberger and Ellen Kay, "Feminism, Men, and Modern Love: Greenwich Village, 1900–1925," in *Powers of Desire: The Politics of Sexuality*, ed. Ann Snitow, Christine Stansell, and Sharon Thompson (New York: Monthly Review Press, 1983), 132. For an argument that the transformation of sexual and social mores after World War I has been overstated by scholars, see James R. McGovern, "The American Woman's Pre–World War I Freedom in Manners and Morals," *Journal of American History* 55, no. 2 (1968): 315–33.

10. Gordon and Bernstein, 671.

11. On how this shift in the definition of sexuality played out in the production of marriage and sex manuals, see Barbara Epstein, "Family, Sexual Morality, and Popular Movements in Turn-of-the-Century America," in Snitow, Stansell, and Thompson.

See also Michael Gordon, "From an Unfortunate Necessity to a Cult of Mutual Orgasm: Sex in American Marital Education Literature, 1830–1940," in *Studies in the Sociology of Sex*, ed. James H. Henslin (New York: Appleton-Century-Croft, 1971), and Walters. For more general discussions of how this change emerged and how it impacted society, see, for example, Steven Seidman, *Romantic Longings: Love in America, 1930–1980* (New York: Routledge, 1991); Kathy Peiss, " 'Charity Girls' and City Pleasures: Historical Notes on Working-Class Sexuality, 1880–1920," in *Passion and Power: Sexuality in History*, ed. Kathy Peiss and Christina Simmons (Philadelphia: Temple University Press, 1989); John D'Emilio and Lillian Freedman, *Intimate Matters: A History of Sexuality in the United States* (New York: Harper and Row, 1988).

12. Gordon, 54.

13. Although none of the books in my sample focused exclusively on contraception, virtually all manuals that dwelled at length on sexual technique advocated gaining access to and information about birth control. In the early 1920s, the influence of eugenics on such discussions was clear-cut, but this was much lessened by the mid-1930s. For an example of how proponents of eugenics discussed birth control, see J. F. Hayed, *The Art of Marriage: A Scientific Treatise* (High Point, N.C.: Book Sales Agency, 1920), 189.

14. Nancy Woloch, *Women and the American Experience* (New York: Knopf, 1984), 382.

15. Wolkoff, 7.

16. Dorothy M. Brown, *Setting a Course: American Women in the 1920s* (Boston: Twayne, 1987), 81.

17. Rosalyn Baxandall, Linda Gordon, and Susan Reverby, eds., *America's Working Women: A Documentary History, 1600 to the Present* (New York: Vintage Books, 1976), 245. See also William H. Chafe, *The Paradox of Change: American Women in the Twentieth Century* (New York: Oxford University Press, 1981).

18. Vern L. Bullough, *Science in the Bedroom: A History of Sex Research* (New York: Basic Books, 1994), 137. See also Beth Bailey, "Scientific Truth . . . and Love: The Marriage Education Movement in the United States," *Journal of Social History* 2, no. 3 (1987): 711–32, for a discussion of how anxiety about how the " 'new freedoms in manners and morals' brought about by urban life would imperil traditional morality and marriage" in the early twentieth century spawned prescriptive college courses, literature, and textbooks (712). Also, it is important to note that a statement about "the changing status of women" should more accurately read "the changing status of white, middle-class women." Although an important and intriguing topic, it is not within the scope of this study to examine how the impossible standards of white domesticity and sexuality depicted in these manuals may have created a different set of norms for poor women or women of color.

19. John Willard Bolte, *How to Stay Married* (Indianapolis: Library Guild, 1934), 41.

20. Ira S. Wile and Mary Day Winn, *Marriage in the Modern Manner* (New York: Century, 1929), 129–30.

21. Anne Enfield, *Recipe for a Happy Marriage* (Syracuse, N.Y.: Bernard J. Gruninger, 1941), 27.

22. Ibid., 53.

23. Bolte, 42.

24. Gladys Hoagland Groves and Robert A. Ross, *The Married Woman: A Practical Guide to Happy Marriage* (New York: Greenberg, 1936), 49. Marital sex manuals in the 1920s and 1930s were, however, far more concerned with the sexual technique and duties of the husband. I found only one manual that drew on the language of food and food preparation to describe male sexual responsibility. See Wilfrid Lay, *A Plea for Monogamy* (New York: Boni and Liveright, 1923): "From a woman's point of view, she is invited by marriage to a banquet, at which she may reasonably expect to find a variety of comestibles all of adult characteristics. If at this banquet she is served by her husband only with milk or pap she is rightly revolted, and will not eat. Milk alternating with pap in successive courses of marital banquet would be cruelty and adequate cause for separation. . . . A man has no right to undertake the erotic support of any woman, and then proceed to starve her and incontinently to fatten himself upon her" (31).

25. See Nicola Humble, "A Touch of Bohème: Cookery Books as Documents of Desires, Fears, and Hopes," *Times Literary Supplement*, 14 June 1996, 15–16.

26. Mary Borden, *The Technique of Marriage* (Garden City, N.Y.: Doubleday, Doran, 1933), 88–92.

27. Ibid., 97–100.

28. Ibid., 100.

29. The concept of marriage manuals as a "site of gender contestation" is Laipson's. See Laipson, 513.

30. Simon Louis Katzoff, *How to Hold Your Husband, or Ten Commandments for a Wife* (San Francisco: Dollar Book House, 1925), 35–36.

31. Bolte, 162.

32. Anne Fisher, *Live with a Man and Love It: The Gentle Art of Staying Married* (New York: Dodd, Mead, 1937), 76–77.

33. Katzoff, 36.

34. Groves and Ross, 104.

35. Paul Popenoe, *Modern Marriage: A Handbook* (New York: Macmillan, 1925), 2, 114.

36. On the impact of Kinsey, Metalious, and *Playboy* magazine, see David Halberstam, *The Fifties* (New York: Fawcett Columbine, 1993). On teenagers, see Beth Bailey, "Rebels Without a Cause? Teenagers in the 50s," *History Today* 4, no. 2 (1990): 25–31.

37. For the argument that historians have overemphasized the way World War II changed gender norms, see Elaine Tyler May, "Rosie the Riveter Gets Married," in *The War in American Culture: Society and Consciousness During World War II*, ed. Lewis A. Erenberg and Susan E. Hirsch (Chicago: University of Chicago Press, 1996). For the kind of analysis May critiques, see Karen Anderson, *Wartime Women: Sex Roles, Family Relations, and the Status of Women During World War II* (Westport, Conn.: Greenwood Press, 1981); Susan Hartmann, *The Home Front and Beyond: American Women in the 1940s* (Boston: Twayne, 1982); Sharon Gluck, *Rosie the Riveter Revisited: Women and World War II Experiences* (Long Beach: California State University, School of Social and Behavioral Sciences, Oral History Research

Center, 1983). For an approach that explores the way the war changed and maintained gender norms simultaneously, see Chafe, 134, and John W. Jeffries, *Wartime America: The World War II Home Front* (Chicago: Ivan R. Dee, 1996).

38. On the political activism of white women in the 1950s, see Harriet Hyman Alonso, "Mayhem and Moderation: Women Peace Activists During the McCarthy Era," in *Not June Cleaver: Women and Gender in Postwar America, 1945–1960*, ed. Joanne Meyerowitz (Philadelphia: Temple University Press, 1994); Birmingham Feminist History Group, "Feminism as Femininity in the Nineteen Fifties?" *Feminist Review* 3 (1979): 48–65; Cynthia Harrison, *On Account of Sex: The Politics of Women's Issues, 1945–1968* (Berkeley: University of California Press, 1988); Susan Lynn, *Progressive Women in Conservative Times: Racial Justice, Peace, and Feminism, 1945 to the 1960s* (New Brunswick: Rutgers University Press, 1992); Leila J. Rupp and Verta Taylor, *Survival in the Doldrums: The American Women's Rights Movement, 1945 to the 1960s* (New York: Oxford University Press, 1987); Amy Swerdlow, "The Congress of American Women: Left-Feminist Peace Politics in the Cold War," in *U.S. History as Women's History: New Feminist Essays*, ed. Linda K. Kerber and Alice Kessler-Harris (Chapel Hill: University of North Carolina Press, 1995). On the way changing gender norms were displayed in popular culture, see Wini Breines, *Young, White, and Miserable: Growing Up Female in the Fifties* (Boston: Beacon Press, 1992); Susan J. Douglas, *Where the Girls Are: Growing Up Female with the Mass Media* (New York: Times Books, 1994); Margaret Finnegan, "From Spurs to Silk Stockings: Women in Prime-Time Television, 1950–1965," *UCLA Historical Journal* 11 (1991): 1–30; Brandon French, *On the Verge of Revolt: Women in American Films of the Fifties* (New York: Frederick Ungar, 1978); Andrea L. Press, *Women Watching Television: Gender, Class, and Generation in the American Television Experience* (Philadelphia: University of Pennsylvania Press, 1991); Nancy Walker, "Humor and Gender Roles: The 'Funny' Feminism of the Post–World War II Suburbs," *American Quarterly* 37, no. 1 (1985): 99–113. On women and employment in the 1950s, see Diane Crispell, "Myths of the 1950s," *American Demographics*, August 1992, 38–45. See also Lois W. Banner, *Women in Modern America: A Brief History*, 2d ed. (New York: Harcourt Brace Jovanovich, 1984), 243.

39. See, for example, Judith Unger Scott, *The Bride Looks Ahead* (Philadelphia: Macrae Smith, 1959), 181.

40. James H. Bossed and Eleanor Stoker Boll, *Why Marriages Go Wrong: Hazards to Marriage and How to Overcome Them* (New York: Ronald Press, 1958), 13.

41. Herbert A. Streeter, *Common Sense in Marriage: A Minister Counsels About Marriage* (Anderson, Ind.: Warner Press, 1958), 106.

42. Scott, 156.

43. Kate Constance, *How to Get and Keep a Husband: A Christian Businesswoman's Answer to One of the Most Perplexing Problems of Our Time* (Philadelphia: Dorrance, 1957), 180.

44. Scott, 154.

45. Clifford R. Adams, *Preparing for Marriage: A Guide to Marital and Sexual Adjustment* (New York: E. P. Dutton, 1951), 156–57.

46. James A. Magner, *The Art of Happy Marriage* (Milwaukee: Bruce, 1947), 57.

47. Le Mon Clark, *Sex and You* (New York: Bobbs-Merrill, 1949), 76.

48. Nino Saitta, *How to Fish Your Man and Chain Your Husband* (New York: Eloquent Press, 1947), 158.

49. Ibid., 159.

50. Alfred Henry Tryer, *Sex Satisfaction and Happy Marriage* (New York: Emerson Books, 1941), 140–41.

51. Théodore Bovet, *Love, Skill, and Mystery: A Handbook to Marriage* (Garden City, N.Y.: Doubleday, 1958.

52. Adams, 212.

53. Streeter, 28.

54. Samuel G. Kling and Esther B. Kling, *The Marriage Guide* (New York: Prentice-Hall, 1950), 130–31.

55. Rebecca Liswood, *A Marriage Doctor Speaks Her Mind About Sex* (New York: Dutton, 1961), 131. Case studies were used in virtually all the 1950s and 1960s manuals in my sample. As a writing technique, "real-life experiences" came to the forefront of 1950s prescriptive and pop psychology literature.

56. Kling, 113.

57. Most marital sex manuals focused on the husband-wife relationship as a sexual relationship, so women's role in providing meals for their children — something which is frequently discussed in cookbooks published in the early to mid-twentieth century — was rarely mentioned.

58. Alex Comfort, *The Joy of Sex: A Cordon Bleu Guide to Lovemaking* (New York: Crown, 1972).

59. Other aspects of our popular culture also demonstrate how food preparation continues to resonate with gendered meanings. The reissue of the original 1950 *Betty Crocker's Picture Cook Book*, for instance, speaks to how Americans seem to hunger *not* for the recipes of the 1950s but for the myth of a nuclear family with a stay-at-home mother to cook and take care of the home and its inhabitants. See Laura Shapiro, "Betty Goes Back to the Future," *Newsweek*, October 19, 1998, 68–69.

5

"The Enchantment of Mixing-Spoons"
Cooking Lessons for Girls and Boys

SHERRIE A. INNESS

The Betty Betz Teen-age Cookbook (1953) informed its readers: "If a girl is reasonably attractive and a good cook as well, she has better odds for marriage than her playgirl friend who boasts that she 'can't even boil water' " (1). "Remember that the good-looking girl who's also a 'good-cooking girl' stands more of a chance of sniffing orange blossoms!" Betty Betz cautioned (1). She was teaching a great deal more than how to cook; she was also teaching girls lessons about gender behavior that were expected to last a lifetime. *The Betty Betz Teen-age Cookbook* is one example of a juvenile cookbook, a popular subgenre of cookbooks that has existed for more than a century. Despite their popularity and prevalence, juvenile cookbooks have been largely overlooked by scholars. Since boys and girls in our culture are regarded as less significant than adults, youth are often left out of the picture when it comes to discussing cooking and its ideology, even though they learn a great deal about cooking at an early age. To understand how adults come to hold very definite ideas about cooking and its relationship to gender, we must turn to girls and boys and the lessons they learn about food and cooking while still young — the same beliefs that they later carry with them into adulthood. Like men's cookbooks, juvenile cookbooks do more than teach how to grill a steak or bake a cake; they demonstrate to boys and girls the attitudes that society expects them to adopt toward cooking and cooking-related tasks. In the first half of the twentieth century, juvenile cookbooks charted the culinary path from the undifferentiated years of early childhood, when both boys and girls were sometimes encouraged to help with small cooking tasks, to later years, when boys were warned to stay out of the kitchen and girls were encouraged to remain there. Juvenile cookbooks are intriguing to study because they teach not only cooking but also sex roles.

The practical need to teach girls (and sometimes boys) about cooking has always existed in human society, and juvenile cookbooks serve as one method of conveying cooking knowledge. In the nineteenth century, juvenile cookbooks, such as Elizabeth Stansbury Kirkland's *Six Little Cooks; or, Aunt Jane's Cooking Class* (1877), were a way to pass down recipes and cooking lessons, primarily to young girls. Such books became more prevalent in the twentieth century when advances in publication and the rising importance of the juvenile book business helped ensure that children's cookbooks were broadly published and distributed. Late nineteenth- and early twentieth-century manufacturers of foods also discovered that juvenile cooking literature was an effective way to hook consumers at an early age, since such literature often featured brand-name foodstuffs from a variety of companies.[1] For many reasons, juvenile cookbooks have become a staple of book publishing companies, both large and small. It is impossible to discuss all these books, but the ones this chapter examines are representative, and although the books I focus on were published between 1910 and 1960, many of my observations are applicable to more recent cookbooks as well.[2]

This chapter does not focus exclusively on cookbooks, since these books were involved in a much larger discourse about juvenile cooking. I study a broad range of texts, from cookbooks to magazine articles about cooking, trying to understand the messages about cooking and gender that were conveyed to children and adults. Unfortunately, this chapter cannot adequately explore the countless intersections between juvenile cookbooks and girls' (and boys') material culture, which includes dolls, toys, books, and numerous other items.[3] More research needs to be done on toys and the entire material culture of girls' and boys' cooking.[4] This chapter focuses primarily on cookbooks and magazines from the first half of the twentieth century — rich resources when it comes to studying how society instructed its youngest members about the gendered nature of domestic cooking. Such sources are valuable because they display many of the same messages about cooking and gender that we discover in cookbooks for adults.

Every Boy and Girl?

It is worthwhile to reflect on the implied readership for juvenile cookbooks. Whether directed at an audience of children or adults, cookbooks are one of the most strongly gendered forms of popular literature (along with romance novels). It is important to understand the process through which a cookbook becomes identified as reading material "for women only" because this strong identification is one reason that domestic cooking remains women's work even today. From their earliest years, children in the first half of the century were indoctrinated to assume that cooking was women's responsibility. Juvenile cookbooks supported and promulgated this belief in many ways, one of the most obvious being that these books targeted girls, not boys, as their "natural" audience; this message was so strongly emphasized by titles and cover art that boys learned that cooking was not an acceptable male activity before they cracked open a single volume.

Although most cookbooks from the first half of the twentieth century did not address both boys and girls in their titles, there were exceptions, including Henrietta Fleck's *First Cook Book for Boys and Girls* (1953); Julia Kiene's *Step-by-Step Cook Book for Girls and Boys* (1956), and *Betty Crocker's Cook Book for Boys and Girls* (1957). Other cookbooks adopted different approaches to acknowledge a co-ed audience, such as one 1920s cookbook dedicated "to every girl and boy who enjoys cooking" (Judson, *Child Life*). Books that mentioned both girls and boys, however, were largely outnumbered by those that addressed only girls: Caroline French Benton's *Little Cook Book for a Little Girl* (1905), Olive Hyde Foster's *Housekeeping, Cookery, and Sewing for Little Girls* (1925), and Maud Murdoch's *Girls' Book of Cooking* (1961). Not just titles showed the overwhelming focus of juvenile cooking literature on girls. A book might be dedicated to a girl, such as Marie P. Hill and Frances H. Gaines's *Fun in the Kitchen* (1927), which was "dedicated to all little girls who love to play house and to make things."[5] Often boys were disregarded completely when cooking was discussed, as in Kate Douglas Wiggin's *Good Housekeeping* article "A Little Talk to Girls on Cookery" (1912). The large number of cookbooks (and other forms of cooking literature) that addressed girls, not boys, supported a culture in which cooking was supposed to be girls' "natural" employment. Boys were taught to view cooking with uneasiness; they were instructed at a young age that their masculinity was imperiled in the most feminine home environment: the kitchen.

Juvenile cooking literature also referred to an implied audience of girls in ways more subtle than referring to "girls" in a title or dedication page. For example, Helen Powell Schauffler's article "The Five-Year-Old Cook" (1926) discussed only a girl's cooking efforts. The article also relied on feminine pronouns to describe young cooks. Similarly, Mae Blacker Freeman's juvenile cookbook was entitled *Fun with Cooking* (1947), a generic title that suggested the book could address both boys and girls. The book's introduction, however, told a different story: "A girl who makes the things in this book . . . gains enough experience to go on to more complicated dishes" (5). Here, it was clear that boys were not part of the intended audience. Most juvenile cooking literature considered the girl to be the cook. In Mrs. S. T. Rorer's article "Cakes and Candies Children Can Make" (1910), she warned mothers to make sure that "each little girl ha[d] an apron, sleevelets, a blank book and a pencil" if she was going to try making candy, even though the article's title referred to children, not just girls (40).[6] Peggy Hoffmann's *Miss B.'s First Cookbook: Twenty Family-Sized Recipes for the Youngest Cook* (1950) prepared young girls to follow in their mothers' footsteps. Hoffmann wrote to her readers that the book would give the beginning cook "a fine chance to help in her own way and will prepare her to be a good cook when she grows up" (n.p.). As these examples demonstrate, juvenile cookbooks often addressed a female audience, even if the books' titles did not make any reference to addressing *only* girls. In such a fashion, the books suggested that girls were "naturally" the ones who should cook.

Juvenile cookbooks also indicated that the "correct" audience was girls by including photographs of just girls. Marie P. Hill and Frances H. Gaines's *Fun in the Kitchen: A Record Cook Book of Easy Recipes for Little Girls* (1927) was decorated with pictures of girls cooking, not boys.[7] *The Betty Betz Teen-age Cookbook* could more accurately be described as *The Betty Betz Teen-Age Girl Cookbook* because the heavily illustrated book pictured only girls cooking (1). When the rare boy was depicted in a juvenile cookbook, he was typically not a cook but a consumer. Henrietta Fleck's *First Cook Book for Boys and Girls* (1953) included numerous pictures of girls cooking and boys consuming what delicacies were dished up. Alice D. Morton's *Cooking Is Fun* (1962) featured a number of pictures of girls making and serving food, but just two pictures of a boy cooking. Mary Blake's *Fun to Cook Book* (1955) featured a cover illustration of a girl cooking. The dominance of photographs or illustrations of girls cooking, not boys, conveyed one underlying message of these books: Girls were the ones who performed the cooking. Boys were the consumers. Girls and boys carried these messages into adulthood, guaranteeing that the majority of women prepared and served food to men, not the reverse.

Food Preferences

Juvenile cookbooks accomplished more than affirming that girls, not boys, should be responsible for cooking domestic meals. The books were a small cog in the much larger machine that instructed children about the complex world of food and cooking and the "correct" gendered relationship they should adopt to food preparation and eating. Even the choice of foods, boys and girls quickly learned, was not an innocent matter of personal preference but an opportunity to display their adherence to what society regarded as "proper" masculine or feminine behavior. Thus, when juvenile cookbooks mentioned the food preferences of boys and girls, the cookbooks also affirmed what was considered desirable behavior for the genders.

According to juvenile cookbooks, boys and girls were supposed to have distinctly different food preferences. Boys, like men, were expected to prefer substantial, hearty foods; girls, like women, were supposed to enjoy sweet, delicate foods. As Julia Kiene observed in her book, *The Step-by-Step Cook Book for Girls and Boys* (1956), "Girls may like to excel in pastries, and so forth, but boys want food that sticks to the ribs" (34). Boys were also expected to have little or no interest in how food appeared as long as it appealed to their taste buds; girls, however, were supposed to be concerned about the appearance and presentation of food. This different approach to foods was emphasized repeatedly in juvenile cookbooks; food appearance was an issue with even the most plebeian of foods: potatoes. One 1920s cookbook observed about creamed potatoes: "Most boys like them because they taste good, and girls choose them because they look pretty" (Harris 18). The relationship of a girl or a boy to the simplest food (whether steak, potatoes, or Jell-O salad) carried symbolic weight. When picking a food, a girl was taught that aesthetics was more important than taste. This belief went beyond creamed potatoes: Women were supposed to be concerned about appearance in all areas of their lives. This concern is one of the main signifiers of femininity. Thus, cookbooks were not just teaching readers how to concoct a Jell-O salad; they were also subtly demonstrating how femininity was constituted.

Creaminess and sweetness were food traits that girls were taught to think of as feminine, and dishes with these characteristics appeared everywhere in juvenile cookbooks; it was implied that girls would take special delight in making and consuming such dishes. Dad and brother might enjoy a slice of coconut cream pie or some other sweet and creamy dessert, but it was clear that such treats were primarily for girls and ladies to enjoy. Creamed dishes were particularly prevalent in cookbooks from the early twentieth century. Caroline French Benton's *Little Cook Book for a Little Girl* (1905) contained recipes for creamed eggs, creamed eggs on toast, creamed codfish, creamed fish, creamed lobster, creamed salmon, creamed oysters, creamed turkey, creamed potatoes, creamed sweet potatoes, and creamed cabbage.[8] Sweet dishes were also given a starring role in juvenile cookbooks. Benton assured her readers that many sweet sandwich combinations were tasty: "All jams and jellies make good sandwiches, and fresh dates, chopped figs, and preserved ginger are also nice" (168). A 1940s cookbook suggested a number of sweet sandwich fillings, such as cream cheese and dates, cream cheese and currant jelly, steamed brown bread and orange marmalade, grape conserve and thin slices of banana, grated sweet chocolate and preserved ginger, chopped prunes with walnuts and lemon juice, and lady fingers filled with chopped figs and whipped cream (Harris 256–57). A slightly later cookbook, *The Teenage Cook Book* (1958), emphasized both creaminess and sweetness in a recipe for "pineapple fluff," which required combining a can of crushed pineapple with eight chopped marshmallows and a cup of whipped cream (Rider and Taylor 68). The same book had a recipe for "frosted lovers' pie": thirty-two marshmallows melted in hot milk, a can of crushed pineapple, whipped cream, and nuts — all poured into a pie crust (92). Such recipes conveyed to young readers what food tastes girls and boys were expected to adopt. Girls were supposed to prefer rich, sweet dishes; boys were supposed to prefer plainer recipes. These gendered tastes continue to serve as one of many ways that boys and girls (and men and women) display their gender identification, even today. When a woman orders a salad for lunch at a restaurant or a man orders pork chops and potatoes, they are doing much more than satisfying their hunger; they are also expressing their gender.

Not only did juvenile cookbooks from the first half of the twentieth century instruct girls about the foods that were most appropriate for their consumption. They also learned that they should enjoy fanciful, imaginative food, and they should fret over making food attractive and decorative. A recipe, girls were taught, could always be made more exotic than its plain Jane elements. A fanciful name helped. In Louise Price Bell's cookbook *Kitchen Fun* (1932), recipes were included for fairy gingerbread (9), Cinderella cake (10), and rainbow dessert (13). But a name was only a beginning. Girls then had to think about the aesthetics of food preparation — something that, at least according to many cookbooks, she should *never* forget if she aspired to be the hostess of the month featured in *Good Housekeeping*. Even *Kettles and Campfires: The Girl Scout Camp and Trail Cook Book* (1928) urged girls to consider the appearance of food: "Camp cooking affords an opportunity to become interested in the esthetics of food combinations and table arrangements and demonstrates that an attractive meal served in an attractive place is eaten with increased relish" (Girl Scouts 6). For a girl, even on a camping trip, cooking was more than serving food; it was an opportunity for her to demonstrate her artistic talents. Cooking let girls demonstrate that they were learning the "correct" feminine habits that they would need as adults.

And there were so many ways for the aspiring young hostess to decorate meals! For example, a recipe for Gelatin Sailboats from the 1930s suggested creating a peach boat using a peach slice, toothpick, and a paper sail to decorate a serving of gelatin (Maltby 258). The same cookbook urged girls to decorate a pudding with a "flower" made of a snipped-up marshmallow and chocolate shavings (261). If these recipes posed insufficient artistic challenges, a girl could try her hand at composing a Candlestick salad, a recipe popular in the 1950s and included in many of the period's cookbooks, like *My First Cookbook* (1959). The cook stuck a banana half into a ring of canned pineapple. A maraschino cherry balanced on top of the banana to imitate the flame, and a bit of red-dyed mayonnaise became the candle's wax (25). Candlestick salad, however, paled in intricacy compared with some recipes. *Better Homes and Gardens Junior Cook Book for the Hostess and Host of Tomorrow* (1963) was chock-full of decorative recipes. Party-surprise sandwiches were "frosted" with cream cheese in order to look like a case, and the "cake" was decorated with olive "flowers" (26). Dressed-up doughnuts had rims spread "with marshmallow cream and roll[ed] in chopped maraschino cherries" (29). "Glittery sugar mallows" were marshmallows dipped in cream and then rolled in colored sugar (38). Intricate recipes like these demonstrated that girls were supposed to think of food as a way to highlight their aesthetic talents. In such a fashion, girls learned that their creative abilities were best focused in the home.

Now that we have explored the food preferences that juvenile cookbooks suggested girls and boys should adopt, let's examine the messages that boys and girls received from these cookbooks about why, when, and what they were expected to cook. These messages varied greatly, creating two codes of behavior when it came to cooking and food consumption. These codes had broad ramifications that went far beyond the kitchen, teaching girls and boys about the gender roles they were supposed to adopt in society at large.

Girls' Cooking

The primary message that is conveyed to girls by juvenile cooking literature is they should have a "natural" affinity for cooking. As Louisa Price Bell points out in a 1943 *American Home* article: "Any sand pile shows what little girls like to do. Witness the long rows of soggy little mud cakes with rock salt icing! The desire to cook is almost as natural to little girls as the desire to play" (80). Girls were supposed to grow up with a "natural" love of cooking, a love that was passed down from mother to daughter. Daughters modeled themselves after mothers, as one 1941 article from *Parents* magazine described: "When you get out your mixing bowl and spoon, have you not smiled when your small daughter did the same going through the make-believe process of beating and stirring just as you did?" (Bell, "Children Like to Cook" 54). Through such rhetoric, girls learned that cooking was not something they had an option about whether or not to pursue. It was assumed that they *would* cook. If they didn't, they endangered much more than their family's health; they threatened to unbalance a culture based on women performing their "natural" duties, whether those were cooking dinner or taking care of children, while men performed their "natural" activities, including working for money and being responsible for law and discipline in families.

Girls also learned that not only was cooking "natural." It was, as Nancy Craig observed, "the supreme key to the greatest of womanly arts: keeping house and family happy" (166). Learning how to cook, juvenile cooking literature suggested, was a responsibility to more than the individual girl or her family; it was a responsibility to all humanity. It was never too early for girls to undertake this responsibility, as one article explained: "So many mothers think cooking is for adults only, or at least should be postponed until their small daughters enter Home Economics class at school. . . . Yet these same mothers will admit that their small daughters are embryo homemakers, that an important part of homemaking is to know how to cook and like it" (Bell, "Some Rainy Afternoon" 80). In 1926, Alice Bradley wrote about the importance of girls learning how to cook so that they would mature into good homemakers: "Mothers often do not realize what a handicap it is to their daughters to get married without ever having had charge of the housekeeping in their own homes for even a limited time. It would be wise for every mother to give her 'teen age' daughter at least one week of housekeeping responsibility this summer" ("When the Children Cook" 98). Early on, girls were taught that cooking was their responsibility. This lesson, even today, has not died out completely. Many wives and mothers — whether or not they have full-time employment outside the home — still feel that it is their responsibility to cook; this belief is hard to shake because it has been woven into the cultural fabric of American society since its earliest years.

Cooking was not just hard work. It was also fun and games (or at least these cookbooks made this promise). Juvenile cookbooks stressed the pleasure of cooking. In Constance Cassady's book *Kitchen Magic* (1932), cooking was referred to as "a sort of magic" (3), and young Ann was invited by her mother to "learn the enchantment of mixing-spoons and pans and things like that" (3).[9] Some writers were even more ebullient when it came to describing the pleasures of cooking. *The Seventeen Cookbook* (1964) informed teenage girls: "Cooking is more than a means to an end: in its most exciting, satisfying form it becomes an end in itself — an expression of one's personality" (v). I think that the most honest comment about the role of cooking in a woman's life came from the book flap of Maud Murdoch's *Girls' Book of Cooking* (1961): "For every girl who wants to be a good cook, this book is an absolute 'must.' Written by a housewife who herself finds cooking eternally interesting in spite of having to do it all the time, it presents the 'how,' 'why,' and 'what' of cooking in an original and exciting way." Cooking might be fun, but it was also a chore that girls were expected to perform almost every day for the rest of their lives. This was one reason that girls' cookbooks were insistent about the delights of cooking, luring girls into performing a task that might be drudgery, not fun.

Finally, girls learned that good cooking skills were essential because they were the best means to attract husbands. Cookbooks taught about cooking, but they also taught how girls should make themselves appealing to boys. The cook who could whip together a stellar banana cream pie or the lightest, moistest chocolate cake was promised more men than she could squeeze into the kitchen. Robert H. Loeb Jr.'s *Date Bait: The Younger Set's Picture Cookbook* (1952) promised to give its female readers "more dates than [they] can handle." *Date Bait* queried: "Does Suzy have all the boys hanging around her place like a school of fish around a worm, just because of a certain cake she bakes? Nothing to it — you can hook those fish in a jiffy" (13). Loeb urged readers to try his cookie and candy recipes, guaranteed to "hook a whale" (13). *The Seventeen Cookbook* was equally insistent that food was the best bait for boys: "To many men (and most teen-age boys) cooking is one of the feminine mysteries, one they can heartily appreciate. With an ever-hungry young man, few things enhance a girl's stock as a girl as swiftly, as surely, as something really good to eat that she made herself" (v). This book emphasized the importance of good cooking for a girl to attract boys. It described a party menu containing "the foods which have proved, survey after survey, to be most popular with boys" (266). "Most of the popular girls we know have one thing in common. In the kitchen, there's a cookie jar — and there's always something in it" (342). Cooking was repeatedly held up as the best way to get a boy; never did these books suggest that boys should use good cooking skills to "hook a girl." Girls learned early that good cooking skills were supposedly the best way to attract boyfriends and husbands. Thus, girls learned that they should cook for boys but not expect boys to cook for them. This was a gender division that boys rarely crossed, and girls were taught that they should not seek to change it because it was society's "natural" order.

Girls learned a host of lessons from juvenile cooking literature that prepared them for their adult roles as the primary preparers and servers of food in domestic homes. Throughout the first half of the twentieth century, juvenile cookbooks remained remarkably consistent. Girls learned that they should cook for the family, since it was their "natural" responsibility. Girls learned that they should enjoy and take pleasure in cooking. And, finally, girls learned that cooking was the best way to catch boys. All of these lessons instructed girls about the domestic roles they should have as adults. But what lessons did boys learn?

"Making Cake Is Not a Man's Job"

The most important lesson boys learned was that cooking was *not* their work. This fact was conveyed to them in many ways, including the dearth of books that were addressed to boys. A few juvenile cookbooks were directed solely at boys, but these books were a minuscule minority compared with the hundreds of juvenile cookbooks addressed to girls. The boys' cookbooks that did exist were careful to build up a different image of cooking than the one found in most juvenile cookbooks directed at girls. Boys' cookbooks needed to stress that cooking was not too feminine. Jerrold Beim's *First Book of Boys' Cook-*

ing (1957) emphasized that its recipes were "for the kinds of things that boys like to eat most. No frills or fuss — just down-to-earth cooking with some fun ideas for good measure" (n.p.). He referred to the kitchen as a boy's "workshop," making it more closely aligned with traditional masculine environments such as garages and tool shops. Beim drew the gender lines in cooking, stating, "The day-to-day cooking for the family is usually done by a woman. But in many families the man is considered the expert when it comes to mixing a salad" (45). Outdoor cooking, according to Beim, was a place where men and boys starred: "Outdoors is where a man can really shine as a cook! When you cook inside, you have usually borrowed the use of the kitchen from your mother. But with outside cooking, boys or men take over completely. The world around you is your kitchen" (63). Like Beim's book, Helen Evans Brown and Philip S. Brown's *Boys' Cook Book* (1959) carefully demonstrated its masculine allegiance by including many "manly" recipes: chili cheeseburgers, steak sandwiches, roast wild duck, fried rabbit, rabbit paprika, buck stew, cannibal steak, broiled pork chops, beef stew, chile con carne, and garlic spareribs. Clearly, the few boys' cookbooks that did exist conveyed to young men that cooking was an acceptable pursuit but only in the right situation (an outdoor barbecue) or when "manly" foods (stew or spareribs, for instance) were being prepared. However, the lack of boys' cookbooks suggested that cooking was not a duty that should concern boys, an attitude that has proved remarkably durable.

Although few juvenile cookbooks existed that were targeted solely at boys, a number of cookbooks mentioned both girls and boys. Alma S. Lach addressed both in *A Child's First Cook Book* (1950). Julia Kiene, the author of *The Step-by-Step Cook Book for Girls and Boys* (1956), was helped by a panel of girls and boys when she tested her recipes. These children's books may have appeared egalitarian, but usually they held different messages for boys and girls. For instance, *Young America's Cook Book* (1938) pictured both boys and girls preparing food. But girls were shown frosting a cake (189) and canning fruits (207), while boys were depicted carving a roast (231), filleting a fish (257), and serving a rabbit casserole for a stag dinner (237). Similarly, in *Betty Crocker's New Boys and Girls Cook Book* (1965), a dozen girls and boys served as consultants, and both sexes were addressed. Even a book such as this featured the boys cooking out over a campfire and grilling steaks, while girls were pictured frosting a cake and making candy. If boys were included in juvenile cookbooks, their presence mandated careful explanation. One book defended its inclusion of boys: "You notice I said boy just as surely as I said girl. For how in the world is a boy going to manage a camping trip or even a one-day picnic in the woods if he doesn't know how to cook?" (Judson, *Child Life* 1). The book later described why one small boy wanted to learn how to cook: "He was a very, very bright boy and he knew perfectly well that if he wanted to go camping and have house parties and all such fun, he'd better learn how to cook a meal by himself" (36). Cookbooks might have included both boys and girls, but the lesson that the children received was about the "correct" gender division between cooking tasks. Boys learned not that they were able to do *all* the cooking but that they were able (and expected) to perform certain tasks. Thus, even when juvenile cookbooks might have appeared to be at their most egalitarian, they still conveyed rigid rules about gender divisions in cooking — divisions that, most likely, carried over to other arenas both inside and outside the kitchen.

Although the majority of juvenile cooking literature left out all mention of boys or carefully delineated what jobs they should perform, a few writers in the first half of the twentieth century supported the idea of boys cooking, even if they would not be grilling a steak. Cookbooks and popular magazines often promoted the idea that both very young boys and girls should learn how to cook.[10] Bertha Gagos wrote in her article "Children Love to Cook" (1949) from *Parents* magazine: "There is a time in every child's life when he or she wants to help in the kitchen" (43). Cooking for the youngest boys was acceptable because it was still a period when their gender was relatively undifferentiated, but some early twentieth-century writers promoted the idea that even older boys should learn how to cook. Bob Davis, for example, wrote in a 1936 article for *Delineator* magazine: "The public schools and all institutions where learning is to be acquired and the younger generation enlightened to take up the responsibilities of living, should include in the curriculum plain cooking for boys. The lad who cannot assemble an edible breakfast in fifteen minutes . . . is unfitted for the responsibilities of matrimony or to pose as the head of a household" (21). Similarly, a cookbook from the 1940s observed, "Both boys and girls should learn to cook, and everybody — boy or girl, young or old — should know something about food values and balanced meals" (Rombauer 13). In 1956, Nancy Craig wrote that boys should learn "that most human of all arts, which is cooking. Certainly if boys grow up, as they have in the past, with a growing contempt for girls' activities and interests, that contempt will abide in some form in adulthood. And if they themselves are not inspired in some way to know, *really* know . . . the womanly art of homemaking (which is nothing less than the art of life itself), then the future of the family is in a state of extreme danger" (194). For these writers, cooking played such a crucial role in the family that both boys and girls should be prepared to cook; such writers, however, were a rarely heard presence compared with the vast majority of observers who argued that young boys did not belong in the kitchen.

More common than writers who suggested that both boys and girls should learn identical cooking skills were writers who suggested that boys, like men, should be prepared to cook, but only in an emergency. For instance, in "Boys and Cookery" (1917), Ladd Plumley urged that boys be taught how to cook because it would help prepare them for a future war, when wartime conditions might mean that women would be missing altogether (178). He also suggested that *all* boys needed to learn how to cook so they would be prepared for the exigencies of daily life: "There is no man anywhere who would not be a more efficient citizen if, in emergencies, he could broil a beefsteak, cook chops, make coffee, bake a pan of biscuits, conjure an omelet, and, yes, mix, knead, and bake a loaf of palatable bread" (179). Plumley, however, made clear that boys needed to be trained for "emergencies," not the daily cooking that was a part of any household's ritual.

This idea that boys should cook but only for a special occasion was reiterated in many early twentieth-century cookbooks.[11] For instance, Caroline French Benton's *Fun of Cooking: A Story for Boys and Girls* (1915) discussed the desirability of boys learning how to cook. In this narrative cookbook, Jack is the son in the Blair family. Although his sisters learn how to cook, he keeps on insisting that cooking is for girls, not boys. His attitude begins to change when he goes camping with his father and recognizes that men and boys need to know how to cook. By the end of the book, Jack concludes, "Emergency cooking is all right; men ought to know how to do that. . . . I'm perfectly willing to cook bacon for breakfast, or scramble eggs, or cook fish for supper, or make a stew" (206). Note that Jack by no means is offering to take over a larger share of the cooking. He also insists that he will not cook desserts and pies, because "making cake is not a man's job" (223). Inez N. McFee's *Young People's Cook Book* (1925) also suggested that both boys and girls should learn how to cook. Boys and men needed to know how to cook, according to McFee, because they would need that ability when "the kitchen goddesses are absent or when they go on long camping trips" (vii). Like Benton's *Fun of Cooking,* McFee's book failed to suggest that boys needed to cook for anything other than an emergency or when they were camping. Another cookbook that discussed the special occasion cooking that boys should perform was Lucy Mary Maltby's *It's Fun to Cook* (1938), a long narrative about two twins, Eleanor Ann and Elsie Jane, who, through the course of the book, prepare various dishes and learn proper etiquette. Although the book did not suggest that it was directed at girls only, most of the book contained menus for a tea party, a bridge luncheon, and similar activities for women and girls. The one chapter in which boys cooked was "Week End at the Lake," when a group of boys decide they want to do the cooking for a weekend, making one woman comment, "I feel very queer about the food arrangements for this trip" (130). In Maltby's book, the boys are not expected to cook except for a special occasion. When they do cook, they prepare "manly" meals such as hamburgers, steak, and broiled steak kabobs. The girls, on the other hand, make recipes like creamed shrimps and eggs on toast, watercress and cream cheese sandwiches, candied sweet potatoes, Canadian bacon, and apple pie.

Another approach to boys' cooking was that cooking literature instructed boys that they should select one specialty meal to prepare, but no more. Boys did not need to claim the broad expertise in cooking that girls had to possess. Louise Price Bell observed in an *American Home* article, "Some Rainy Afternoon" (1943), "Let your children cook as often as they want to; encourage them all you can. This applies to boys as well as girls. There is nothing a man is prouder of than his skill over the kitchen range. One little boy I know can make a mean waffle, another is an expert at a secret hamburger concoction, a third at baking powder biscuits" (80). Thus, boys were trained to be experts at a limited task, but girls were not given the choice to possess such limited skills; they, after all, were being trained to be the central cooks in families. Boys were being trained to be what one book called "happy amateurs in the kitchen" (Gossett and Elting, n.p.). This philosophy lingers to the present when a father or brother might be content to specialize in spaghetti sauce or grilled hamburgers; mothers and sisters are seldom offered this opportunity. Armed with his single specialty, a man transforms himself into an expert. Equipped with hundreds of recipes that she must use night after night, a woman becomes a drudge, perceived as possessing no true sense of the epicurean heights that may be reached with food (something males, presumably, understand).

Finally, the other important message that boys learned was that cooking was easy, so easy that any boy could do it, if he so desired. One 1940s article from *House Beautiful*, entitled "Making a Cook Out of Butch," informed readers, "Take our word for it — any boy who can read can cook. What's more, he'll love to" (225). The attitude that good cooking requires nothing more complicated than reading and following a recipe is the same attitude that has defined women's domestic responsibilities (no matter what they might be) as easier than men's. In America, a stereotype has persisted that women complain too much about their "easy" household tasks, including cooking. Juvenile cookbooks support the belief that cooking is much easier than women make it out to be — plus, it is enjoyable. Thus, they have no legitimate right to complain about their burden of the household tasks.

Of Easy-Bake Ovens . . .

We have found that juvenile cookbooks and cooking articles in the first half of the twentieth century sent different messages to girls and boys. Boys were instructed that — if they learned to cook at all — they should become knowledgeable about only a few limited items. For them, cooking was an optional pursuit, something they could choose to do, but no juvenile cookbook suggested that boys should take over the majority of household cooking responsibilities. On the other hand, girls were taught that cooking was one of the most joyous tasks they would perform in their households; it was something that they should perceive as a pleasure. Girls should also remember that cooking was a sacred responsibility to the family. Boys and girls were taught different ideas about the role of cooking in their lives, and these ideas about the gendered nature of cooking have lingered up to the present. More girls than boys participate in daily cooking in the household. Although more boys cook today than in earlier decades, many boys still perform relatively limited cooking chores, far more limited than the responsibilities of most girls.

To understand the gendering of food, cooking, and cooking culture, we cannot focus only on adults; we must also scrutinize childhood, exploring how girls and boys learn at an early age that cooking is "girls' work." Studying how children learn the gendered nature of cooking (and many other responsibilities) is a task that mandates going farther afield than cookbooks. The whole culture of childhood cooking, from cookbooks to toys, needs to be explored in more depth. Thus far, scholars have skimmed the top of a huge field. Even the simplest of toys is playing a more important role than we might first assume. What does it mean that the toy I craved most as a child was a Betty Crocker Easy-Bake oven? (My mom never bought me one, which is probably why I became a professor.) I now recognize that something as "simple" as an Easy-Bake oven is more complex than it first might appear. Analyzing the "simple" history of play ovens and other toys modeled after kitchen appliances and how such toys have been marketed to girls could be a subject for extensive study, and countless other items that form juvenile cooking culture deserve scholarly attention. It is too rich a field to overlook.

Notes

1. For example, General Mills promoted its products to young readers in *Betty Crocker's New Boys and Girls Cook Book* and its *Cook Book for Boys and Girls*. For other juvenile cookbooks that promoted brand-name foods, see Blake and *My First Cookbook*.

2. Additional juvenile cookbooks include Clark; Fletcher; Fryer; Harben; Johnson; Lach, *Let's Cook*; Miles; Robins and Wilberforce; Rudomin; Schloss; Schulz; Sedgwick; and Watson.

3. Other studies of girls' material culture include Formanek-Brunell; Seiter; and a number of the essays in the anthology edited by West and Petrik. Heininger et al. contains references to girls' material culture in the nineteenth century.

4. For anyone curious about cooking culture, toys are a particularly fascinating area to study because of the prevalence of food-related toys (tea party sets, toy ovens, toy kitchen utensils, to name a few) and the long-lasting popularity of such toys across generations. As cultural critic Ellen Seiter observes in her book *Sold Separately: Children and Parents in Consumer Culture* (1993), "The product categories of girls' toys have remained remarkably stable since the twenties: vacuum cleaners, ovens, strollers or shopping carts, kitchen sets, doll houses" (74). Why?

5. Directing juvenile cookbooks at an audience composed primarily of girls was not limited to the twentieth century. In earlier centuries, this was even more likely to be true. For example, Harriet J. Willard addressed *Familiar Lessons for Little Girls: A First Book of the Art of Cookery* (1886) specifically to "young girls selected from the poorer districts in a large city." Her book did not discuss the possibilities of boys cooking.

6. Another example of a book that had an implied audience of girls was Clara Ingram Judson's *Cooking Without Mother's Help: A Story Cook Book for Beginners* (1920), in which the two children learning how to cook from their mother were both girls. Louise Price Bell's *Kitchen Fun* (1932) was identified on the cover as "a cook book for children." Despite this claim, the book was directed solely at girls. A small girl was portrayed on the book's cover. On the title page, a girl was shown reading a cookbook; boys did not appear anywhere in Bell's work. In Mary Blake's *Fun to Cook Book* (1955), new cooks were urged to wear aprons over their dresses (6).

7. Both Mae Blacker Freeman's *Fun with Cooking* (1947) and Peggy Hoffmann's *Miss B's First Cookbook* (1950) included pictures of girls cooking, not boys. *Let's Have Fun Cooking* (1953) also included pictures of girls only.

8. Similarly, Louise Price Bell's *Jane-Louise's Cook Book* included recipes for creamed chicken, salmon, crab meat, beets, carrots, celery, onions, creamed peas, spinach, and string beans.

9. Florence Harris's cookbook, *Patty Pans* (1929), started off with a picture of a girl in a kitchen reading a cookbook, and the caption read, "It is fun to work in a

kitchen." Similarly, Fay Lange wrote, "Cooking is fun for the pigtail set. It is important play for my daughter, Carol, when she makes her famous chocolate stacks, company butterscotch pie, or other dishes for the family."

10. A number of popular articles pointed out the desirability of girls and boys cooking. See Bonneville; Bradley, "When the Children Get Supper"; "Children Can Cook"; Gillespie; "In This Kitchen, Cooking Is Child's Play"; Jacobs; H. Lange; LaRoche; LeBron; Moore; Rose; Shouer; "Small-Fry Cooks"; and "Why Don't You Cook Dinner?"

11. Articles that addressed specifically boys and encouraged them to cook included "Cub Chefs"; "Kid Kapers"; MacFadyen; Patterson; Patton; Pfeiffer; and Silver.

Works Cited

Beim, Jerrold. *The First Book of Boys' Cooking*. New York: Watts, 1957.
Bell, Louise Price. "Children Like to Cook." *Parents* May 1941: 54+.
———. *Jane-Louise's Cook Book: A Cook Book for Children*. New York: Coward-McCann, 1930.
———. *Kitchen Fun: Teaches Children to Cook Successfully*. Cleveland: Harter, 1932.
———. "Some Rainy Afternoon." *American Home* Dec. 1943: 80–82.
Benton, Caroline French. *The Fun of Cooking: A Story for Boys and Girls*. New York: Century, 1915.
———. *A Little Cook Book for a Little Girl*. Boston: Estes, 1905.
Better Homes and Gardens Junior Cook Book for the Hostess and Host of Tomorrow. New York: Meredith Press, 1963.
Betz, Betty. *The Betty Betz Teen-age Cookbook*. New York: Holt, 1953.
Blake, Mary. *Fun to Cook Book*. Los Angeles: Carnation, 1955.
Bonneville, Jane Burbank. "Our Children Can Manage Meals." *Parents' Magazine* Sept. 1996: 48–49.
Bradley, Alice. "When the Children Cook." *Woman's Home Companion* Aug. 1926: 98+.
———. "When the Children Get Supper." *Woman's Home Companion* Apr. 1923: 100+.
Brown, Helen Evans, and Philip S. Brown. *The Boys' Cook Book*. Garden City, N.Y.: Doubleday, 1959.
Cassady, Constance. *Kitchen Magic*. New York: Farrar and Rinehart, 1932.
"Children Can Cook." *Parents* Jan. 1954: 56–59.
Clark, Garel. *The Cook-a-Meal Cook Book*. New York: W. R. Scott, 1953.
Craig, Nancy. "Introduction to the Womanly Arts." *House Beautiful* Dec. 1956: 166+.
Crocker, Betty. *Betty Crocker's New Boys and Girls Cook Book*. New York: Golden Press, 1965.
———. *Cook Book for Boys and Girls*. New York: Simon and Schuster, 1957.
"Cub Chefs." *Woman's Home Companion* July 1949: 120–22.
Davis, Bob. "Come into the Kitchen, Boys." *Delineator* July 1936: 20–21.

Fleck, Henrietta Christina. *A First Cook Book for Boys and Girls*. New York: Alumni Offset, 1953.

Fletcher, Helen Jill. *The See and Do Book of Cooking*. New York: Stuttman, 1959.

Formanek-Brunell, Miriam. *Made to Play House: Dolls and the Commercialization of American Girlhood, 1830–1930*. New Haven: Yale University Press, 1993.

Foster, Olive Hyde. *Housekeeping, Cookery, and Sewing for Little Girls*. New York: Duffield, 1925.

Freeman, Mae Blacker. *Fun with Cooking*. New York: Random House, 1947.

Fryer, Jane Eayre. *East Steps in Cooking for Big and Little Girls; or, Mary Frances Among the Kitchen People*. Philadelphia: Winston, 1912.

Gagos, Bertha. "Children Love to Cook." *Parents* Jan. 1949: 43+.

Gillespie, Myrtle Cook. "Let Them Cook!" *Parents* Mar. 1948: 52+.

Girl Scouts of the United States of America. *Kettles and Campfires: The Girl Scout Camp and Trail Cook Book*. New York: Girl Scouts, 1928.

Gossett, Margaret, and Mary Elting. *Now We're Cookin'; the Book for Teen-Age Chefs*. 1948. Irvington-on-Hudson, N.Y.: Harvey House, 1968.

Harben, Philip. *The Teen-age Cook*. New York: Arco, 1957.

Harris, Florence La Ganke. *Patty Pans: A Cook Book for Beginners*. 1929. Boston: Little, Brown, 1941.

Heininger, Mary Lynn Stevens, Karin Calvert, Barbara Finkelstein, Kathy Vandell, Anne Scott MacLeod, and Harvey Green. *A Century of Childhood, 1820–1920*. Rochester, N.Y.: Strong Museum, 1984.

Hill, Marie P., and Frances H. Gaines, eds. *Fun in the Kitchen: A Record Cook Book of Easy Recipes for Little Girls*. Chicago: Reilly & Lee, 1927.

Hoffmann, Margaret Jones. *Miss B.'s First Cookbook: Twenty Family-Sized Recipes for the Youngest Cook*. Indianapolis: Bobbs-Merrill, 1950.

"In This Kitchen, Cooking Is Child's Play." *House and Garden* Feb. 1955: 58–59.

Jacobs, Margaret Moore. "Let 'em Can and Cook." *American Home* July 1937: 47+.

Johnson, Constance. *When Mother Lets Us Cook*. New York: Moffat, 1908.

Judson, Clara Ingram. *Cooking without Mother's Help: A Story Cook Book for Beginners*. New York: Nourse, 1920.

——. *Child Life Cookbook*. New York: Rand McNally, 1926.

"Kid Kapers." *American Magazine* Mar. 1954: 57.

Kiene, Julia. *The Step-by-Step Cook Book for Girls and Boys*. New York: Simon and Schuster, 1956.

Kirkland, E. S. [Elizabeth Stansbury]. *Six Little Cooks; or, Aunt Jane's Cooking Class*. Chicago: Jansen, 1877.

Lach, Alma S. *A Child's First Cook Book*. New York: Hart, 1950.

——. *Let's Cook*. Chicago: Child Training Association, 1956.

Lange, Fay. "Cooking Can Be Play." *American Home* Mar. 1955: 80.

Lange, Helen Dickinson. "Our Young Cooks." *American Cookery* Jan. 1942: 275+.

LaRoche, Betty Gregory. "Mothers Share Tips on How to Bring Up a Good Cook." *Farm Journal* Jan. 1962: 56–57.

LeBron, Marion. "Invite Them into the Kitchen." *Parents* Apr. 1944: 32+.

Let's Have Fun Cooking: The Children's Cook Book. Chicago: Moody, 1953.

Levenstein, Harvey A. *Revolution at the Table: The Transformation of the American Diet.* New York: Oxford University Press, 1988.

Loeb, Robert H. *Date Bait: The Younger Set's Picture Cookbook.* Chicago: Wilcox and Follett, 1952.

MacFadyen, R. Byron. "Teach Your Boy to Cook." *Good Housekeeping* Aug. 1929: 100+.

McFee, Inez N. *Young People's Cook Book.* New York: Crowell, 1925.

"Making a Cook Out of Butch." *House Beautiful* Oct. 1948: 225–26.

Maltby, Lucy Mary. *It's Fun to Cook.* Philadelphia: Winston, 1938.

Miles, Betty. *The Cooking Book.* New York: Knopf, 1959.

Moore, Shirley. "I Want to Cook." *American Home* Feb. 1954: 75–76.

Morton, Alice D. *Cooking Is Fun.* New York: Hart, 1962.

Murdoch, Maud. *The Girls' Book of Cooking.* New York: Roy, 1961.

My First Cookbook. Sugar Land, Tex.: Imperial Sugar, 1959.

Patterson, Sterling. "Shall We Join the Ladies?" *Better Homes and Gardens* Oct. 1936: 107+.

Patton, Patty. "Make Your Child Welcome in the Kitchen." *Parents* Oct. 1956: 104–5.

Pfeiffer, Sarah Shields. "He Might Like Cooking!" *Parents* Feb. 1946: 47.

Plumley, Ladd. "Boys and Cookery." *American Cookery* Oct. 1917: 177–79.

Rider, Dorothy, and Betty Taylor. *Teenage Cook Book.* Boston: Meador, 1958.

Robins, Elizabeth, and Octavia Wilberforce. *Prudence and Peter and Their Adventures with Pots and Pans.* New York: Morrow, 1928.

Rombauer, Irma S. *A Cookbook for Girls and Boys.* Indianapolis: Bobbs-Merrill, 1946.

Rorer, Mrs. S. T. "Cakes and Candies Children Can Make." *Ladies' Home Journal* 15 Dec. 1910: 40.

Rose, Dorothy E. "Junior Chefs." *Parents'* June 1951: 53+.

Rudomin, Esther. *Let's Cook Without Cooking.* New York: Crowell, 1955.

Schauffler, Helen Powell. "The Five-Year-Old Cook." *Good Housekeeping* Dec. 1926: 78+.

Schloss, Ezekiel. *Junior Jewish Cook Book.* New York: Ktav, 1956.

Schulz, Charles M. *Peanuts Cook Book.* New York: Scholastic Book Services, 1969.

Sedgwick, Ursula. *My Learn-to-Cook Book.* New York: Golden Press, 1967.

Seiter, Ellen. *Sold Separately: Children and Parents in Consumer Culture.* New Brunswick: Rutgers University Press, 1993.

The Seventeen Cookbook. New York: Macmillan, 1964.

Shapiro, Laura. *Perfection Salad: Women and Cooking at the Turn of the Century.* New York: Farrar, Straus and Giroux, 1986.

Shouer, Louella G. "Never Too Young to Bake." *Ladies' Home Journal* Oct. 1949: 204–5.

Silver, Roy R. "L.I. High School Boys Excel as Chefs; Cook Dinner as Culmination of Course." *New York Times* 25 May 1958: L57.

"Small-Fry Cooks." *Look* 26 Jan. 1954: 56–57.

Watson, Jane Werner. *Susie's New Stove: The Little Chef's Cookbook.* New York: Simon and Schuster, 1950.

West, Elliott, and Paula Petrik, eds. *Small World: Children and Adolescents in America, 1850–1950*. Lawrence: University Press of Kansas, 1992.

"Why Don't You Cook Dinner?" *Sunset* Feb. 1956: 131+.

Wiggin, Kate Douglas. "A Little Talk to Girls on Cookery." *Good Housekeeping* May 1912:689–92.

Willard, Harriet J. *Familiar Lessons for Little Girls: A First Book of the Art of Cookery*. Chicago: Sherwood, 1886.

Young America's Cook Book: A Cook Book for Boys and Girls Who Like Good Food. New York: Scribner, 1938.

Home Cooking

Boston Baked Beans and Sizzling Rice Soup as Recipes for Pride and Prejudice

JANET THEOPHANO

As much recipes for living as formulas for cooking, cookbooks serve as forums for the discussion of the conduct of life. Even the most pragmatic of books alludes to both a moral world and an aesthetic to be tended. Although their most salient function is to provide instruction in the domestic arts, cookbooks and household manuals have been used by women to examine and shape their own and others' lives.[1]

The corpus of books I examine are from rare book collections at the University of Pennsylvania's Van Pelt Library, the Historical Society of Pennsylvania, Radcliffe's Schlesinger Library, Winterthur, and my own collection. They span four centuries and represent cultures from nearly every part of the globe. This chapter will illustrate the ways that women have used cookbooks — and the terms of kitchen practice — as a vehicle for constructing, defending, and transgressing social and cultural borders.[2] My argument is not that women conformed to the images and ideals they and others constructed, but that they found them useful points of departure for reflection. It is a commonplace that prescriptive literature does not necessarily represent the "reality" of the period in which it was written or reflect the ways women actually behaved. None of the cookbooks I discuss are meant to suggest typicality. What is remarkable is that women of diverse backgrounds have chosen the genre as a suitable place to probe issues of cultural identity.

In dedications, prefaces, and introductions, as well as with recipes and titles and other explanatory material, the cookbook writers told their stories. Some books were elaborate, if not implicit, explorations of identity — of self, of other women, and of home, community, and country. These probings sometimes supported and sometimes challenged the status quo. (*The New Housekeeper's Manual* [1873] by Catharine Beecher and Harriet Beecher Stowe is one such text.) More than a few authors were critical of accepted social and cultural mores. Other texts offered modest prefaces in keeping with prevailing norms about women's public demeanor, social disruptions disguised by unassuming rhetorical strategies. (Amelia Simmons's *American Cookery* [1796], the first cookbook written by an American, is an example.) These introductions, large or small, encoded images of the "feminine," some of which were sanctioned by an authoritative culture while others were in opposition to normative standards. What the cookbook authors put forward as "feminine" was entangled with other social features: race, class, ethnicity, and religion among them.

Because gender embraced other features of social life, the discussion of women's responsibilities in these texts was also a site for an "autobiographical presence," "self-reflection," and "political commentary."[3] In these texts, women debated the merits and flaws of customary culinary practices that highlighted and demarcated social and cultural boundaries. The texts — neither univocal nor without ambivalence and contradictions — encoded messages that defined, defended, and transgressed cultural boundaries.

Even while cookbook writers valorized women's work and embraced an expanding consciousness and community of women through an increasingly literate readership, in the process other women were, just as often, *excluded* from the community that the authors defined. It was not only prominent author-cooks, such as Amelia Simmons, the Beechers, Irma Rombauer, and Julia Child, whose work informed and shaped the changing images of American women and cultural standards from the late eighteenth through early twentieth centuries, but the vernacular writing of women whose works remained unpublished or printed in limited quantities for community charitable and fund-raising purposes.[4]

Poetry and Beans: *The Presbyterian Cookbook*

Notable published authors, such as the Beechers, provided guides for the household, and "the care of servants," to facilitate the work of some women — primarily white, Anglo-Saxon, and middle class — or to champion liberation from arduous kitchen responsibilities. Ordinary women made use of their receipt and cookery books in similar, albeit vernacular ways. In some instances, they emulated the famous authors whose works they read by attempting to write books of their own; in other cases, they preferred to model themselves after the ideals of womanhood these printed texts described, without striving to become authors themselves. If nothing else, the compilation of recipes or the editing of printed texts offered women a site in which they could "write" their own books, their own lives and histories. Through these texts, women developed lineage and community affiliations and identified themselves as members of a community of women. Bequeathing one's book to next of kin bound women of one generation to the next. Their "modest presences" were assertions of the self that embedded them in a cultural context and social network.[5] They defined community and those who were outside it.

Beginning with the American Civil War, women used their recipes to raise money for charitable causes. Through the compilation and sale of church and community cookbooks, women funneled the proceeds into hospitals, poor houses, missions, churches, synagogues, and orphanages.[6] As women continued their humanitarian efforts and their household labors, they engaged in what Anne Goldman calls "sotto voce" debates about their own and others' proper place in society.[7]

In 1873, the Ladies Society of the First Presbyterian Church of Dayton, Ohio, "hastily compiled and published" *The Presbyterian Cookbook*, a "small collection of recipes for plain household cooking." As ordinary housewives, they "begged indulgence for the manner of their writing"[8] — they had, after all, never written for publication before. In this slender volume, published locally, we find a recipe that gives directions for "Cooking Beans" reprinted from *Moore's Rural New Yorker*. Innocently enough, the recipe is in verse:

COOKING BEANS

If, my dear Rural, you should ever wish
For Breakfast or dinner a tempting dish

Of the beans so famous in Boston town,
You must read the rules I here lay down.

. . . .

Then if, in the pantry, there still should be
That bean-pot, so famous in history,
With all deference bring it out,
And if there's a skimmer lying about,
Skim half of the beans from the boiling pan
Into the bean pot as fast as you can;
Then turn to Biddy and calmly tell her
To take a huge knife and go to the cellar;
For you must have, like Shylock of old,
"A pound of flesh," ere your beans grow cold;
But, very unlike that ancient Jew,
Nothing but pork will do for you.

. . . .

Like an island of pork in an ocean of beans;
Pour on boiling hot water enough to cover
The tops of the beans completely over,
Shove into the oven and bake till done,
And the triumph of Yankee cookery's won! (53–54)

In denoting the proper code for making beans—itself a symbol of the New England elite—the poem alludes to improper conduct, that of Shylock, that ancient Jew, whose pound of flesh was taken in the form of usury, the stereotypical behavior of the Jew. Pork, the forbidden food of Jews, is in this instance the delectable and necessary—the centerpiece—ingredient in cooking beans, the quintessential Bostonian dish. What more compelling way to show the dangers of the foreign than to contrast a preferred food in one culture with the tabooed food of another? At the same time, the poem's mention of "the bean-pot, so famous in history," mythologizes an artifact that is a symbol of the New England agrarian roots of American culture. The poem's placement in the text signals another feature of the women's cultural life. Not only did the reference to Shylock highlight the differences between Christians and Jews, and between Americans and foreigners, but it also displayed the Presbyterian women's erudition. Quotations from venerated literature, such as Shakespeare's plays, often graced the pages of nineteenth-century cookery books. White Anglo-Saxon Protestant women were expected to be familiar with elite literature as a reflection of their respectability and refinement. In this cookbook they found a forum for their own cultural commentary about contemporary issues, in particular, the perceived threat of foreign incursions through immigration. Although the poem itself may not have been written by a woman, its deployment in the local cookbook acknowledges the concerns of many women in this community about racial matters.[9]

It is no surprise that homegrown, grassroots cookbooks that serve humanitarian goals are reflections of very particular and parochial concerns. The charitable effort is meant to serve a local community or, in some cases, a proselytizing mission far from home. In service to their own cause, the fundraisers celebrate their own culture and community while, at best, ignoring other communities and, at worst, denigrating them. This is not to demean women's many successful charitable efforts on behalf of other groups as well as their own. Still, it is ironic that in engaging in charitable activity to benefit their own group, the compilers of the *Presbyterian Cookbook* invoked negative images of Jewish cultural otherness and difference.

Ordinary women attended to and commented upon the political and social issues of their time. Attitudes toward cultural difference, in this case anti-Semitic expressions, could be promulgated in their quotidian writings and disseminated in local circles. Women who were barely literate could use such artifacts of daily life as the cookbook to express their fears about ethnic, cultural, and religious differences and the negative impact that things foreign could have on American life.

Cooking in Translation: *How to Cook and Eat in Chinese*

If American women were using the venue of the cookbook to express their views on social and cultural life, and to protect cultural and class boundaries through the codification of kitchen practice, a few foreign-born women found the cookbook a handy genre for crossing the very cultural, linguistic, and social boundaries established in household advice literature by women such as the Beecher sisters and Mrs. Putnam.[10]

One immigrant woman who used the cookbook to cross cultural boundaries was Buwei Yang Chao, who in 1945 published *How to Cook and Eat in Chinese*.[11] On the surface, it is an effort to educate American women about Chinese civilization by introducing them to Chinese food and cooking. Betty Fussell eloquently said, "Eating is the primary act of translation. One ingests the world of things and articulates a world of ideas."[12] Chao's book is such an act of translation. It interprets Chinese home cooking for an American kitchen and alludes to the thorny processes of acculturation and assimilation — another act of translation — for newly immigrated families.[13]

Chao, in her brief introduction, states: "I am ashamed to have written this book. First, because I am a doctor and ought to be practicing instead of cooking. Secondly, because I didn't write the book" (xii). In these opening sentences, she sets the stage with the problematics of her cookbook enterprise — an enterprise that implicates the process of immigration. The difficulties she and her family experienced in writing the cookbook are similar to the difficulties that they encountered in their new country. Both required learning how to adapt familial patterns and relationships learned in one cultural setting to another.

We are enlightened by her statement that she "ought to be practicing [medicine] instead of cooking" when Chao tells us that she "grew up with the idea that nice ladies should not be in a kitchen" (xii). With this disclaimer, she underscores her socioeconomic class as a physician, a mark of rank. She also tells us that she is a wife and mother. All these personal characteristics will be deployed in her efforts to gain the American reader's attention and trust. Though she is Chinese, Chao draws attention to the personal characteristics of middle-class marriage and motherhood that she shares with her reading public; she has the expertise of a native, the long experience of cooking for a family, and social standing. In making these claims for cultural knowledge and authority, she distinguishes herself from the ordinary immigrant.

Chao would also have us understand that there is a distinction between Chinese and Japanese cultures. With broad anti-Asian sentiment in the United States following World War II, it was imperative for her to differentiate and distance herself from the Japanese. When she tells us why she learned to cook despite her class prerogative not to do so, we discover her own anti-Japanese attitude. She claims, "I never stirred an egg until I went to college — the Tokyo Women's Medical College. I found Japanese food so uneatable that I had to cook my own meals" (xii). This statement signals the painful relationship between Chinese and Japanese during this period as clearly as a declaration of hostilities. In this, and again later, in the title of a recipe, i.e., "Bomb Tokyo," Chao alludes to Chinese sentiments toward Japan and the enduring effects of war on a culture and country (xiv).

Besides learning how to cook while in Japan, Chao undertook a study of regional Chinese cuisine. While her husband, a philologist, surveyed regional dialects in China, she learned how to cook its specialties. "I like to talk to strangers and I wanted to learn more about my country. I learned about many of the local customs and recipes in this way" (xiii). Her interest in cooking and her interest in learning about her own culture were united in this journey, a culinary pilgrimage in her homeland, a country that was to dramatically change.

Armed with the cultural authority she had accrued on this expedition, Chao used her expert knowledge to make a path into American homes via the dinner table. She intelligently views the intimate knowledge of food and language, and the activities of eating and speaking, as deeply initiating one into a culture, and, conversely, preventing outsiders from crossing borders. To be an insider is to know how to speak and how to eat. By bringing an "authentic" version of Chinese food and Chinese ways of eating into American homes, Chao is likewise crossing a cultural boundary. She has chosen the alimentary canal as the road to understanding.

In addition to her own attempts to create alliances with an American audience, she is aided by a notable American and winner of the Nobel Prize for Literature, Pearl S. Buck, whose devotion to issues of Sino-American relations won her a place in history. In her preface, Buck argues that Chao's book is a contribution to world peace and suggests that the author should be nominated for a Nobel Peace Prize. Buck sees Chao as a cultural mediator: "For what better road to universal peace is there than to gather around the table where new and delicious dishes are set forth, dishes which, though yet untasted by us, we are destined to enjoy and love? I consider this cookbook a contribution to international understanding" (xi).

But Buck is careful to attend to her intended Anglo audience. She states her loyalty and identity first and foremost as that of an American housewife. "I am trying to write this preface as an American housewife who is daily responsible for the meals of a large family and for occasional guests as well. . . . I have steadily remembered that I now live in the United States and that I am limited to American meats and vegetables, fats and fruits. It is as an American woman therefore that I should like to say that it seems to me this is a perfect cook book" (x). By allying herself primarily with American women, Buck's testimonial to the usefulness of the book for an American kitchen becomes credible. More than that, as a renowned expert on Chinese culture, Buck is both attesting to the cuisine's authenticity and speaking on behalf of the American readers who regard her as a fellow national. Her dual role enables Buck to act as a cultural broker for Chao, her text, her cuisine, and her culture.

Reviewers such as Clementine Paddleford agree with Buck's assessment of the authenticity of Chao's cuisine. With Chao as a guide you may "walk right though China's kitchen door . . . while she is cooking and you sit there with your mouth watering."[14] Furthermore, according to the Literary Guild review on the book's dust jacket, "With nothing more exotic than a bottle of soy sauce and a copy of *How to Cook and Eat in Chinese* you can turn out dishes that are easy on the ration points, amusing to cook and satisfying to eat." Americans can cook foreign foods and remain patriotic. This style of cookery is in keeping with the reduction of meat and milk products touted by governmental agencies. At this time, in service of the war effort, American anthropologists such as Margaret Mead and Ruth Benedict, sociologists such as John Bennett, and nutritionists were encouraging Americans to model their eating habits after other cultures' cuisines. Some of these peasant diets required little meat, fat, and vegetables and sustained hard-working and vigorous populations.

On the dust jacket, we are told that "the recipes she [Chao] concocts, and there are hundreds in this book, haven't a spoonful of anything in them that you cannot get right here in the United States; but they are true Chinese dishes. Some of them call for ingredients found only in Chinatowns, but usually the author marks these 'optional.' For a very few recipes, Chinatown ingredients are indispensable. (Incidentally such ingredients can be bought by mail.) In short, the great majority of the recipes require only items obtainable in any American food store." Thus, according to the dust jacket, readers can venture as far from home as they are able or as far as they dare. They can buy exotic products and never step foot into the Chinese community. The cuisine presented by Chao allows Americans to travel without ever leaving home. It is up to the reader to decide how far she will go on her voyage to cultural understanding. In this process, the only person to cross cultural boundaries is Chao!

At the same time that Chao is infiltrating the cultural borders of her new country, she is reserving for Chinese their rightful place as insiders to their culture, a place that few Americans may inhabit. It is through a knowledge of cooking and eating practices that Chao guards her *own culture's* borders. To be Chinese, her readers must know how to eat. She cautions Americans:

The greatest difficulty is that you do not feel natural when you eat Chinese food in American. You feel you are missing something essential. You do not feel that you are eating a meal. It is not ch'ih-fan. Now when I say "you" I mean "we" of course. So far as *you* are concerned, I would recommend first concentrating on preparing one dish or so in your usual scheme of meals and then try occasionally community eating as a lark. When you know how to shovel rice or congee gracefully over the edge of your bowl and leave a clean bowl at the end of your meal, then you are doing better than even some American old-timers in China, and we will feel that you belong. (13)

Chao is explicit about who constitutes "we" and "you." Americans who are not familiar with the rules of Chinese table etiquette are beyond the pale. To understand the people and its culture, one has to grasp their civilities. In the intricacies of eating politely may be found the door to their culture. In order to be an "insider," her readers must know how to eat rice from a bowl, sip tea from a cup, and be hospitable.

Chao is clear that what Americans have learned to eat in restaurants labeled as Chinese dishes is as foreign to the Chinese as American food. In a step-by-step fashion Americans may slowly adapt to Chinese patterns of eating. Chao encourages the reader, "The next step you may take in eating in Chinese may be to have all food Chinese but served and eaten with the framework of an American meal. In China, especially when there are foreign guests not used to Chinese ways of eating, this is sometimes practiced and is called 'Chinese meal foreign eaten.' Each guest is served individually and there is no common dish or dishes you eat directly out of." According to Chao, if nonnatives are willing to learn both the methods of cooking and eating, they, like Pearl S. Buck, may be considered "fellow provincials" (xiv). Americans may have no difficulty enjoying Chinese cuisine, but they may stumble when invited to partake from a common bowl. To eat from the same dish as others is to symbolically share a bond or an identity.

Throughout the book, Chao takes us on a journey — in time and in space — and repeatedly lets us know that we are the outsiders to this culture. In her descriptions of meal systems, we learn the difference between a meal — "fan, a period of rice" — and a snack — "tien-hsin, something to dot the heart" (3). We also learn about customary behavior at the end of a banquet when heavy foods are served. "This is the time to serve rice or congee if you can still eat anything. But most experienced eaters can, because they know the program beforehand and know the motto of 'Ten, jen, hen!' It means something like: Await, avoid, attack! That is you wait and avoid eating too much of everything, but when something really good comes, attack!" (6). Chao describes the etiquette specific to these occasions in a spirit of frivolity and playfulness. Dignitaries and outsiders are often accommodated at these large and formal occasions. Hospitality is paramount. Formality is high; expectations of intimacy are low. Only those familiar with the meal systems are knowledgeable and socially competent enough to override the decreed presentation. They may do so without censure. By the same token, those who do not know the sumptuary regulations are exempt from criticism.

On such occasions Chao, it seems, is lenient about an outsider's lack of insight into Chinese protocol. Lack of familiarity with Chinese conventions is understandable. Yet when it comes to family gatherings, Chao's tolerance of difference wanes. In a comparison of Chinese and American meals, the latter do not get a favorable review:

Many visitors to China or even long-time residents who never eat a Chinese meal except when invited to a formal dinner with "courses" have no idea what a totally different affair a Chinese family meal is. The typical family meal has several dishes all served at the same time. In families, in shops, and on the farm, people eat together, and share a little of several different dishes, and never have one dish belonging to one person. . . . The result is you feel you are all the time carrying on a friendly conversation with each other, even though nobody says anything. I wonder if it is because the American way of each eating his own meal is so unsociable that you have to keep on talking to make it more like good manners. (5)

Commensality in China, then, represents a profoundly different decorum than American etiquette. The intimate and intense *sharing* of food that marks family borders in China is absent from the American conventions, she concludes negatively. Food and its proper distribution during meals is the medium of this message. Speech merely interferes with proper conduct, which is focused on the manner of ingestion itself. The integrity of the family unit is symbolized by partaking of a collective meal from communal bowls. Talk is cheap. It cannot replace the solidarity that is engendered by sharing food from a single bowl.

Chao's description of eating at home and eating outside the home, how, when, and with whom, is a masterful ethnographic account of food consumption in Chinese society. Her focus in these descriptions is on customs and manners as well as food content. She points to each culture's share of seemingly odd behaviors and then, with rhetorical elegance, mocks western conceptions of appropriate demeanor. On differences in the techniques of eating Chao offers the following advice:

Certain hot foods are best when very hot. The technique for eating them is to draw in air over a narrow opening so as to hasten evaporation and diffuse the flavor. This is most effective when the air roughens the surface of the liquid. That is why hot soup, hot soup-noodles, hot congee, etc., are best when sucked in with as loud a noise as possible. Here again, I feel an inner conflict when I remember how I was taught that in foreign countries one must drink soup as quietly as possible. On the other hand, I can never bring myself to blow my nose in public, as people do in America, since this operation tends to be much louder than eating noodles and sounds much less inviting. (12–13)

Chao turns the world upside down to make nonsense out of our understandings of proper conduct. By contrasting American health habits with the logic of Chinese eating strategies she refocuses her social lens on Americans and Europeans.[15] Perhaps we can see ourselves as equally, if not less, "civilized" than the culture with which Americans are compared. Her sensitivity to the differences between Chinese and American commensal patterns reflects her own reminiscence of a childhood in both cultures. The experience of growing up among missionaries left a bitter aftertaste: "Americans who have lived long in China, especially those who have mixed with the Chinese, like to shovel-eat their rice even when they have returned and eat in American-Chinese restaurants. On the other hand, missionary-educated Chinese students hesitate to go Chinese before Americans because when they learned American manners of eating American food, they acquired the feeling that they are also good manners for eating any food. I share some of this feeling myself, because I was partly missionary-educated myself" (13). Chao recognizes what anthropologists have called "going native." When westerners eat Chinese food in American settings using Chinese manners, they show off their erudition, sophistication, and expertise in cultural matters. How well traveled they are! What prestige accrues to those who have lived in far-off lands and can adroitly maneuver themselves in several cultures. However, unlike their western counterparts, Chinese, inculcated in Anglo decorum by colonizing missionaries, do not enjoy the same reputation. They learned painfully how much better the manners of the white world were, for they are used everywhere. Missionary teachers imparted a sense not only of cultural difference but of cultural superiority. The westerners who traveled widely were not immigrants; they were adventurers and were acknowledged for their competencies in several cultures. What is most contradictory in this view is that foreign-born "immigrants," who adapt to multiple cultural settings and move comfortably among them, are not counted as competent by their adopted country. Consequently, Chao, as do many immigrants, lives in two worlds — her adopted country and the China of her memory and of her research and reconstruction — and not fully in one or the other.

Her collection of recipes is an evocation of the past, a nostalgic representation of regional cuisine. Although some foods have vanished in the trauma of the war and postwar period, her culinary repertoire is an account of war and its hardships on a people, circumstances that contemporary Chinese in China now face. The misery of her compatriots is expressed in the Proustian reminiscence of a meal of which she is deprived by relocation and that the Chinese themselves no longer have: "Hearing from friends and relatives about hardships at home and meeting those who have only recently come abroad make me feel how unreal some of those nice-eating things of the good old days seem to be. What's the use of talking about drinking golden, hot millet congee when you cannot get enough gray, gritty rice to eat?" (xiv). In a culinary mnemonic she traverses a landscape and recaptures a pristine past. In her narrative account of war through recipes we learn the new names given to familiar and traditional regional recipes: "Bomb Tokyo" is the title of a recipe — recently renamed in Chungking — for rice toast in soup, a variety of Mongolian Pot; "Depth Charging," the retitled "dropped eggs," consists of a couple of raw eggs poached in a "big pot" of hot soup (xiv). What terror and subversion compelled the renaming of such delectable family fare! At the same time, *How to Cook and Eat in Chinese* wants to evoke a way of life that no longer endures, a way of life that exists, perhaps, only in the author's imagination, an imagination born of dislocation and memory. Chao recounts folklore and history in her re-creation of Chinese regional cooking. "In the time of the Emperor Hsuan Tsung (eighth century A.D.), litchi 'nuts' had to be relayed by fast horses from Szechwan to Chang-an in modern Shensi to please his favorite courtesan. Recently, they have been flown from Canton to Shanghai. But on the whole, even in peacetime, most of the juicy peaches of Hopeh or Shantung are known only in their small locality, at least so far as knowledge of the juice trickling up your wrist is concerned" (19). Since the sensate world re-created in cookbooks begs recovery or discovery, it is, at best, only imitative. As with other memoirs and reminiscences," cookbooks appear to belong to the literature of exile, of nostalgia and loss."[16]

Still, Chao's book is more than a memoir. It is also an anatomy of culinary, cultural, and linguistic patterns. Both author, Chao, and foreword writer, Hu Shih, view the book as a grammar of techniques and methods. Linguistic analogies are profuse and pervasive. Shih praises Chao's abilities as a linguist to surmount cultural borders with the creation of a terminology American women can understand in order to teach them how to prepare Chinese cuisine. Yet, interestingly, and perhaps with particular Chinese modesty, Chao claims not to have written the text; it was written for her, in this case by her daughter and husband. The tensions of writing the book refer as well to this family's transition to another cultural and social world, an experience similar to other emigrating families. Chao explains, "You know I speak little English and write less. So I cooked my dishes in Chinese, my daughter Rulan put my Chinese into English, and my husband, finding the English dull, put much of it back into Chinese again" (xii). "Mushrooms Stir Shrimps" was changed to "Shrimps Fried with Mushrooms" and then changed back again to sound more Chinese. "The Salted Stews the Fresh," a favorite dish in Shanghai, consisting of salted and fresh pork clear-simmered together (19), was finally left in its original Chinese form. Perhaps Professor Chao thought that the recipes would appear more authentic and quaint to American readers if their titles were literal translations of the Chinese. Rulan, it seems, would have preferred adapted — more modern — titles for the book's English-speaking audience to signal her family's successful acculturation to American society.

Chao credits her daughter with writing the book, but not without cost. "I don't know how many scoldings and answering-backs and quarrels Rulan and I went through" (xii). In her critique of the generational strains caused by writing the book, Chao is also speaking to the strains and stresses to which generational relationships are subject in a new country. Chao says, "If kind friends — too many, who helped too much, to thank adequately here — if they had not come to the rescue to get the book done in a last midnight rush, the strained relations between mother and daughter would certainly have been broken. You know how it is with modern daughters and mothers who think we are modern" (xiii–xiv).

The fictional works of Amy Tan, Gish Jen, Denise Chong, and Maxine Hong Kingston[17] describe the trials of the mother-daughter relationship in detail, but the few words Chao uses to describe her situation are, in some ways, adequate. "And it is even more delicate with a mother and daughter, both having had mixed experiences of eating, cooking, and speaking and writing" (xiv). Multiculturalism, acculturation, and assimilation become issues troubling mother and daughter. In her book, the older woman recounts some of her journeys to different countries as proof of her sophistication and modernity, while, according to her mother, the younger woman views her parent, in this new milieu, as traditional and unworldly. Yet, despite their cultural differences and the stresses of writing the book, the bond between mother and daughter is affirmed. Their identities are confounded in the text at least on one occasion. One wonders if the following reminiscence, which is a footnote to the recipe for "Steamed Rice: Changsha Style . . . often used as a drink served individually, like thin congee" — belongs to mother or daughter (191). "This was my favorite drink when I lunched at school in Changsha, because all dishes in Changsha tasted so hot. — Rulan" (191). Has Rulan taken the opportunity to share — in her mother's book — her *own* memories of China, or is she embellishing the directions with stories of Chao's childhood told to her by her mother? In her role as translator Rulan may have decided to use her editorial prerogative to add a personal touch to the recipe with this memory. Perhaps she signed it as her contribution to her mother's book rather than as her own reminiscence.

Like many children of immigrant parents, Rulan acts as a cultural mediator/translator for her mother in the larger society and as such assumes an authoritative position vis-à-vis her parent. In this case the mother-daughter relationship is complicated by several border experiences, not the least of which is generational and complementarity of knowledge. Chao, the mother, knows how to cook; Rulan, the daughter, knows how to write. The enterprise requires negotiating authority within the boundaries of the household as well as outside it.

If writing the book created tension between Chao and her daughter, about her husband's contribution she has this to say: "Next, I must blame my husband for all the negative contributions he has made toward the making of the book. In many places, he has changed Rulan's good English into bad, which he thinks Americans like better. His greatest contribution is even more negative. . . . The only recipe that is really his own is Number 13.1, Stirred Eggs, which I let him write out himself. But he was so long-winded about it that I had to stop him from trying any other dish" (xiv). He begins his recipe with unprecedented formality in this list of ingredients." Obtain: 6 average-sized fresh eggs (for this is the maximum number of eggs I have cooked at one time); 50 c.c. fresh lard, which will approximately equal the content of 4 level tablespoonfuls; 1 plant of Chinese ts'ung (substitute scallion if ts'ung is unobtainable) about 30 cm. long by 7 mm. in average diameter" (133). Professor Chao, the linguist, writes out — with extraordinary scientific accuracy — a recipe Mrs. Chao claims is the simplest and most basic of Chinese dishes. The procedural directions are equally precise. "Either shell or unshell the eggs by knocking one against the another in any order" (134). The footnote Professor Chao adds to his text belabors — almost comically — the process of breaking the eggs: "Since, when two eggs collide, only one of them will break, it will be necessary to use a seventh egg with which to break the sixth. If, as it may very well happen, the seventh egg breaks first instead of the sixth, an expedient will be simply to use the seventh one and put away the sixth. An alternate procedure is to delay your numbering system and define that egg as the sixth egg which breaks after the fifth egg" (135).

He continues his rules for making eggs by warning the reader about the obvious next step. "Be sure to have a bowl below to catch the contents. With a pair of chopsticks, strike the same with a quick, vigorous motion known as 'beating the eggs.' This motion should, however, be made repeatedly and not just once. Automatic machines, aptly named as 'egg-beaters,' have been invented for this purpose. Make cross sections of the ts'ung at intervals of about 7.5 mm., making 40 sections altogether. Throw in the ts'ung and the measured amount of salt during the final phase of the beating" (135). Professor Chao's instructions resemble the analytic parsing of a sentence more than the writing of a recipe. However, we realize that there is some tongue-in-cheek humor embedded in the recipe text when Professor Chao volunteers evidence of his linguistic expertise to the reader: "To test whether the cooking has been done properly, observe the person served. If he utters a voiced bilabial nasal consonant with a slow falling intonation, it is good. If he utters the syllable *yum* in reduplicated form, it is very good. — Y.R.C." Her husband's efforts as a communicator of cooking techniques simply confirm Chao's sensibility that gender domains are sacrosanct. Men should not be in the kitchen. Even a professional woman such as she is better placed there than a man. Of her decision to use a particular orthographic and phonetic system for transliterating Chinese words she says: "Chinese words are given in the Wade system to which my husband is opposed" (xvi). If her husband, a famous philologist, can intrude upon her kitchen *and* try to determine the language used in her cookbook, then she, in her role as the family's cook, can be an interloper in the realm of linguistics. In the very act of writing about the tension between them, however, she challenges her husband's authority in his domain of expertise and inverts the norm of women's subordination and deference to their husbands.[18]

Postscript

It was not only "celebrity-reformers" like the Beecher sisters, who self-consciously published their views on society, but ordinary women who in their own charitable enterprises scripted a social world that accepted no intruders.[19] Employing their culture's elite literature in the service of their everyday cookbook gives weight and authority both to their kitchen practices and to their beliefs about social and cultural differences.

The Presbyterian ladies' selection of speech in a different register — a poem — that eulogizes a New England agrarian past marks the limits of culinary, and thus cultural, acceptability. Nonnative women, as did many others, also used what was close at hand as a way of crossing borders or patrolling them. Buwei Yang Chao's book is most obviously an account of difference, as it is an attempt to re-create a cuisine and a culture. In both instances, women from various classes, cultural origins, and political persuasions found the cookbook a place to circumscribe or cross social and cultural borders, to martial the persuasive force of the kitchen to gain support for their beliefs and causes. In each case, the author evoked a sense of "place" as an ideal with which to conform, whether "place" was a physical locale, a memorialized past, or a social location. The regional China of Chao's memory and the glorified New England of the Presbyterian ladies' poem each commemorate a place, a time, and the genius of a people.

In the process of commemorating a place through its food, culinary practices are codified. For this reason, in writing a recipe book the author is able to embed status, rank, and power in its rules. Because it is born of memory, the food and the place are matchless in their re-creation. Consequently, cookbook writers are able to claim expertise whether they are describing the preparation of "Sizzling Rice Soup" or Boston baked beans. Explicitly about disseminating knowledge, the texts, depending upon the reader, may create a gap as often as a bond. The very act of inscribing cultural and social differences in food preparation may link author and reader or create a wedge in the form of an "us" and a "them" or a "we" and a "you."

If cookbooks are about the losses of exile and the trauma of expulsion, they are also opportunities for nostalgia, travel, voyeurism, and emulation. They are subtle ways of marking insider and outsider status in social and cultural life. If all these books are about exile in its broadest sense, they are also about exclusion and inclusion. They are about the ways women write a place into being: to defy, delimit, manipulate, and infiltrate social, cultural, and geographical boundaries. And they do so in everyday places like the homely cookbook.

Notes

The research for this work was partially funded by the University of Pennsylvania Research Foundation. I would also like to thank Kristine Rabberman and Jeff Shultz especially for repeated readings and helpful suggestions. For their thoughtful comments on earlier drafts of this chapter, I would like to thank Monique Bourque, Janet Golden, Janet Tighe, and Elizabeth Toon.

1. For earlier work on household advice literature, the pioneering work of Mary Ryan is an example. See Mary P. Ryan, *The Empire of the Mother: American Writing about Domesticity, 1830–1860* (New York: Harrington Park Press, 1985). My own work on cookbooks includes *Household Words: Women Write from and for the Kitchen* (Philadelphia: University of Pennsylvania Libraries, 1996), an exhibition of materials from the Esther B. Aresty Collection of Rare Books on the Culinary Arts,

Van Pelt Dietrich Library; and "A Life's Work," in *Fields of Folklore: Essays in Honor of Kenneth S. Goldstein*, ed. Roger Abrahams (Bloomington, Ind.: Trickster Press, 1995), 287–99.

2. Kathryn Kish Sklar, in *Catharine Beecher: A Study in American Domesticity* (New York: Norton, 1973), has noted the role played by such prominent women as Catharine Beecher and Harriet Beecher Stowe in writing for American women through the genre of household advice manuals, as have Jeanne Boydston, Mary Kelley, and Anne Margolis in *The Limits of Sisterhood: The Beecher Sisters on Women's Rights and Woman's Sphere* (Chapel Hill: University of North Carolina Press, 1988).

3. Anne Goldman's analyses of the embedded autobiographies in cookbooks by Cleofas Jaramilla and Fabiola Cabeza de Baca seeks to expand the concept of auto-biography in *Take My Hand: Autobiographical Innovations of Ethnic American Working Women* (Berkeley: University of California Press, 1996). Her insights informed my interpretation.

4. For a discussion of the role that community cookbooks have played in documenting local history and defining community, please see Anne L. Bower, ed., *Recipes for Reading: Community Cookbooks, Stories, Histories* (Amherst: University of Massachusetts Press, 1997).

5. Goldman, *Take My Hand*, 4.

6. Jan Longone, " 'Tried Receipts': An Overview of America's Charitable Cookbooks," in Bower, ed., *Recipes for Reading*, 18.

7. Goldman, *Take My Hand*, xxvii.

8. Ladies of the First Presbyterian Church, *Presbyterian Cookbook* (Dayton, Ohio: Historical Publishing Company, 1873), 7.

9. I am using the category of "race" to define Jewish cultural and ethnic identity in keeping with nineteenth-century ideology and usage.

10. Mrs. Putnam, *Mrs. Putnam's Receipt Book and Young Housekeeper's Manual* (Boston: Ticknor and Fields, 1852).

11. Buwei Yang Chao, *How to Cook and Eat in Chinese* (New York: John Day, 1945). Page numbers appear in the text.

12. Paper presented at Food: Nature/Culture, a social research conference at the New School University, New York, November 5–7, 1998.

13. See, for example, Maxine Hong Kingston, *The Woman Warrior* (New York: Vintage Books, 1977).

14. Book jacket excerpt of review by Clementine Paddleford.

15. Chao tells us quite early on in the book that she uses the term *American* to denote Americans and Europeans (xv).

16. Arjun Appadurai, "How to Make a National Cuisine: Cookbooks in Contemporary India," *Society for Comparative Study of Society and History* (1988): 18.

17. Amy Tan, *The Joy Luck Club* (New York: Ivy Books, 1989); Gish Jen, *Mona in the Promised Land* (New York: Vintage Books, 1996); Denise Chong, *The Concubine's Children* (New York: Penguin, 1996); and Maxine Hong Kingston, *The Woman Warrior*.

18. For this point, see Chong; Hong Kingston; Jen; Pang-Mei Natasha Chang, *Bound Feet and Western Dress* (New York: Doubleday, 1996); for an anthropological

perspective, see Margery Wolf and Roxane Witke, eds., *Women in Chinese Society* (Stanford: Stanford University Press, 1975); Rubie S. Watson, "Named and the Nameless: Gender and Person in Chinese Society," *American Ethnologist* 13.4 (1986): 619–31; Jean Lock, "Effect of Ideology in Gender Role Definition: China as a Case Study," *Journal of Asian and African Studies* 24.3–4 (1998): 228–38.

19. Thanks to Elisa New, associate professor in the Department of English at the University of Pennsylvania, for this term.

Processed Foods from Scratch

Cooking for a Family in the 1950s

ERIKA ENDRIJONAS

Buy processed foods but cook from scratch; be creative but follow directions precisely; accommodate all family members' preferences but streamline the food purchase and preparation process; work part-time but be a full-time homemaker; and do it all with little or no training: such were the contradictory messages delivered to American women by their cookbooks in the 1950s. Like the cookbook authors themselves — ranging from socialites like Amy Vanderbilt to home economists like Meta Given to fictional characters like Betty Crocker — these cookbooks, in all their complexity, both reflected and molded the texture of women's lives.

The late 1940s and 1950s witnessed the emergence of not only a reinvigorated consumer culture and a child-centered culture but also a food-centered culture. Convenience or processed foods, which promised to save women tremendous amounts of time in the kitchen, were a growing phenomenon. Time saved on household tasks through technology meant more opportunities for women's personal development. Such development was tempered, however, by powerful messages that women should not neglect their domestic obligations to the family.

Contrary to historical precedents, as Americans' incomes rose during the postwar years, their expenditures on food increased rather than decreased. Scholar Karal Ann Marling contends that "the percentage of the average American family's income spent on food was going up as total income rose because consumers were willing to pay more for processing."[1] Although family budget expenditures on food were a small percentage of the overall 240 percent increase in expenditures on household items,[2] one cookbook estimated that most families spent one-third of their budget on food.[3]

Processed food was both a symbol of a burgeoning manufacturing economy and an important indication of technological advancement. Americans did not necessarily eat more, but they did purchase more food items, which theoretically increased the variety of foods they consumed and sped up the cooking process.[4] Cookbooks reflected this shift toward processed foods. For example, cookbook author Katharine Johnston noted that frozen food was "once a luxury, [but] is now almost a necessity."[5] Blanche Firman wrote, "Frozen vegetables are God's own gift to the busy housewife," as such foods offered the perfect combination of variety and speed.[6]

Simply put, processed foods presented women with a choice. The demand for women to rededicate themselves to their domestic pursuits, particularly cooking, appeared at the same time as did the proliferation of processed foods in the marketplace. Cookbooks promised that home-baked goods were the key to emotional stability and a show of love within the family at the same time that advertising and a consumer culture bombarded women with new types of processed food.

During World War II, processed foods, though limited in variety, had been a boon for women because they simplified cooking. "Brown 'n' Serve" rolls, cake mixes, and other packaged foods that needed little if any preparation meant that assembling a meal required less imagination and less time. The consequence, according to historian Glenna Matthews, was that processed foods "were closer to being ready-to-eat than anything before. And the level of skill that housewives needed to bring to cookery declined further."[7] This de-skilling of daily cooking became even more pronounced during the 1950s.

According to cookbook author Ruth Ellen Church, "No matter how many prepared foods we have with us, there's still plenty of cooking to be done."[8] *Betty Crocker's Good and Easy Cookbook* heralded the convenience of processed foods, although it did call for a moderate approach to their use. "Take advantage of all the fine modern timesavers—the prepared mixes, ready-to-eat cereals, canned and frozen fruits and juices to interchange with the fresh."[9] One author even provided her readers with a list of convenience foods to have on hand.[10] Moreover, Michael Reise offered that "packaged food cookery is virtually foolproof. You can count on good results."[11]

The definition of what constituted "good" was certainly debatable. As Matthews noted: "The nadir of American cookery came in the fifties. This was the heyday of prepared food and the cream-of-mushroom-soup school of cuisine whereby the cook could pour a can of this product over anything that was not a dessert and create a culinary treat according to the standards of the day."[12] Novelist John Keats captured this speedy approach to cooking in describing one of his central character's attempts to make dinner: "Mary took down a prepared spaghetti dinner from her shelves, a can of peas, and, casting around for dessert, decided on mixed fruit. She emptied the spaghetti and the peas into saucepans, put the saucepans on the stove; emptied the canned fruit into a bowl and put the bowl in the refrigerator."[13] Contrary to Keats's negative reaction to this approach to cooking, processed foods and meals consisting of such foods were lauded by Americans.

Processed food supposedly meant shorter hours in the kitchen, too. Unfortunately, the food itself only sped up one part of the process of producing a meal. "Cooking and meal cleanup," asserts historian Phyllis Palmer, "occupied the largest segment of time in a housewife's weekly schedule."[14] Thus, food preparation time may have been shortened, but the meals still required assembly, and both preparing and serving meals created dirty dishes.

Thus, a new definition of what constituted "home-cooked meals" was born in the postwar years, and homemakers were charged with finding the balance between convenience and taste and duty.

Creativity and Constraint

In the 1950s, cooking presented women with a paradox: cooking was viewed as an outlet for creativity; however, this creativity was encouraged in very structured, controlled ways. Additionally, while women were expected to express their creative energies through their cooking, this creativity was subordinate to the need to be of service to the family.

Popular psychologists postulated about the importance of creativity for women: "Housewives had to repossess the duties from which they had been displaced and to revive such lost arts as canning, preserving, and interior decorating. If the woman who viewed cooking as a pedestrian task rededicated herself to becoming a gourmet chef (and a food chemist), what had once been a tiresome chore could be transformed into a creative adventure."[15]

There was merit to this advice; cooking can be creative, and cookbooks encouraged this creativity in various ways. In fact, cookbooks encouraged women to be creative cooks by emphasizing the way in which food could be viewed as a work of art. Gwen French suggested that when using her cookbook, a woman would "know the pure, creative joy of cooking; [she] will be a real artist."[16] Helen Corbitt asserted that salads "should be a thing of beauty, fresh, chilled, and delectable to eat."[17] According to Marling, for many people, the visual pleasure of food was actually more important than the taste. Moreover, she argues that the 1950s witnessed a renewed emphasis on "decorative cooking," which originated in the nineteenth century. "Reform-minded cooking schools . . . aimed to elevate the feminine work of the kitchen to a science — or a fine art. The artfulness of table presentations, it was thought, stimulated the salivary glands and thus aided digestion."[18]

Food that was aesthetically pleasing was thus presented as a pleasure both to create and to consume. William Kaufman noted that "women look to cooking more and more as a real outlet for their creative and artistic drives."[19] According to *Woman's Day Collector's Cook Book*, "The modern housewife . . . need not be a student of architecture to create delectable tidbits. . . . Here are pastries as simple as you choose . . . on which you may lavish your creative artistry."[20] One cookbook author even suggested that cooking had "become a creative, highly respected art."[21] In this same vein, Janet McKenzie Hill suggested in her cookbook that "baking bread, making cakes, cookies . . . is . . . the best part of cooking. Surely it satisfies a creative urge, for. . . . [it] is a work of art — the art of cooking."[22] Feminine culinary prowess was evidenced most clearly by women's cake-making abilities. According to Marling, cakes were "the ultimate in aesthetic fare. The cake was food as sculpture, frosted in living color. It was a test of mother love and womanly competence."[23]

Suggestions for creativity with food were often specific and direct. Many cookbooks encouraged women to broaden their family's palates. Such expansion was to be accomplished by the introduction of a wide variety of foods and menu plans. However, experimentation and openness to new recipes were presented to women in some cookbooks as if the women were children. For example, the authors of the *General Foods Kitchens Cookbook* lectured: "You know how children hang back from a food they haven't seen before. Do you sometimes hesitate to undertake a dish with a strange name, a new ingredient, or one that requires a process or technique you haven't tried before?"[24]

The tone of this message is hardly surprising. Such language demonstrated a prevalent assumption that women needed precise directions for cooking. True to the nature of the culture at this time, women were expected to follow the directions given; thus their creativity and experimentation had an element of control to it.

For example, in the *Betty Furness Westinghouse Cookbook*, women were told, "Create pleasure, excitement at your house — make bread. You may feel timid about it but if you follow directions, it will be o.k."[25] One author warned women not to "jay walk" when cooking by stressing the need both to be prepared and to follow directions precisely.[26] Similarly, Ruth Bean urged her readers: "Try these recipes exactly as given, and use the correct-size pans" before straying from the instructions as given.[27]

In other words, a self-confident cook was one who strictly and obediently followed directions. Jean Mattimore and Clark Mattimore argued that women must follow the directions exactly, and this included reading the recipe twice through before starting: "That's what it takes to make a good pie — that and the ability to resist the impulse to experiment."[28] Susan Adams Mueller presented the following "deal" to homemakers in her cookbook: "If you conscientiously follow every detail and master each design . . . you will have the fundamentals of all good cooking at your finger tips."[29] In *Recipes for Good Eating*, the authors insisted, "Follow the directions to the letter and your family [will] exclaim, 'The best pie crust you ever made!' "[30]

In a more extreme example, the authors of the *Basic Cook Book* asserted that women should treat most recipes as an "order."[31] Mildred Knopf stated quite firmly that women were to follow each step meticulously "because the recipes that follow are set forth in such a way that you have only to follow one direction at a time . . . and try not to look ahead."[32] One cookbook even provided a strict timetable for women to follow that left only a minute or two to complete the assigned tasks:

7:15 Heat water for coffee
7:16 Prepare grapefruit
7:20 Set table
7:23 Make French sandwiches
7:29 Make coffee
7:30 Serve breakfast[33]

While this timeline may seem rigid to the experienced cook, a novice might have benefited greatly from such precise directions.

In fact, the written format of most cookbook recipes was such that a woman would know the necessary ingredients, cooking temperatures, and required utensils before beginning the cooking process, which made follow-ing directions that much easier. Whereas nineteenth-century cookbook au-thors often left vital information or critical steps out of recipes on the assump-tion that the recipe reader would be familiar with basic cooking techniques, twentieth-century cookbook authors offered explicit ingredient lists and cook-ing directions. Following a trend begun in England by such cookbook authors as Isabella Beeton and Fannie Farmer, Americans began to standardize the way in which recipes were written.[34] Renowned food author M. F. K. Fisher traced the development of this modern concept of recipes, which increasingly left nothing to chance. This need for simplification and clarity, notes Fisher, means that "a good recipe, for modern convenience, should consist of three parts: name, ingredients, method."[35] Moreover, the recipe title should be "descriptive," and the ingredients listed in the order of their use, their exact amounts, and what types of cooking pans will be used.

Following directions in the 1950s, however, meant that if women failed to do so, they had no one to blame but themselves for any cooking disaster. According to James Beard, "The fact that today's cook, especially in our country, commands such a vast variety of ingredients makes her potential achievement in the kitchen so much the more inspiring, and her failures, when made through carelessness or indifference, so much less excusable."[36] Elsie Masterton insisted that women should "make it [their] business to see that it's perfect every time," because past successes were no guarantee of future outcomes.[37]

Implicit is the idea that as long as women followed directions, failures would not occur. The authors of the *Basic Cook Book* believed that "a depend-able cookbook on the kitchen shelf is the best form of insurance against cooking failures."[38] But following directions was only one part of this insur-ance policy. Josie McCarthy wisely recommended that all ingredients be gathered and accessible before one started the meal to avoid "scurrying to the cupboard, fumbling in the back of the refrigerator, or discovering that there is one important ingredient missing."[39] This taught women the art and impor-tance of being prepared when cooking. The only drawback of such "insur-ance" advice was that proper preparation in no way guaranteed complete success. Sometimes egg whites simply do not whip and dough does not rise; thus, cookbook directions did not always ensure success and were far from foolproof.

An interesting corollary to this "insurance" concept is that when and if women made mistakes, they were obligated to "make it up" to their families. Thus, there was consistent pressure to stick to historically successful recipes at the same time that they were being encouraged to experiment and taught to fear losing their family's interest in food to boredom. Meta Given insisted that it was a woman's job to keep her family "interested in protective food which must be eaten every day."[40] Proper menu planning and a sense of imagination on the part of women were presented by Given and most cookbook authors as ways in which women could avoid their family's food dissatisfaction.

In fact, many cookbooks suggested that sugar in various forms was a pacifier and remedy for almost every food situation.[41] Consequently, dessert, potentially one of the most creative aspects of cooking, was presented as a way to rescue a poor meal. Julie Kiene advised women that a good dessert was the best way to "salvage an improperly balanced dinner . . . [and a home-maker] would be wise and popular if [she took] the time to provide suitable desserts."[42] According to Agnes Murphy, "A dessert is the cook's last chance to prove her proficiency."[43] Similarly, Mattimore and Mattimore asserted that "men judge a woman's cooking ability by her apple pie."[44]

Kiene and other authors also suggested that filled cookie jars were symbols of motherly affection. However, it was made clear in countless cookbooks that cookie jars were specifically to be filled with home-baked goodies. Ruth Neumann asserted that treats should be made "from scratch because . . . while cake and cooky [*sic*] mixes have their place and are excellent, they still cannot come up to the delectable perfection of the old-fashioned variety. I hate to see our children missing out on the pleasures of old-fashioned baking, too."[45]

Josie McCarthy echoed this emphasis on old-fashioned cooking in noting that many of her recipes were "old-fashioned, slow to make, but to [her] mind, worth the trouble."[46] Church suggested that women who relied too heavily on packaged or frozen foods would lose "the sense of achievement and pride that there is in mixing and baking a dinner from scratch."[47] *General Foods Kitchens Cookbook* admonished women "not to neglect the cooking you yourself do from scratch. It's pleasant."[48]

Service to one's family also called for the application of creativity to more than just meal preparation. To fill the extra time supposedly created by processed foods and ever-advancing appliances, women were encouraged to provide a "special touch" by making small additions to improve their family's day. This included posting the breakfast menu to increase family appetites, providing elaborate place settings for breakfast, including individual vases of fresh cut flowers, and hauling out fancy tablecloths for everyday meals.[49] Additionally, Betty Crocker advised, "Brighten the days for your children with simple treats. A little extra thought on your part can make the plainest between-meal snack an adventure to build happy memories."[50]

Creativity also meant economizing work. Many cookbooks suggested that women spend their "spare" time wisely on Saturday baking or cooking for the week ahead. Louella Shouer advised women that "making a jar of French dressing should be a weekly habit. A cake or cupcakes . . . could be on your Saturday program, too."[51] These tips actually helped women do all of their necessary baking by encouraging them to dispense with this time-consuming activity in a block of weekend time.

Finally, Brett Harvey's interviews with 1950s homemakers aptly revealed that the concern for creativity, in tandem with the desire to satisfy their family's need for interesting cuisine, led many women to spend enormous amounts of time on silly dishes. As one woman recalled, "And the cooking! I actually remember a recipe which called for making flowers out of mashed potatoes molded into Bartlett pears, with cloves for the stems, and glazed with egg whites." Another housewife, describing the ways in which she filled her days, said, "I took care of the house, did fancy knitting and strange cooking — you know, puff pastry — I canned, made pickles, lots of bread."[52]

Satisfaction Guaranteed

The connection between domesticity, cooking in particular, and personal satisfaction for women was common in the postwar period. While many women did gain satisfaction through domestic work, cookbook rhetoric often exaggerated the connection between domesticity and satisfaction. In *Martha Deanes Cooking for Compliments*, Marian Young Taylor aptly articulated this projected ideal in her preface: "Modern psychiatrists tell us that happy is she who reaps satisfaction from the work she does. Including her cooking — of which she will average some 50,000 hours of her married life!"[53] Church stated, "We must not meekly succumb to the trend toward feeding our families completely ready-made dishes. . . . We'd be robbing ourselves and our families of great pleasure. For us there is joy in creating appetizing dishes."[54]

Several cookbooks drew a parallel between women's personality development and their domestic duties as if they were two sides of the same coin. According to Florence Arfmann, "Women have got today's sense of values; they put as much emphasis on personality as on perfectionist housekeeping."[55] Another cookbook suggested that a woman's personality could be judged by the appearance of her table at mealtime. "Setting the table, like preparing a stage set, is fun, whether it is done just for your family or for your most elaborate entertaining. It is at your table that you have an opportunity to express your personality."[56]

Women's effectiveness and personal satisfaction in the kitchen was not judged solely by their efficiency or cooking abilities. Appropriate attire for women in the kitchen was subject to debate in postwar cookbooks, many of which described a connection between women's clothes and their family's appetite and happiness. In the twenty-seventh edition of *Settlement Cook Book*, published in 1945, the advice given to women about their kitchen clothing had not changed from the Depression-era version of this cookbook: "Jewelry should not be worn in the kitchen. Wear a cotton wash dress or a cover-all apron with a pocket for a handkerchief. Have a small hand-towel that buttons on to the band of the dress or apron. Have two pot holders, fastened together with tape and attach to dress or apron. Wear washable cap that covers the hair."[57]

By contrast, Betty Crocker recommended that women should wear nice clothes and makeup in the kitchen while doing their cooking chores because it would enhance their families' enjoyment of their food. It was also assumed that women would feel better, more satisfied with their efforts if they took great care in how they dressed and groomed themselves. "Every morning before breakfast, comb hair, apply makeup and a dash of cologne. Does wonders for your morale and your family's, too! Think pleasant thoughts while working and a chore will become a 'labor of love.' "[58] In the same vein, Ida Bailey Allen noted in her cookbook, "Stay-at-home wives, young and older, are discarding house dresses and cover-all aprons. The replacement? Swirls, colorful sunbacks, play suits with button-on skirts." She advised women to "learn to look and feel dainty as you work."[59]

In short, the *Settlement Cook Book* viewed cooking as substantial work, for which washable uniforms were the most appropriate attire. However, at a time when women were encouraged to find satisfaction in even the most mundane tasks, Betty Crocker's suggestions may have been more helpful.

Beginning Bride, Beginning Cook

Perhaps the most striking contradiction during this period was the issue of women's state of preparedness for their homemaker duties. Why, if the culture informed women that their "natural" role was to be wives and mothers, did they appear to be so inadequately prepared? Simply put, cookbooks assumed no knowledge on the part of beginning brides, which is why so many of them equated the term "bride" with "beginner."[60]

Missing in historical and other literature is a discussion of the apparent generation gap with respect to cooking. Evident from all of these texts, however, is the implication that women were not learning how to cook from their mothers. To this end, Marling asserts that "Betty Crocker became the substitute mother to a generation of motherless exurbanites."[61] In fact, women were expected to remake themselves in Betty Crocker's image as the quintessential wife and mother.

According to Marjorie Heseltine and Ula M. Dow, "That girl is lucky who has had the opportunity to master a few basic dishes in a kitchen where someone else was responsible for the meal as a whole."[62] French lamented her own lack of training: "Gentle reader, this is a cookbook like no other cookbook. It is a book I wish someone had written when I was a bride."[63] Hale MacLauren also described her own knowledge of cooking as limited as a young woman: "I knew there were eggs and I knew there were lemons. It was reasonable to believe I could boil an egg or extract the juice from a lemon. Beyond this I had never thought to go."[64] Blanche Firman's reason for writing her cookbook was to compensate for her daughter-in-law's apparent lack of training in homemaking. "Peggy was bewildered by all the troubles of housekeeping and really wanted to know how to run a house happily and feed her family."[65]

According to Levenstein, in 1951, 58 percent of women believed that they were not better cooks than their mothers.[66] Many women had not learned as girls growing up in the home how to cook. No single explanation can adequately or accurately account for this phenomenon. Marling suggests that postwar women "missed 'the apprenticeship of the stove' which had once equipped their mothers and grandmothers and great-grandmothers before them with basic culinary skills."[67] Neither Harvey nor the women she interviewed mentioned learning to cook from their mothers. In fact, in most instances, the women interviewed indicated that they had taught themselves to cook with the help of cookbooks.

Often it was assumed that women, regardless of age, only learned how to cook once they were married. The requisite first poorly prepared meals were considered a rite of passage for newlyweds. Fisher humorously offered that "for a long time I believed that the first pangs of connubial bliss brought with them a new wisdom, a kind of mystic knowledge that slipped with the wedding ring over all the fingers of the bride, so that at last and suddenly and completely she knew how to boil water."[68]

Hill stated that young girls' attendance in the kitchen was "fairly casual" and only incidental. She insisted that "most young women learn to cook only when they have a home of their own. There are too many skills for girls to learn as they grow up, and cooking is often neglected."[69] Hill, however, offered no explanation for this. Even cookbooks like the *Time Reader's Book of Recipes* that made references to an oral tradition of cooking knowledge passed through the generations approached cooking as though women were completely ignorant of it.[70]

The idea that brides did not know how to cook may have been rooted in fact. As sociologist Marjorie DeVault notes in her work on food preparation within the family, rarely did mothers actually explain cooking or any household function explicitly. One plausible explanation for this is that mothers may have assumed that cooking could be learned through observation. Wilma Lord Perkins, for example, mentioned learning to cook through observation in the *Fannie Farmer Junior Cookbook*.[71] DeVault, too, relates the following example: "She never sat down and said, 'OK, this is how you do such and such.' She may have done that with something like baking cookies, but not everyday meals. . . . So I think if I picked things up at all it would be osmosis. And then kind of adapting, you know, things that I remember her cooking."[72]

It would be shortsighted to assume that learning to cook is simply about preparing food. Cooking requires not only the physical preparation of meals but also the ability to juggle food needs and tastes, a skill learned only through practice. Women's cooking duties were as much about providing sustenance as they were about satisfying their family's needs and desires. DeVault insists that women have been socialized to accommodate the tastes of each family member.[73] Many cookbooks published in the 1950s articulated this responsibility. For example, the author of the *Betty Furness Westinghouse Cookbook* suggested, "It is a wise homemaker who can anticipate the appetites of her family and provide them with homemade candy just at the time they feel they want it the most."[74] Included in this accommodation is having to adjust menus to meet the needs of all family members, a task involving a significant amount of work for women. In describing the complexity of women's cooking duties, French stated that women "may have had to cope with capricious, finicky or excessive appetites."[75]

Thus, women's household duties included accounting for other family members' tastes while balancing very real budget and time limitations. Their success at these tasks further ensured that future generations of women would be expected to perform at the same level and with the same dedication. What is most striking is the unconscious nature of it. One of the women DeVault interviewed thought nothing of her complicated shopping needs, which included accommodating her vegetarian children and her husband's meat and processed food desires. "It's not a hassle. I mean, I don't think it's outrageous. . . . Everybody has food preferences."[76] According to DeVault, this type of work is largely invisible. The ability to do such balancing acts has been attached to women's gender role, and the end result is that women have had expectations placed upon them on the basis of their ability to complete such tasks.

Accommodating a variety of food desires within the family required an ample supply of food, and one large aspect of homemakers' work was shopping for groceries. Supermarkets were a revolutionary aspect of the growth of suburbia whereby women could supposedly purchase all the goods they needed in one central location. However, the supermarket, instead of being a benefit to women, to some extent, actually represented the devaluation of their time, for twenty years earlier, stores were full service establishments where women placed orders and store employees filled them.[77] Conversely, the author of the *Silver Jubilee Super Market Cook Book* suggested that "before the advent of the supermarket, when Mrs. America wished to buy her groceries, meats, fruits and vegetables, she had to ask the storekeeper or clerk for every item she wanted."[78]

Grocery shopping involved the complex task of stocking kitchen shelves both efficiently and economically. For Mary L. R. Taylor, women were to avoid waste by "calculating the family appetite, then buying to meet its needs; second, by using all the food paid for."[79] She even included a sample grocery list to stock the larder for not only the first meal after getting married but for the first week of food as well. Given advised women not to shop at one store; instead, they should go to all available stores to get the best deals possible.[80] Mary Grosvenor Clark advised women to "make a habit of reading a food market report in your daily paper, and before settling down to plan meals, glance through the day's bargains."[81] While going from store to store permitted the purchase of food at the best price, it also represented a further devaluation of women's time in food procurement.

Lily Wallace viewed marketing, especially the first time, as a "big adventure." For Wallace, it represented the "serious side" of women's realization of the home and kitchen they've dreamed of their entire lives.[82] It was also an opportunity to get out of the house. One woman interviewed by Harvey thought her shopping trip out to be a time of comradeship with other women: "My one outing of the week was to go to the Safeway for groceries — we'd go in a group, a bunch of women, in a carpool."[83] Some cookbooks, however, discouraged women from shopping with each other, for such excursions might lead women to buy unnecessary items simply because their friends were buying them. Others believed that women were incapable of concentrating on their lists and requisite menu plans if friends were along. The author of *Anybody Can Cook* insisted that when women "Trot, Trot, Trot" to the market they should "Be systematic," otherwise they might "come home without the two or three things [they] may need most."[84] Depending upon one's approach and disposition, according to one author, marketing could be "a confusing and exhausting task, or it [could] be a new adventure every day."[85]

In sum, the job of cooking encompassed more than simply putting three meals a day on the table. It involved servicing other family members and expending large amounts of energy to ensure that their likes and dislikes were satisfied when preparing those meals. When Betty Friedan wrote about "work expanding to fill the time," she was referring, in part, to the intersection of technology and the expectations placed upon women. The Depression and the shortages of World War II were but a memory in the 1950s. Grocery shelves were filled with growing numbers of processed foods, and women's work supposedly was lightened by the advent of appliance technology. Women's work, however, was still significant and largely invisible.

Cooking was presented to women in the 1950s as one element of their nurturing function within the family, not as work that could be shared. Nutrition expert Adelle Davis insisted upon the importance of good, healthy food in caring for the family, and she articulated the connection between food preparation, nurturing, and the family's health in her cookbook: "When she hears her physician praise the beauty of her children, when she sees her husband, young beyond his years, succeeding because of his energies, when she feels the surge of vibrant health in her own body, she will realize that . . . she has shouldered her tasks and has seen to it that good health has come from good cooking."[86] The tone of her rhetoric is a powerful reminder of the awesome responsibility women had to their families in the postwar period. Neither she nor many other women at the time took that responsibility lightly.

Notes

1. Karal Ann Marling, *As Seen on TV: The Visual Culture of Everyday Life in the 1950s* (Cambridge: Harvard University Press, 1994), 220.

2. Elaine Tyler May, *Homeward Bound: American Families in the Cold War Era* (New York: Basic Books, 1988), 165.

3. Marjorie Heseltine and Ula M. Dow, *The Basic Cook Book* (Boston: Houghton Mifflin, 1947), 13.

4. Harvey Levenstein, *Paradox of Plenty: A Social History of Eating in Modern America* (New York: Oxford University Press, 1993), 101, chaps. 7 and 8.

5. Katharine Johnston, *Deep-Freezing for the Housewife* (London: Sir Isaac Pitman and Sons, 1959), iii.

6. Blanche C. Firman, *Peggy Put the Kettle On: Recipes and Entertainment Ideas for Young Wives* (New York: Exposition Press, 1951), 99.

7. Glenna Matthews, *"Just a Housewife": The Rise and Fall of Domesticity in America* (New York: Oxford University Press, 1987), 203.

8. Ruth Ellen Church, *Mary Meade's Kitchen Companion: The Indispensable Guide to Modern Cooking* (New York: Bobbs-Merrill, 1955), 33.

9. *Betty Crocker's Good and Easy Cookbook* (New York: Simon and Schuster, 1954), 4.

10. Lily Haxworth Wallace, *Just for Two Cookbook* (New York: Bramhall House, 1952), 65.

11. Michael Reise, *The 20-Minute Cook Book* (New York: Crown, 1953), 2.

12. Matthews, *"Just a Housewife,"* 211.

13. John Keats, *Crack in the Picture Window* (Cambridge: Riverside Press, 1957), 59.

14. Phyllis Palmer, *Domesticity and Dirt: Housewives and Domestic Servants in the United States, 1920–1945* (Philadelphia: Temple University Press, 1989), 56.

15. William Henry Chafe, *The American Woman: Her Changing Social, Economic, and Political Roles, 1920–1970* (New York: Oxford University Press, 1972), 206.

16. Gwen French, *Anybody Can Cook* (Boston: Little, Brown, 1954), 12.

17. Helen Corbitt, *Cookbook* (Boston: Houghton Mifflin, 1957), 42.

18. Marling, *As Seen on TV*, 221–22.

19. William I. Kaufman, ed., *Cooking with the Experts: Over 400 Simple, Easy-to-Follow, Taste-Tempting Recipes Selected by Television's Best Cooks* (New York: Random House, 1955), vii.

20. *Woman's Day Collector's Cook Book* (New York: E. P. Dutton, 1960), 263.

21. Ida Bailey Allen, *Ida Bailey Allen's Cookbook for Two* (Garden City: Garden City Books, 1957), 1.

22. Janet McKenzie Hill, *Cooking for Two* (Boston: Little, Brown, 1951), 190.

23. Marling, *As Seen on TV*, 224.

24. Women of General Foods, *General Foods Kitchens Cookbook* (New York: Random House, 1959), 3.

25. Julia Kiene, ed., *Betty Furness Westinghouse Cook Book* (New York: Simon and Schuster, 1954), 315.

26. Allen, *Cookbook For Two*, 8.

27. Ruth Bean, *All-in-One Oven Meals* (New York: Bramhall House, 1952), 9.

28. Jean Mattimore and Clark Mattimore, *Cooking by the Clock* (New York: Ace Books, 1948), 50.

29. Susan Adams Mueller, *Susan Adams' How-to-Cook Book* (New York: A. A. Wyn, 1951), 14.

30. Proctor and Gamble Company, *Recipes for Good Eating* (1945), 17.

31. Heseltine and Dow, *Basic Cook Book*, 55.

32. Mildred Knopf, *The Perfect Hostess Cook Book* (New York: Alfred A. Knopf, 1959), xiv. See also Mattimore and Mattimore, *Cooking by the Clock*, esp. chap. 1, which gives explicit directions for how to use the book.

33. Allen, *Cookbook for Two*, 49.

34. M. F. K. Fisher, *With Bold Knife and Fork* (New York: G. P. Putnam's Sons, 1968), 18, chap. entitled "The Anatomy of a Recipe."

35. Ibid., 23.

36. James Beard, *The Fireside Cookbook: A Complete Guide to Fine Cooking for Beginner and Expert Containing 1,217 Recipes and Over 400 Color Pictures* (New York: Simon and Schuster, 1949), 11.

37. Elsie Masterton, *Blueberry Hill Cookbook* (New York: Thomas Y. Crowell, 1959), 2.

38. Heseltine and Dow, *Basic Cook Book*, 4.

39. Josephine McCarthy, *Josie McCarthy's Favorite TV Recipes* (Englewood Cliffs, N.J.: Prentice-Hall, 1958), 1.

40. Meta Given, *The Modern Family Cook Book* (Chicago: J. G. Ferguson, 1953), 14.

41. During World War II, Americans found it as difficult to ration sugar as they did to ration meat and butter. Sugar was rationed until 1947. Levenstein, *Paradox of Plenty*, 85, 96.

42. Kiene, *Betty Furness Westinghouse Cook Book*, 315.

43. Agnes Murphy, *The American Everyday Cookbook* (New York: Random House, 1955), #1308.

44. Mattimore and Mattimore, *Cooking by the Clock*, 169.

45. Ruth Vendley Neumann, *Conversation-Piece Recipes* (Chicago: Reilly and Lee, 1962), 207.

46. McCarthy, *Favorite TV Recipes*, 2.

47. Church, *Kitchen Companion*, 11.

48. *General Foods Kitchens Cookbook*, 3.

49. See, for example, *Betty Crocker's Good and Easy Cookbook*, 4; and Mueller, *How-to-Cook Book*.

50. *Betty Crocker's Good and Easy Cookbook*, 226.

51. Louella G. Shouer, *Quick and Easy Meals for Two* (New York: Bramhall House, 1952), 2.

52. Brett Harvey, *The Fifties: A Women's Oral History* (New York: HarperPerennial, 1993), 117, 52.

53. Marian Young Taylor, *Martha Deanes Cooking for Compliments* (New York: M. Barrows, 1954), 9–10.

54. Church, *Kitchen Companion*, 13. See also Amy Vanderbilt, *Amy Vanderbilt's Complete Cookbook* (Garden City, N.Y.: Doubleday, 1961).

55. Florence Arfmann, ed., *The Time Reader's Book of Recipes* (New York: E. P. Dutton, 1949), 4.

56. Ada B. Lothe, Breta L. Griem, and Ethel M. Keating, *The Best from Midwest Kitchens* (New York: Gramercy, 1946), 7.

57. Mrs. Simon Kander, ed., *The Settlement Cook Book: The Way to a Man's Heart* (Milwaukee: Cramer-Krassett, 1945), 4.

58. *Betty Crocker's New Picture Cook Book* (New York: McGraw-Hill, 1959), 5.

59. Allen, *Cookbook for Two*, 1, 48.

60. See, for example, Kiene, *Betty Furness Westinghouse Cook Book*; Carol Truax, ed., *Ladies' Home Journal Cookbook* (Garden City, N.Y.: Doubleday, 1960); *General Foods Kitchens Cookbook*; Heseltine and Dow, *Basic Cook Book*; and Beard, *Fireside Cookbook*. This is by no means an exhaustive list.

61. Marling, *As Seen on TV*, 209.

62. Heseltine and Dow, *Basic Cook Book*.

63. French, *Anybody Can Cook*, ix. See also McCarthy, *Favorite TV Recipes*, esp. chap. 4.

64. Hale MacLauren, *Be Your Own Guest: Once-A-Week Cooking* (Boston: Houghton Mifflin, 1952), 3.

65. Firman, *Peggy Put the Kettle On*, 11.

66. Levenstein, *Paradox of Plenty*, 124–5. The women beginning their families in the 1950s were raised during the Depression and World War II. There are no references to anyone other than the mother cooking for the family as these women were growing up.

67. Marling, *As Seen on TV*, 208–209.

68. M. F. K. Fisher, *The Art of Eating: "How to Cook a Wolf"* (New York: World, 1954), 207.

69. Hill, *Cooking for Two*, v.

70. Arfmann, *Time Reader's Book of Recipes*, 5. See also Marguerite Gilbert McCarthy, *The Cook Is in the Parlor* (Boston: Little, Brown, 1949); *General Food Kitchens Cookbook*; and Carli Laklan and Frederick-Thomas, *Gifts from Your Kitchen: A Collection of 300 Recipes with 300 Wrappings* (New York: M. Barrows, 1955).

71. Wilma Lord Perkins, *The Fannie Farmer Junior Cook Book* (Boston: Little, Brown, 1946), introduction.

72. Marjorie L. DeVault, *Feeding the Family: The Social Organization of Caring as Gendered Work* (Chicago: University of Chicago Press, 1991), 106.

73. Ibid., chaps. 2, 5, and 6.

74. Kiene, *Betty Furness Westinghouse Cookbook*, 441.

75. French, *Anybody Can Cook*, 230.

76. DeVault, *Feeding the Family*, 87.

77. Nona Glazer, "Servants to Capital: Unpaid Domestic Labor and Paid Work," in Naomi Gerstel and Harriet Engel Gross, eds., *Families and Work* (Philadelphia: Temple University Press, 1987), 236–55.

78. Edith Barber, *Silver Jubilee Super Market Cookbook* (New York: Super Market Publishing, 1955), xi.

79. Mary L. R. Taylor, *Economy for Epicures: A Practical Menu and Recipe Book* (New York: Oxford University Press, 1947), 2.

80. Given, *Modern Family Cook Book*, 49.

81. Mary Grosvenor Clark, *The Best Cookery in the Middle West* (Garden City, N.Y.: Doubleday, 1956), 317.

82. Wallace, *Just for Two Cookbook*, 64.

83. Harvey, *The Fifties*, 122.

84. French, *Anybody Can Cook*, 22.

85. Hill, *Cooking for Two*, 3.

86. Adelle Davis, *Let's Cook It Right: Good Health Comes from Good Cooking* (New York: Harcourt, Brace, 1947), 563.

Freeze Frames

Frozen Foods and Memories of the Postwar
American Family

CHRISTOPHER HOLMES SMITH

Frozen Memories

Like many icons of American popular culture that we have witnessed since
the end of World War II, the "TV Dinner" is defined by the fact that its
packaging is remembered, even if its content is largely forgotten. The "TV
Dinner" slogan was originally coined for a product distributed in 1954 by the
Swanson division of the Campbell Soup Company (fig. 8.1). Despite its name,
the Swanson TV Dinner was not necessarily intended to be consumed in front
of the television set, but was conflated with TV in order to denote similarly
modern notions of sophistication and prosperity. In this respect, both TV and
the TV Dinner gave material expression to the nation's desire to celebrate the
end of scarcity through a postwar lifestyle of leisure. Even before Hitler began
to terrorize Western Europe, the rapidly growing frozen foods industry in the
United States had confidently promised American consumers, particularly
women, a level of domestic efficiency and freedom that previously they could

Fig. 8.1. History in the making: Swanson TV Dinners, circa 1957. Used by permission of Vlasic Foods International.

only imagine. The simple genius of the TV Dinner slogan was to create a brand identity around the household appliance that most clearly represented how the spoils of victory were to be translated into radically revised social relationships back home. In other words, the TV Dinner made the postwar society's transition from the rigidity of old-style labor to the mobility of new-fangled diversion as garishly literal as tail fins on a souped-up hot rod. The strategy proved so successful that almost immediately *every* frozen dinner product on the market became colloquially known as a "TV Dinner."

Even though the current product box no longer sports the original "TV Dinner" terminology, Swanson's initial stroke of ingenuity continues to reap significant rewards, as three million TV Dinners are still consumed each week in the United States, generating about $300 million in annual sales for Vlasic Foods International, the company that currently controls the label. In addition, Vlasic's recent press material proudly notes that "the original Swanson aluminum tray, retired in 1987 in place of a microwavable tray, resides in the Smithsonian."[1] But what insights into the TV Dinner's social history get lost despite the product's official cultural commemoration? Answering this question via an investigation of the gendered aspects of the American frozen foods industry will be the chief objective of this chapter. From the premise that TV Dinner nostalgia is symptomatic of our simplification of Cold War Americana, I argue that the discourses that introduced frozen foods to the nation's housewives actually indicate that a far more complex set of gender relations existed at the time. An underlying component of my analysis will illustrate how various attempts to bolster the definition of masculinity within the domestic sphere are paradoxically the most central yet least expressed elements of postwar kitchen culture. The object for frozen foods proponents at the time revolved around teaching women how to use the new products to convince men that they were gaining ground in American society, even as they appeared to be losing it.

Corporate executives at Vlasic would be the first to say that finding a compelling answer of their own to the riddle of the nation's continued taste for TV Dinners is paramount to the sustained health of their business. Not too long ago, Vlasic was not an independent corporation, but rather an unappreciated assortment of misfit brands loosely connected under the Campbell Soup umbrella. After being spun off from the food giant in 1998, these businesses consolidated under the Vlasic banner and began a fitful journey toward profitability. As it galvanized itself for the pursuit of Wall Street's fickle ardor, the publicly owned company based its future viability on the re-launch of the Swanson TV Dinner, an asset that it had gained in its divorce from Campbell.

Vlasic's brain trust immediately identified Swanson as a classic underperformer. While the brand could still lay claim to the cultural cachet granted by the nation's unwavering nostalgia for the 1950s, it was gradually losing market share, nonetheless; according to the most recent statistics, Swanson controls only 9 percent of all frozen dinner sales.[2]

In order to bolster its rather unimpressive position in the frozen dinner pecking order, Vlasic is betting that the aging baby-boomer generation will regard TV Dinners not merely as sustenance for their bodies, but also as a legacy of innocence and wonder that they can pass on to their children. Vlasic's optimism comes not so much from wishful thinking, but from painstaking consumer surveys. In a company press release announcing a new media campaign for TV Dinners, Murray S. Kessler, President of Swanson Frozen Foods, summarized how his company envisioned turning residual knowledge of their product into renewed public interest: "What parent doesn't remember having a Swanson dinner growing up? . . . Consumers and parents told us they had fond memories of growing up and enjoying the dinners because they were a treat. It was special picking what dinner to have, eating it in front of the television, and of course eating the dessert first. We will bring these types of memories into the present and share them with new generations."[3] Thus, in January 1999, Swanson launched a $300 million television ad campaign under the banner "Make New Memories with Swanson." The series of thirty-second commercials, all of which were developed by Young and Rubicam New York, began circulation with a spot called "Betty the Babysitter."[4]

The commercial depicts a wife and husband going out on a date in the family car, leaving their two daughters at home where they are about to be served a Swanson dinner by Betty, their caretaker for the evening. The viewer's gaze begins on the father's jovial face as he sits behind the wheel of the automobile, but attention is quickly diverted from him as the camera pans to the laughing countenance of the mother. The off-screen narrator begins to read aloud the mother's thoughts: "Tonight while you were out, your kids were in the trusted care of Betty the babysitter. You know they ate well, because Betty made new Swanson boneless fried chicken dinners." This scenario prompts the children's mother to recollect being fed TV Dinners by her own childhood babysitter. As the narrator recounts the evening's events, sepia-toned images of the mother's "past" roll across the screen: "Your kids ate the brownies first, they devoured the tender all-white meat and the crispy coating, with less than perfect table manners, and they finished the mashed potatoes with their fingers. Oh, like when you were a kid, you didn't eat a Swanson dinner the same way . . . with Joan, the babysitter."

The legacy that the "Betty the Babysitter" commercial constructs is one specifically geared toward female consumers, one which promises to revisit and memorialize those revolutionary mid-century moments when American women began to eschew the vertically anchored norms of motherhood for an assortment of more socially mobile lifestyles. In the commercial, these memories create a hermetically sealed world of timeless pleasure. From a child's standpoint, this is all well and good, but from an adult's it is somewhat misleading. A more ambivalent reception of these images arises when one considers that the commercial's vision of a collective feminine heritage seems to expunge even the least suggestive twinge of regret from the mother's reminiscence (and even minimal resentment on behalf of the father). This allows the memories that Swanson packages within the new-and-improved TV Dinners to be as free of guilt as they are of fat. This is critically important, since any mother will tell you that theirs is a responsibility that is perennially wracked by feelings of inadequacy. As Susan Douglas argues acerbically, "no matter what you do, you can't ever be good enough as a mother. If you don't work, you're a bad mom, and if you do work, you're a bad mom. . . . The tightrope walks are endless."[5] Certainly, Douglas would agree that many real-life mothers today are not altogether happy about the emotional and economic costs attendant to finding childcare. Yet, since the vast majority of women want nothing so much as a break from their jam-packed schedules of career and family rearing, the idea of a night on the town is a seductive one. So, what Swanson constructs with "Betty the Babysitter" is a vision of a fancifully self-assured femininity in which nurturing melds comfortably with self-indulgence, abandonment simulates connection, and an unproblematic past foreshadows a carefree present.

The commercial also attests to how the depiction of the American woman across generational divides has been, and continues to be, critically important to the marketing strategies of the frozen foods industry. Interestingly, the effort to position frozen foods as an integral element of American kitchen culture has produced an inextricable connection between women and their television sets. In 1958, for example, the Television Bureau of Advertising (TvB) conducted a survey designed to catalogue the modern accoutrements found in TV-owning households. Upon tabulation of the survey's results, Norman E. Cash, the president of TvB, wrote, "television's most avid viewers are also the heaviest users of frozen foods."[6] Demographic information on American housewives was a key pillar of Cash's study. For example, TvB found that, "households in which the housewife is under 50 account for four out of five freezer storage facility households. . . . This also shows the pattern for television. . . . It seems significant that housewives in households equipped with freezer storage facilities spent triple the time viewing television as reading newspapers (152 minutes on the average day vs. 50 minutes)."[7] In 1999, Swanson's "Betty the Babysitter" commercial represents another chapter in the frozen foods industry's exhaustive inquiry into feminine domestic behavior. However, it is significant to note that what the commercial does not transmit along the cultural conduit between its fictive female characters and their audience is a more nuanced historical understanding of how the TV Dinner and frozen foods in general were subjects within a heated argument over what it meant to be a woman or a man in 1950s America.

Frozen Foods and the Construction of Postwar Femininity

Frozen foods began to penetrate the general consumer market in the roughly half-decade prior to World War II, only to be delayed by the conflict. When the war began to wane and V-J Day flickered promisingly on the horizon, the frozen foods industry began to elicit, and often solicit, large amounts of coverage in the business, general interest, and women's press as a fundamental aspect of postwar life. However, as Lynn Spigel has documented with regard to television's introduction to the American home, while frozen foods promised unprecedented culinary efficiency, and thus an entirely novel way of imagining the duties of heterosexual womanhood within the nuclear family, they also stirred up pronounced anxieties related to personal health, the perceived dangers embodied by the commodities of mass culture, and the terminal disruption of traditional family life.[8] Much like the arrival of television, the advent of the new market for frozen foods required that families, especially housewives, learn a diffuse corpus of rules to facilitate the incorporation of these products into the home. Toward this end, a panoply of articles and handbooks emerged to disseminate this range of expectations and conventions to the curious public.

For its part, the frozen foods industry worked feverishly to capitalize on its profit potential by promulgating knowledge of its markets and how to exploit them. These efforts resulted in frozen foods becoming one of the big "growth" stories in the business press throughout the postwar period. As *Business Week* reported in its February 2, 1946, issue regarding the industry's market penetration: "The per capita consumption figures . . . are heartening to the packer in that they spread before him a vast panorama of opportunity to expand at the expense of other segments of the food industry, processed and unprocessed. And small as they are, they mirror a phenomenal growth in recent years . . . people are eating more than twice as much frozen fruits and vegetables as they ate in 1940."[9]

In order to continue experiencing this bonanza, the frozen foods industry had to successfully negotiate contradictory ideals of postwar American femininity. At different moments within this undertaking, the desired notion of the "feminine" was alternately packaged within images of the glamorous, the matronly (fig. 8.2), and even the hypersexualized pin-up (fig. 8.3). Studying the tensions between these disparate representations comprises the primary focus of the upcoming analysis. A few questions drive this project: What options for self-creation and self-care were available to women within predominant frozen foods discourses and imagery? How did frozen foods discourse promote new definitions for what it meant for the American family to practice the virtue of "freedom" in postwar society? How were these opportunities for self-redefinition constrained and enabled by traditional and emergent patriarchal norms? To answer these questions, I have examined a broad range of reports on the frozen foods phenomena from the perspective of both the industrial and popular press. On the industrial side, I have looked through every issue of the frozen foods industry "bible," *Quick Frozen Foods*, from 1945 to 1959 to understand how the packers and their retailers conceptualized their target market and how to reach it. I have augmented these accounts by collecting reports on the industry from business magazines such as *Nation's Business*, *Business Week*, *Fortune*, and *Forbes* as well as periodicals like the *Journal of Home Economics*. I also have looked at descriptions of how the frozen foods industry was made known through general interest magazines like *Collier's*, *Time*, *Newsweek*, *Commonweal*, *Harper's*, the *Atlantic*, the *New Yorker*, and the *New York Times Magazine*. To ferret out how women were specifically instructed to respond to the advent of frozen foods merchandising, I also carefully perused articles and advertisements in homemaker's magazines such as *American Home*, *House Beautiful*, *Better Homes and Gardens*, *Good Housekeeping*, *Ladies' Home Journal*, and *Parents*. Finally, for the broadest possible perspective, I read several of the most well-known books on the frozen foods industry and home freezing that circulated widely at the time.

Coming into the Cold: Heated Hype Heralds the New Industry

Recounting the overlooked role of women in the frozen foods story requires us to indulge the "Great Man" philosophy of traditional historiography and

Fig. 8.2. Service with a smile. Used by permission of *Frozen Foods Digest*.

Fig. 8.3. Miss Foil Kraft: The hostess of better foods. Used by permission of *Frozen Foods Digest.*

backtrack to the narrative's most widely acknowledged beginning. The frozen foods industry owes much of its initial growth to the inventiveness of Clarence Birdseye, whose legacy in frozen foods circles is monumental. Though he was not the first to strike upon the idea of quick freezing as a means of food preservation, Birdseye did inaugurate feasible methods of packaging a wide variety of products for the retail trade. Eventually, he became emboldened enough with his tinkering to go into business, first through his General Seafoods Company and then through its sister operation, the General Foods Company, which specialized in frozen fruits and vegetables. These operations garnered such immediate success that the Postum Company bought out Birdseye in 1928 for the tidy sum of $22 million.[10]

Soon other companies hit the trail blazed by Birdseye and, despite the hard times of the Great Depression, by 1935 the frozen foods industry had become a nationwide juggernaut. By 1938, *Quick Frozen Foods* began monthly publication, serving as a further catalyst for promoting the industry. Due to a severe lack of freezer space in local groceries, frozen foods' initial growth stemmed from institutional, rather than retail sales,[11] yet these relatively limited points of distribution set the stage for the industry's prolonged expansion. Many pundits of commerce began to regard frozen foods as an inexorable phenomenon with no hurdle seeming too great for the industry to surmount.

Such reports began to assume a quasi–Manifest Destiny tenor, with frozen foods figured as a primary agent through which humankind could begin to conquer the limits of the natural environment. Indeed, the upheaval of the normal progression of the calendar loomed as frozen foods' primary gift to society. As *Fortune* announced to its readers in June 1939, "quick freezing at once does away with the space-time limits of perishable-food distribution. With frozen foods, neither season nor geography has any meaning, for strawberries in December are exactly the same as strawberries in June, and its just as easy to serve the rich fruits of the tropics field-fresh on a breakfast table in Maine as it is to serve blueberries."[12]

American women were to be the cultural gatekeepers who would usher this amazing new world of suspended animation into the domestic sphere. In one article symptomatic of this widespread belief, *Commonweal* pronounced loftily that "when the average housewife now prepares her Christmas dinner, she can serve strawberries and cream along with her turkey and cranberry sauce. She can enable her guests to enjoy corn-on-cob with an almost cornfield freshness. All of these products will be just as fresh as when harvested the summer before, but not as young."[13] In the summer of 1943, Birdseye heralded the coming of the frozen foods age at a meeting of the Institute of

Food Technologists in St. Louis. At that gathering, Birdseye predicted that: "Instead of bins of tomatoes, spinach and other 'fresh' vegetables," the postwar grocery "will have a series of low-temperature self-service cabinets. There the housewife even in the remote village will find frosted cooked vegetables, including tropical and Arctic delicacies. When she gets home, she will put them in the frosted food compartment of her post-war refrigerator."[14] That same summer, *Collier's* reporter David O. Woodbury made frozen foods the subject of his "Your Life Tomorrow" column, commenting upon their ability to flatten distinctions between both geographic locations and economic status. Woodbury forecast that, "A month's supply of fresh foods always at hand in your own kitchen in bewildering variety; menus that include ready-cooked specialties actually prepared by famous chefs in London, Rome or Paris — these are but two of the advantages that the new 'deep-freezing' system will bring into every postwar home."[15] By the end of the year, *Fortune* also described deep freezing's ability to broaden the range of the traditional American palate.

Thus, to imported cheeses, oils, nuts, and *pâté de foie gras*, we may add such an exotic pantry as East Indian *rijsttafel* with its dozens of strange ingredients; delicate tropical fruits that heretofore couldn't stand shipping but had to be consumed directly from the tree or bush; fish unheard of except by ichthyologists; meats, game, poultry, and whole foreign meals, precooked and quick-frozen, ready for the table after the usual defrosting and warming up. Because these things can be produced so cheaply abroad, it is possible to bring them on our market profitably in their quick-frozen form even over tariff walls.[16]

By the start of World War II, however, this utopic vision of globalization had not completely lived up to expectations. Not enough families outside of the rural regions had access to home freezing equipment to make frozen foods a fact of everyday life. In the short term, the gap between the demand for frozen foods and technological capacity was filled by the so-called frozen locker industry. These facilities were huge, warehouse-style, communal freezers where individual families could rent locker space.

Although construction of freezers was suspended during the war, the increasing inevitability of victory and the swelling ranks of frozen foods proselytes caused demand for the new appliances to escalate dramatically. Making the modern notion of natural abundance a reality for American women represented a major investment opportunity for all aspects of the frozen foods industry, none more than the manufacturers of home freezers. Widespread accounts of the ease, quality, and long-term economic efficiency of home freezing — regardless of family size[17] — mitigated much of the consumer caution against the new technology. Still, reassuring the public was an ongoing effort for the industry. As part of this project, discourses surrounding the public dissemination of home freezers paid particular attention to their ability to shrink the disparity in quality of life between the have's and the have-not's.[18] One of the most stalwart advocates of the new "freezing way of life" was journalist and home freezer owner Boyden Sparkes. In his 1944 book *Zero Storage in Your Home*, Sparkes wrote glowingly of an American Shangri-La of social equality to be ushered in by the age of home freezers. He described the new appliances as possessing the

inherent power to make the phrase, "American standard of living," connote to a greater degree than ever before an enviable standard. Millionaires who have learned how to use it eat better than they could without it — not merely in wartime; any time! . . . [And] with this instrument in mass production, poverty-stricken areas in this nation should shrink to a smaller proportion of the whole than ever existed in any civilization. The potential greatness of this machine, the family-size food freezer, is its power, when ably used to make us really free; free from want, free from the usual fears of security — and, I dare say free from envy![19]

The promulgation of interest in home freezers and the frozen foods market near the end of the war by people like Sparkes presaged the postwar rise of the role of "experts" in the struggle over public opinion. Throughout this period, "whether in medicine, child rearing, or even the intimate areas of sex and marriage, expertise gained legitimacy as familiar, 'old-fashioned' ways were called into question."[20] As one might expect, while Sparkes and other champions of frozen foods trumpeted the egalitarian benefits of a burgeoning mass culture, more conservative voices in this mushrooming punditocracy had different ideas about what these trends signaled for the future well-being of American civilization.

One of the most strident of the dystopian voices within the mass culture debate was Philip Wylie. Wylie is well known for his 1942 polemic, *Generation of Vipers*, in which he railed against what he perceived as an unholy alliance between women, big business, and — in an updated version of the manuscript thirteen years later — the castrating effects of television culture.[21] He also made himself audible in the rancor over frozen foods in the mid-1950s. Wylie's most caustic attack against the likes of TV Dinners came in an *Atlantic* article bluntly titled "Science Has Spoiled My Supper." In his diatribe, Wylie attacked women's magazines for instructing an entire generation of women to shun the "from scratch" cooking techniques perfected by his elderly mother-in-law. He maintained that the women's magazine approach to cooking left "appetite unquenched and merely serves to stave off famine." As he closed his essay, Wylie reserved his most poisonous barbs for the quick freezing folks, contending that " 'deep-freezing' . . . has rung down the curtain on American cookery. Nothing is improved by the process. I have yet to taste a deep-frozen victual that measures up, in flavor, to the fresh, unfrosted original. And most foods, cooked or uncooked, are destroyed in the deep freeze for all people of sense and sensibility."[22]

Thus, for all of the excitement stirred up by enthusiastic advocates like Sparkes, the frozen foods industry had to struggle throughout the postwar period against various arguments about its complicity with the "homogenization" of American cultural values and the dissolution of traditional social authority. Hints as to how they overcame these obstacles can be gleaned from the testimony of the industry's female "fans." Indeed, merely a few months after Wylie's article appeared, *House Beautiful* ran a mock "love letter" extolling one woman writer's adoration for the new food industry in a fanciful article entitled, "Dear Food Industry—I Love You": "This is a letter I've been wanting to write for years. I don't think I've ever told you how much I admire you, how big and fine and bold, imaginative and exciting you are. You might have thought I didn't really appreciate all your care and thought of me. Long before now I should have made it clear. Like any woman happy in love, you've made me feel like a queen. . . . A queen with a whole retinue of tireless servants on call 24 hours a day, every day in the year, at the wave of a can opener."[23] Yet, by the missive's end, such love-sick idolatry short-circuits in the name of a feminine desire for self-actualization: "Honestly, I don't mind your doing my work for me. You can go right on scrubbing the vegetables, peeling the carrots, washing my rice in seven waters, simmering the beef bones. You can hand me the basics. But I'm selfish. I want to retain the fun of creation."[24]

In this struggle to satisfy the conflicting wishes of American consumers, the frozen foods industry worked on several fronts. In the first instance, the home freezing advocates maintained their original proposition that mass culture was a democratic force because it offered more individuals more freedom of choice, rather than limiting such options to the privileged few. In this regard, frozen foods were envisioned as meshing comfortably with a wide range of lifestyles, from the traditional husband and wife couple raising children in the bucolic simplicity of the country to the modern, unmarried female executive living the high life of the city. Interestingly enough, despite frozen foods' populist intentions, all of its mythic lifestyles were ones of material privilege.

An editorial in the March 1949 issue of *Quick Frozen Foods* demon-strates, as well, the degree to which the packers were cognizant of the tradi-tional notions of individuality that they had to appease within the minds of their potential customers. The magazine's editors claimed that "home made foods are on the downgrade every year and yet, even though housewives want to do it quickly there still lingers a nostalgic yearning in every woman's heart to retain that home made, fresh touch. Here, frozen foods supply the happy answer for they are fresh, not canned, and satisfy the American home-maker that she is serving fresh foods."[25] Almost simultaneously with this proclama-tion, women's magazines, rather than bemoaning frozen foods as the end of the amateur chef's ability to infuse her culinary creations with individuality, instead advised their readers to consider the relatively bland seasonings of most frozen foods as their opportunity to express their unique sense of taste. As *House Beautiful* confided to its readers in 1951:

The real secret in making ready-made foods acceptable is knowing how to glamorize them in their preparation. The only safe course for the food manufacturer is to "play the middle of the road" — to season for the common-denominator taste — bland, unstartling, careful. Using mass-produced foods just as they come out of the can or the package is not the way to endear them to gourmets. Just as it is practical to simplify *haute couture* recipes downward in the interests of labor saving, so is it practicable to elaborate upward ready-made foodstuffs to obtain stimulating variety and sophistication and richness.[26]

The ease of prepared frozen foods promised that the gastronomic whim of each family member and household guest could be catered to as conveniently as an evening at a neighborhood restaurant — without the cost. One *American Home* writer exclaimed: "Behold the housewife of the future! After the matinee, she dashes back from town, inserts a few coins in the slot machine at the station, gets a steak for dinner for Hubby, hot dogs for Junior, creamed chicken for Sis, and a salad for herself. Once home, she shoves them in the radar oven, sits down to hear Junior's spelling. Before he can spell 'cat,' dinner is ready and the family sits down to eat."[27] This quotation points to how the packers and their backers promoted frozen foods by constantly stressing traditional notions of natural abundance and individual freedom with freezing technology's unrivaled efficiency. Not surprisingly, then, by the end of the war home freezers and their wares were repeatedly depicted in ads as the modern version of a mythic cornucopia that refashioned the traditional notion of the country's bountifully feminine heartland for a new stage of patriarchal moder-nity (fig. 8.4).

However, this new vision of an old concept had to take account of the

Fig. 8.4. Frozen abundance. Used by permission of Amana Appliances.

real changes that World War II had made in the lives of American women, who now spent more hours working outside of the home than they ever had before. In October of 1948, Elizabeth Sweeney, editor of the household equipment section for *McCall's* magazine, gave a speech before members of the Eastern Frozen Foods Association in New York City that spelled out women's desire to use frozen foods as a bulwark against lost time. She summarized her talk in an article for the *Journal of Home Economics* in January of the following year:

American homemakers . . . want and badly need time-savers in meal preparation. More American women are working today than ever before. They are women who get meals for families despite a day's work outside their home. They appreciate a product that is ready to cook, or half cooked to start with. They are willing to pay for that convenience. They can afford to pay for it because, though economic necessity is the single biggest reason for the increased number of working women, the net result is a higher-than-average family income. Frozen foods fill a need.[28]

The availability of more types of work for women beyond the standard positions as maids and nannies, also inspired a mass exodus from the servant class, prompting a shortfall in hired household help. As a result, wealthy "hostesses who would never have considered serving anything but fresh foods turned to frozen ones because they were so much more simple to prepare."[29] Their less fiscally endowed sisters followed suit for exactly the opposite reason; for them, frozen foods meant that even they could enjoy the luxury of having "1001 servants in their kitchen."[30]

To further quell the anxieties fomented by this blurring of the traditional boundaries of "women's work," the supporters of frozen foods articulated home freezing as a vital tool in the maintenance of the Cold War ideal of domestic security. This meant acknowledging the permanence of women's expanded employment outlook, and its necessity, while simultaneously reassuring men that they stood to be the primary beneficiaries of these radically new trends. A quotation from Sparkes' book offers a hint at what these arguments sounded like to "Joe Paycheck":

Actually, there is almost no hope that the United States or any other nation can develop an economy in which fifty weeks of pay-roll work can be guaranteed generally, along with a high standard of living. . . . Suddenly, I think, the pay-roll worker is going to discover that his wife really can help him make a living without leaving home; that is his children, too, can contribute to the making of the family living, to the maintenance of family security — and do this with lasting benefit to themselves. On this ground the food freezer seems to me to be unique in a whole line of conveniences that have come to us out of our industrial power . . . with a freezer the whole family can help make the living.[31]

Home freezing and frozen foods served as the perfect arbiter between American men and women who sought to ease the tensions that existed between
them over their shifting roles in the American home. Several years later, Edith
Ramsay echoed this viewpoint in her own exaltation of the manifold benefits
of home freezing: "Never has a household task reached the glamorous stage
so fast as that of home freezing. Many a housewife who has had a taste of it
declares she'll preserve this way and only this way. . . . Because the cabinet is
a real investment, not just another ten-quart kettle, the man of the house gets
interested too. Man has never been one to stand over the hot canning kettle —
but freezing is such a simple and interesting process he likes to help."[32]
Frozen foods promised men the economic helm of the family — even if it
meant that they were no longer solely responsible for breadwinning and
wealth production. Women were promised the benefit of convenience, even as
the predominant images that represented them within the new idea of leisure
still depicted them serving their families within the American home.[33]

Packaging the Female Consumer

Freedom for the fifties family was a function of the American housewife's
productive capacity. Frozen foods and home freezers became key components
of this Cold War Magna Carta. The degree to which married women could
convince their husbands that frozen foods were both tasty and a boon to the
household budget was the extent to which they could begin cutting down the
time spent on food preparation for the sake of more enjoyable activities. In
House Beautiful, Florence Paine provided a hypothetical example of such a
camouflaged act of sedition featuring a fictitious "Dad's weakness for fresh
asparagus." She suggested to her female readership that "when asparagus is at
its peak in flavor, and selling at a favorable price, you can buy it in quantity,
freeze it, and convince Dad further that he didn't make a mistake when he
invested in a freezer."[34] Clearly, this sort of tactic did not fully liberate women
from patriarchal control, but it did increase their ability to exert influence over
decision making inside the home.

Rather than frame this compromised position as a losing proposition for
their female audiences, women's magazines offered married women information that would empower their efforts to make frozen foods and home freezers
seem attractive to their husbands. In fact, the magazines were quite self-
conscious about their role as a member of the expert class. As Paine wrote in
another article, "the shape of most postwar things is still pretty hazy. But by

dint of practical freezing experience and much leg work, *House Beautiful* can now disperse the controversial mists surrounding the future of quick freezing."[35] In the text that followed, Paine outlined nine different "revolutionary" promises likely to result from the inception of the frozen foods era, and pictured twelve home freezing units for her audience to contemplate. Other articles, like one in *Good Housekeeping* in March 1949, instructed women on how to select the type of freezer that best suited their family's needs.[36] Ruth Carson reserved a significant portion of her "Cooking with Cold" feature in the January 4, 1947, issue of *Collier's* to offer "Some 'Don'ts' for the Housewife" with regard to freezing, storing, and reheating frozen foods.[37] Myrna Johnson gave similar tutelage in her article "What Would Grandma Say!" in the May 1947 issue of *Better Homes and Gardens*.[38] In the May 1950 issue of *Parents*, Gail Wentworth testified to all the doubting members of her readership as to the ability of frozen foods to be the crux of a week's worth of sophisticated home dinner menus.[39] An entirely different cadre of experts counseled the American housewife on the virtues of frozen foods through the American Home Economics Association's *Journal of Home Economics*. In a symposium published in May 1948 this periodical provided educators with the knowledge necessary to instruct future homemakers on everything from fruit and vegetable freezing and frozen meat preparation, to packaging frozen foods and the intricacies of frozen poultry.[40] A few months earlier, in the spring of 1947, one of that symposium's most sought after participants had instructed readers of *House Beautiful* on "How to Get Weeks Ahead in Your Cooking."[41]

All of this instruction may seem overwrought in hindsight, but, at the time, it was a crucial part of the industry's survival. Quite simply, if women were not taught how to guarantee the quality of the frozen product for their families, low cost and time management would not be enough to give the industry a more secure niche in the public mind. Sweeney argued in the *Journal of Home Economics* that the entire industry, from the producers to the retailers, needed to take women's desire and need for specific instructions on the use of their products seriously or risk losing their confidence. She chastised producers to recognize that: "Women do need as concise and complete information on labels as food manufacturers long ago learned was required for satisfaction in the use of all food products. A program of 'use' education with storekeepers is a critical essential."[42] And as Tressler warned the industry in his segment of the *Journal of Home Economics* frozen food symposium: "If a housewife buys a package of frozen fruit or vegetables which lacks flavor or has an undesirable flavor, she is not likely to buy that brand again. And if her own frozen fruits and vegetables do not have desirable flavors, she will soon question the desirability of home frozen products."[43] These quality concerns indicate a sign of the frozen food industry's maturation process, however, and not its demise. Indeed, what they indicated above all else was the increased need for the industry to be proactive in the development of meaningful relationships with its female customer base. In short, the frozen foods packers and distributors, as businesses that once could rely solely on the national advertising presence of the Birds Eye brand "and only a few regional advertisers," now needed to think seriously about their new "No. 1 problem . . . marketing."[44]

This would prove to be a difficult issue for an industry that had long been a largely unregulated field ripe for exploitation by profit-minded speculators. The dizzying amount of product roll out from these fledgling enterprises often presented the homemaker with a litany of "sound-alike" brands to choose from.[45] As more big-name canning companies began to enter the frozen foods market,[46] dominant players began to emerge from amid the clutter, yet the overall picture at the postwar grocery store remained muddled. Even more puzzling to the consumer was the fact that these brands increasingly began to offer products that had never been sold in frozen form before. Some of these products—like frozen orange juice in 1948,[47] frozen waffles in 1951,[48] and frozen bread by 1953[49]—helped cement the staying power of the industry. Others—like frozen packaged rabbit chops—provided temporary bursts of interest, only to either fade over the long haul or recede to small regional markets.[50] The issue of "quality" became paramount amid this carnivalesque milieu of foodstuffs, as many untrustworthy packers foisted inferior products on customers for the sake of fast money. Periodically, the unscrupulous dealings of a few had a deleterious impact upon the entire industry, and a stern process of "natural selection" hit the frozen foods market as "consumers soured somewhat on all frozen foods because the quality of a lot of the fly-by-night brands was poor."[51]

In 1947, for instance, due in no small part to the downturn in overall sales, *Quick Frozen Foods* announced to the industry in an editorial that "The Time Has Come to Advertise Frozen Foods." In the article the editors of the magazine called for a national ad campaign designed to educate the consumer as to the virtues of frozen foods, especially with regards to quality: "The impression must be created that frozen foods . . . are of consistently good quality, and that they may be bought with confidence."[52] As a result, in the beginning of the 1950s much of the new advertising within the industry began to emphasize the safety and reliability of frozen foods packaging. At the same time that they pushed for uniform standards of quality management, the packers tried to retain the notion of magic within their wares. In a lengthy editorial in February 1948, the editors of *Quick Frozen Foods* made this belief in hocus-pocus abundantly clear when they implored their constituents to

SELL QUICK FREEZING! Sell the fundamental idea behind our system of food preservation, the idea of suspended animation. . . . This is the great, exciting and dynamic theme upon which the whole industry rests. . . . IT IS ALL THE INDUSTRY HAS TO SELL! The worst rut into which the industry can fall is to get into the attitude of allowing Mrs. House-wife to compare a can of peas and a package of frozen peas on a price basis. *The industry must recapture that mysterious charm that intrigued the public imagination at the beginning.*[53]

It does not seem as if packers made it a point to advertise the method of quick freezing per se, but they did strive to preserve and develop new ways of conveying the "magical" aspects of frozen foods through a wide range of packaging and advertising schemes. These campaigns revolved around the predominant social themes of the day, and all of them figured the female consumer as a prize to be fought over and captured amid the clutter of other-wise indistinguishable brands (fig. 8.5). The principle behind these efforts concerned the idea that if women were not sure as to a brand's veracity, or when they were simply perusing the grocery aisles with no clear plan in mind, then "impulse" sales would ultimately decide whether a product was plucked from the refrigerated display cases (fig. 8.6). Alluring package design became a crucial way to seduce and corral the female consumer. Notions of conve-nience and ease also became built-in features of a product's packaging (fig. 8.7). This theory of "impulse" buying represented the industry's new em-phasis on catering to customers' emotions rather than to their ability to make a rational decision. As Mary Beth Haralovich noted, by the late 1950s, "with high competition in the consumer product industry, it was no longer adequate to determine the conscious needs of the homemaker. . . . Instead, market researchers sought to uncover the unconscious processes of consumption."[54]

Advertisements within the frozen foods industry were not simply ethe-real constructs, but were also firmly grounded within many of the important social trends of postwar domestic life. Many packers, for example, used their advertising to echo the unprecedented number of youthful marriages. In 1950, Snow Crop pitched its frozen concentrated orange juice with its brand mascot — a polar bear — depicted as a bride walking down the aisle toward the altar. The Downyflake brand of breading products also made the notion of wedded bliss explicit in one of their ads from 1958. Thinly veiled connota-

How to make sure the <u>big</u> one doesn't get away!

Your *biggest* catch, after all, is Mrs. Cash Customer. Landing *her* is just as important as hauling in and processing the finest catch.

How does she buy? Oftentimes by brand preference. But just as often it's by *eye* when she's "fishing around" in her favorite market.

Marathon packaging can catch her roving eye . . . make her reach for your sea food . . . dig down for cash just as surely as you bring fish up from the deep.

To make sure the good fish *in* your package "look good enough to eat" *on* your package, see the Man from Marathon. He can show you how to bait your customer-catching hooks with brilliantly printed Marathon overwraps and cartons. He also has the answer to the right combination of cartons and machines that smooth and speed your production operations. Write Marathon Corporation, Dept. 639, Menasha, Wisconsin. In Canada: Marathon Packages Limited, Toronto.

MARATHON
PACKAGES
SELL BRANDS · PROTECT PRODUCTS · SPEED PRODUCTION

Fig. 8.5. Baiting Mrs. Cash Customer. Used by permission of *Frozen Foods Digest*.

Fig. 8.6. Frozen foods manufacturers banked on fancy packaging as a surefire way to drive revenue. Used by permission of AlliedSignal Corporation.

Fig. 8.7. Freedom means convenience. Used by permission of *Frozen Foods Digest*.

Fig. 8.8. Nostalgic notions of homemaking remained a central pillar of the typical frozen product sales pitch. Used by permission of *Frozen Foods Digest.*

tions of child-rearing were also hinted at repeatedly by frozen food producers, retail freezer manufacturers, and package designers. Impulse sales advocates figured the American homemaker as an individual hungry for the respect and adulation of her family as reward for her service providing abilities (fig. 8.8). Frozen foods manufacturers even paid glancing attention to the alleged problem of juvenile delinquency by positioning their products as a calming influence that would tame even the most unruly ruffians. Even after the delinquency furor subsided by the end of the decade, the frozen foods industry continued using youthful iconography — though in a more idealized form — as part of its ongoing effort to connote "quality, safety, and trust."

The packers also followed fashion trends, like the new focus placed upon feminine glamour (fig. 8.9). This sort of representation is noteworthy since it does not picture the female model in the type of domestic context considered "normal" at the time. Douglas underscores how the mid-century iconography of glamour may have proved temporarily disruptive to traditional gender codes in her description of the Camelot era of the Kennedy administration. Specifically, Douglas explores how the chic sensibility of the First Lady, Jacqueline Kennedy, instituted a new kind of feminine possibility for young girls and women to emulate. Douglas suggests that, "Jackie was tradition and modernity, the old femininity and new womanhood, seemingly sustained in a perfect suspension. She was a wife and a mother, but she also worked outside the home. She deferred to her husband, but at times she outshone him."[55] Given this complex gendered environment, the frozen foods industry tried to cater to all sorts of definitions of femininity. Frequently, ads like the aforementioned one for the Milprint packing company attempted to tether the more renegade possibilities of Cold War chic with captions pointing towards the time-honored notion of "family." Clearly, not every troublesome aspect of these glamorous representations could be contained so neatly by the status quo.

For all of their apparent efforts at containing the image of the new American woman, the packers also betrayed a desire for someone less inhibited than the perky sort of hausfrau depicted in the family-oriented ads — one who was unabashed about the sex appeal percolating beneath her cooking apron. Many packers and refrigerator manufacturers made such salacious heroines mascots for their companies. Two of the most widely circulated of these icons were "Boston Bonnie" for the Boston Bonnie Fisheries (fig. 8.10), and "Jenni Genetron" for the refrigerants division of the Allied Chemical Corporation (fig. 8.11). Even more sophomoric ads simply featured scantily clad women showcasing various packaging products as silly captions made a double en-

Fig. 8.9. In the postwar era, frozen fish sticks were considered chic. Used by permission of Milprint Packaging Company.

Fig. 8.10. Frozen foods manufacturers developed an assortment of risqué iconography in order to market their wares. Used by permission of Fishery Products International, Ltd.

Fig. 8.11. Jenni Genetron: The happy face of the technologically adept housewife. Used by permission of AlliedSignal Corporation.

tendre of their bodies (fig. 8.12). Placed in the context of the Cold War, some might have conjectured that these ribald representations constituted a subversive discourse that undermined the normalized female sexuality deemed appropriate to domestic preparedness in the atomic age. Elaine Tyler May has suggested, for example, that the discourses of normalization that urged marriage and motherhood upon all women in the 1950s, especially those who worked outside the home, functioned within this Cold War context to "infuse domestic roles with national purpose."[56] It's hard to find hints of hawkish patriotism in ads like that featuring "Miss Foil Kraft — The Hostess of Better Foods," found in *Quick Frozen Foods* in September 1954 (fig. 8.13) — unless the uses of her coquettish foil apron included protection against gamma rays! These cheesy images, hatched from the self-indulgent minds of men, amply demonstrate how women and their depiction of sexual desire helped sell frozen foods throughout the Cold War in ways that were completely unpredictable.

Conclusion

In hindsight it appears that at roughly the very moment when TV Dinners assumed the status of popular mythology, frozen foods began to diminish in significance as unlikely symbols for American women's enhanced sense of civic and domestic freedom. Part of this cultural decline stems from the escalating political momentum of the women's movement in arenas other than the home. Eventually, the sort of liberties that postwar women celebrated and participated within via the arrival of frozen foods came to be regarded as disturbingly naïve and childlike by subsequent generations of feminists. Not surprisingly, contemporary marketing efforts for TV Dinners — like the "Betty the Babysitter" commercial — have little choice but to infantilize and simplify these products' more intricate role in the development of the feminist consciousness found in 1950s suburbia. Unfortunately, this process of infantilization is one of the primary mechanisms for the marginalization of popular culture's important social commentary.

Frequently, these powerful discourses of historical erasure take the form of humor. Indeed, the luxury of laughter afforded by the punch line of the standard TV Dinner quip is borrowed from the essentially bankrupt belief that everything else we have been inspired to produce during the latter half of the twentieth century has been profoundly grave and meaningful. Such a belief, in itself, is laughable.

Fig. 8.12. Many of the industry's slogans left nothing to the imagination. Used by permission of *Frozen Foods Digest*.

Fig. 8.13. As politically incorrect as this ad may seem by today's standards, it and others like it signaled the realization of social progress for members of the postwar generation. Used by permission of *Frozen Foods Digest*.

I hope that by taking a more serious account of the way in which the frozen foods industry used various representations of domestic life to help construct the hopes and dreams of postwar American women — and mitigate an ideological backlash from traditionally minded men — I have reversed our tendency to make light of this process, at least somewhat. Perhaps, if we pause long enough to recollect what small vestige of freedom American women found in the unassuming TV Dinner, we will be inspired to memorialize much more about that aspect of our collective heritage than a trifurcated aluminum tray.

Notes

I would like to thank my colleagues in the Media and Cultural Studies Department at the University of Wisconsin — Madison, especially Dr. Michele Hilmes, for giving me crucial suggestions for the revision of this chapter. I would also like to thank Dr. Sherrie A. Inness for her patient and insightful commentary on my ideas. This chapter is dedicated to my fiancée, Salaam, who inspired and supported me throughout my research and writing.

1. "Swanson Launches First Television Campaign in 10 Years: 'Make New Memories With Swanson,' " *prnewswire*, 11 January 1999, *http://www.prnewswire.com/cgibin/stories.pl?ACCT=105&STORY=/www/stor.../000084209* Consider as well this made-for-Hollywood scene orchestrated on March 30, 1999, in honor of "the former poultry company executive who invented the TV Dinner": "Kneeling before a bank of cameras, Gerry Thomas, 77, placed his handprints in a block of wet cement, along with an imprint of the Swanson brand's classic aluminum dinner tray, on the fabled courtyard outside Mann's Chinese Theater. . . . The ceremony was presided over by Hollywood's honorary mayor, Johnny Grant, who hailed Thomas as the father of 'the longest-running television hit that until today hasn't been properly recognized.' " Steve Gorman, "TV Dinner Inventor Honored in Hollywood," Reuters Newswire, 31 March 1999.

2. Constance L. Hays, "A Makeover for the TV Dinner," *New York Times*, 25 July 1998, Sec. D, 1.

3. *prnewswire*, 11 January 1999.

4. Kevin Lowery, phone interview by author, 19 February 1999; "Betty the Babysitter," prod. and dir. Young and Rubicam New York, 30 seconds, 1999, videocassette. I am grateful for the courteous assistance of Mr. Lowery, vice president for public affairs, Vlasic Foods International, and Kathleen Ruane, vice president for corporate communications, Young & Rubicam New York, who graciously granted me a videotaped copy of the commercial.

5. Susan J. Douglas, *Where the Girls Are: Growing Up Female with the Mass Media* (New York: Times Books, 1994), 282–83.

6. Norman E. Cash, "Television's Most Avid Viewers Are Heaviest FF Users," *Quick Frozen Foods*, March 1958, 260.

7. Ibid.

8. Lynn Spigel, *Make Room for TV: Television and the Family Ideal in Postwar America* (Chicago: University of Chicago Press, 1992).

9. "Frozen Foods: A New Horizon," *Business Week*, 2 February 1946, 30–42.

10. E. W. Williams, *Frozen Foods: A Biography of an Industry* (Boston: Cahners Books, 1963), 2.

11. J. D. Ratcliff, "The Big Freeze," *Collier's*, 14 August 1937, 26.

12. "Quick Frozen Foods," *Fortune*, June 1939, 63.

13. Ross L. Holman, "Frozen Freshness," *The Commonweal*, 20 February 1942, 432.

14. "Post-War Grocery Store," *Science News Letter*, 12 June 1943, 182.

15. David O. Woodbury, "Your Life Tomorrow," *Collier's*, 28 August 1943, 16.

16. Quoted in "Tomorrow's Menu," *Reader's Digest*, February 1944, 15.

17. "No Family Is too Small for a Freezer," *House Beautiful*, January 1946, 52–53. See also Lenore E. Sater, "It's Time to Know About Freezing," *Parents*, August 1945, 136–37.

18. In one of the first postwar articles on the "walk-in" style of home freezers, readers were told that the units would insure them the type of abundance befitting the court life of ancient royalty. The story claimed that "In the time of Lucius Licinius Lucullus (110–57 BC), five hundred peacock tongues were considered a dainty entree — at a cost of \$10,000 per couvert. The food you can have from your own frozen food locker would make Lucullus green with envy and at considerably less than ancient Roman prices!" "Treasure Room for Gourmets," *House & Garden*, November 1945, 126–27.

19. Boyden Sparkes, *Zero Storage in Your Home* (Garden City, N.Y.: Doubleday, Doran, 1944), 3.

20. Elaine Tyler May, "Explosive Issues: Sex, Women and the Bomb," in *Recasting America: Culture and Politics in the Age of Cold War*, ed. Lary May (Chicago: University of Chicago Press, 1989), 156.

21. Spigel, 61.

22. Philip Wylie, "Science Has Spoiled My Supper," *Atlantic*, April 1954, 45–47. Several months later, when the letters responding to Wylie's essay were published, opinion was predictably mixed across and within gender categories. Some men, echoed Wylie's standpoint; others shared the gratitude that the women in their lives had for how frozen foods had made their lives easier. Many older women stood by their memories of the "good old days." Many younger women lashed back at Wylie, choosing to "bless" the advent of frozen foods. Some said that frozen foods were not the problem, but faulty techniques in preparation. This latter opinion surely brought affirmative nods from the many women's magazine editors who had spilled so much ink over the years instructing American women how to get it right! "*Atlantic* Repartee," *Atlantic*, July 1954, 16–18.

23. Poppy Cannon, "Dear Food Industry — I Love You," *House Beautiful*, January 1955, 74.

24. Ibid., 102.

25. "Frozen Food Era Is Coming In!" *Quick Frozen Foods*, March 1949, 93.

26. "Is Your Grandmother Standing Between You and Today's Freedom?" *House Beautiful*, March 1951, 150.

27. Joseph L. Nicholson, "Melt Your Dinner," *American Home*, February 1947, 141.

28. Elizabeth Sweeney, "What We Have Found out About Frozen Foods," *Journal of Home Economics*, January 1949, 26.

29. E. J. Kahn, Jr., "The Coming of the Big Freeze," *New Yorker*, 14 September 1946, 73.

30. Jean Harris, "You Have 1001 Servants in Your Kitchen," *House Beautiful*, March 1951, 74. Sparkes also believed that "for the woman who is not only housewife but also schoolteacher, stenographer, sales woman, or in some other way a money earner, the freezer offers a release from the necessity of daily cooking. . . . *This means that in some households cooking can become a process no longer requiring the year-round presence in the kitchen of a full-time cook, hired, or 'married' "* (emphasis added, 9). A wry essay published in a 1958 issue of the *New Yorker* depicted servants as the last bulwark against frozen foods. So in many respects, frozen foods *simulated* the presence of these people as a productive means of obfuscating the fact that they were making them *obsolete* in the domestic production of traditional comforts. "Hall on Cooking," *New Yorker*, 22 February 1958, 27–28.

31. Sparkes, 58.

32. Edith Ramsay, "Buying and Caring for Home Freezers," *American Home*, April 1947, 152.

33. As Mary Beth Haralovich has suggested, "the economic responsibility for class status lay with the father while the mother was addressed through emotional connotations associated with homemaking." Mary Beth Haralovich, "Sit-coms and Suburbs: Positioning the 1950s Homemaker," in *Private Screenings: Television and the Female Consumer*, ed. L. Spigel and D. Mann (Minneapolis: University of Minnesota Press, 1992), 126.

34. Florence Paine, "You'll Eat Better with Less Work," *House Beautiful*, January 1946, 122.

35. Paine, "How Quick Freezing Will Affect Your Future Life," *House Beautiful*, January 1945, 53.

36. Helen W. Kendall, "You Manage Better with a Freezer," *Good Housekeeping*, March 1949, 183.

37. Ruth Carson, "Cooking with Cold," *Collier's*, 4 January 1947, 51.

38. Myrna Johnson, "What Would Grandma Say!" *Better Homes and Gardens*, May 1947, 68.

39. Gail Wentworth, "Short Cuts with Quick Frozen Foods," *Parents*, May 1950, 86.

40. Donald K. Tressler et al., "About Frozen Foods and Freezing Them," *Journal of Home Economics*, May 1948, 233–40.

41. Donald K. Tressler and Lucy Long, "How to Get Weeks Ahead in Your Cooking," *House Beautiful*, December 1947, 154.

42. Sweeney, 26.

43. Tressler et al., 233.

44. "Frozen Foods Enters Selling Era," *Business Week*, 4 January 1947, 28–32.

45. For instance, in the fall of 1946, E. J. Kahn, Jr., noted that "Among Birds Eye's many, many rivals are Bird Valley and Blue Bird. The long list also includes

Chilld Quic, Col-Pac, Cold Gold, Deepfreeze, Fresh Froze, Fresh Frozen, Freshzest, Friidegs, Frigidettes, Frigidfruit, Frigifood, Frospac, Frozest, Froz-N-True, I-C-Kold, Igloo, Kol-Pac, Kold Pak, Kold Kist, Pelfreez, Pictsweet, Redyquik, Sno-Dipt, Snow Cap, Strat O Freez, Zer-O-Pak, Zero-Pack, Zeroseald, and Honest George" (77).

46. "Frozen Foods: A New Horizon," *Business Week*, 2 February 1946, 42.

47. "Comeback for Frozen Foods," *Business Week*, 19 March 1949, 23.

48. *Quick Frozen Foods*, May 1951, 48–49.

49. Paul W. Kearney, "Cold Bread Is Hot News," *Nation's Business*, December 1953, 58–60; "Fresh Frozen Bread," *Science News Letter*, 18 April 1953, 243; "Now It's Frozen Bread," *Business Week*, 11 April 1953, 44–46.

50. "Frozen Rabbit Chops Are Gaining a Place in the Cases," *Quick Frozen Foods*, November 1952, 45.

51. *Business Week*, 19 March 1949, 23.

52. "The Time Has Come to Advertise Frozen Foods," *Quick Frozen Foods*, March 1947, 122.

53. "How Will the Industry Advertise?" *Quick Frozen Foods*, February 1948, 42 (emphasis added).

54. Haralovich, 125.

55. Douglas, 38.

56. May, 159.

She Also Cooks

Gender, Domesticity, and Public Life in Oakland, California, 1957–1959

JESSICA WEISS

"Woman's place is still in the home — no matter how many other places she finds herself in the world's eye." This was the opening line in Oakland journalist Kay Wahl's long-running column in the *Oakland Tribune*. Entitled "She Also Cooks," the column appeared first on November 3, 1957. Wahl profiled a concert musician and provided her favorite recipe. Accompanying the piece was Wahl's miniature sketch of a woman standing in front of a roast turkey, about to orchestrate a meal with the bow of her violin. From its inception, "She Also Cooks" showcased East Bay women and illustrated that they could balance both public and private life. Each week's installment included the trademark sketch and a brief interview with an accomplished local woman, and always closed with a recipe.

"She Also Cooks," which ran from 1957 to 1964, epitomizes the ambiguous, transitional gender constructs of the 1950s and early 1960s, deepening our understanding of the complexity of postwar notions of gender by moving the discussion from the broad trends and prescriptions of the national media to a local community, in this case, Oakland, California. Here we can hear the actual voices (albeit fashioned for public consumption) of women who combined public life — careers or full-time civic or philanthropic volunteer activity — with family life in an era supposedly defined first by domesticity and then by a sudden groundswell of feminism. Wedged in a section called "The Feminine Sphere" amidst the more predictable mix of society notes, club news, and wedding announcements, Wahl's column blithely merged the domestic and nondomestic aspects of postwar middle-class women's lives. The column offers a unique opportunity to analyze the educations, occupations, and views of the women whom Wahl interviewed. As a culinary time capsule, "She Also Cooks" provides a look at what upper-middle-class American women cooked and how they talked about cooking as the 1950s drew to a close. These recipes and interviews illustrate the ways in which American women not only participated in public life in the postwar era but also paved the way for gender role change and the feminist revival of the 1960s and 1970s.[1]

Women's historians have revised the conventional interpretation of gender ideology and female possibilities in the 1950s. Reexamining Betty Friedan's "feminine mystique," which until recently dominated discussions of women's experience in the 1950s, we now realize that Friedan's seemingly exhaustive discussion of women's magazines constituted, as historian Joanne Meyerowitz convincingly argues, "only a piece of the postwar cultural puzzle." The rest of the puzzle shows overlooked evidence of "domestic ideals in ongoing tension with an ethos of individual achievement that celebrated nondomestic activity, individual striving, public service, and public success." More than one image of womanhood flourished.[2]

"She Also Cooks" adds another piece to the puzzle of gender ideals in the 1950s. It uncovers a group of civically active women as they were portrayed in their local newspaper and the ways they defined women's roles. Primarily, Wahl sought to rescue the publicly active woman from aspersions of androgyny and nondomesticity. Moreover, Wahl and the women she interviewed sustained a belief in what one historian has called a "female ethic" that stemmed from women's nurturing role and backed their claims for women's activity outside the home. The columnist and those she interviewed insisted that women at all stages of the life cycle had a public role to fulfill, be it via self-expression, social service, or employment. Part and parcel of that viewpoint was a relaxed approach to convenience cooking that enabled the cook to spend less time in the kitchen and still find preparing meals an outlet for creativity.

Between November 3, 1957, and November 15, 1959, Kay Wahl featured 104 women in her column. The majority of the women were East Bay residents or former inhabitants. Wahl focused on prominent women, many whose names she gleaned from *Who's Who*. Given the focus on fame and accomplishment, it's not surprising that they were a highly educated group. Sixty-two attended college and thirty-three had gone on to graduate or professional school including nine doctors of philosophy, five medical doctors, and four juris doctors. Wahl preferred to write about women in conventionally male fields — medicine, law, and architecture, for instance. Thirty-five percent of those interviewed fell into that category. She also heavily favored women who had achieved renown in the arts — fiction, theater, film, music, or painting — interviewing twenty-three women in this field. Other women whom she interviewed ran the gamut of small business owners, local politicians, and clubwomen.[3]

While the occupations and professions of the women Wahl included were diverse, the population was not. In two years Wahl wrote up only one African American woman, a singer named Elmerlee Thomas. Judging by surname, most of the Oakland women tapped for their views on women's roles and quick and easy recipes were white Anglo-Saxon Protestants with a handful of white ethnic women — Italian, Jewish, Armenian American — sprinkled in. Wahl's focus was the middle- or upper-class woman who worked to provide an outlet for talent or intellect. No assembly-line workers or file clerks appear on her roster. Yet Wahl's preference for querying prominent women does provide some interesting historical side notes. The musician's wife, Mrs. Dave Brubeck, author Beverly Cleary, and comedienne Phyllis Diller were all swept up in Wahl's embrace. Brubeck provided a recipe for cheesecake; Cleary cooked creamed potatoes with fresh rosemary; and Diller, formerly an Alameda housewife, contributed an "offbeat" recipe for tomato pudding, a concoction that called for canned tomatoes, stale bread, and brown sugar.[4]

Three-quarters of the women interviewed were mothers over forty. The largest single category within that age group were the twenty-one grandmothers. One age group formed a conspicuous minority among the interviewees — young women in their twenties; Wahl questioned only five. In the thick of the baby boom, it is likely that many of these women were occupied with rearing small children. Through Wahl's column, then, we glimpse a very particular subset of postwar East Bay women — highly educated, successful, middle-aged or older, and white. These women — married middle-class mothers and grandmothers, most of whom came of age in the 1920s and 1930s — and the column that preserved their achievements, words, and recipes for posterity prompt further questions and suggest new ways of understanding gender change in the 1950s. A close look at Wahl's column restores a generation of women usually ignored in discussions of the 1950s to the narrative of the postwar transformation of women's roles.[5]

By featuring working women, Wahl's column tapped into the postwar trend of increasing women's employment. Women's labor force participation accelerated even in the midst of a decade of affluence and family building. Since married women and mothers were the conspicuous participants in this marked growth of the female labor force, Wahl's subjects were by no means unique. Indeed, the sharpest increase in employment rates during those years is to be found among middle-class women. This fact makes Wahl's column of particular historical utility — revealing as it does the views of participants in what constitutes a major transformation in the contours of middle-class women's lives.[6]

Wahl took for granted this transition; it was her starting point. Based on women's changing lives, her concerns were twofold. First, she wanted to reassure readers in the throes of gender role change that careers did not dilute femininity. Second, she hoped to smooth the path of acceptance for those women on the forefront of these changes, encouraging other women to follow. Above all, Wahl insisted that the career woman was feminine and indeed still domestic, not the masculinized competitor depicted in postwar propaganda.

"There isn't a woman in the world who doesn't have a favorite recipe," Wahl declared, and her column supported her declaration. Recipes for macaroni and cheese, marrow balls with broth, and melon stuffed with shrimp made her case; women with interests outside the home could and did cook. Busy volunteer Mrs. W. H. Oliver, who chaired the volunteer branches of Oakland's Children's Hospital, a full-time commitment, had "her favorite recipe (like almost every other woman in the public eye)." Wahl maintained, "Today, women are doing their best to rock the world — but they aren't giving up their place in the home." According to Wahl, careers and public service did nothing to diminish women's domestic proclivities and were, therefore, no threat to the nation's family life.[7]

Homes and marriages were safe from neglect, Wahl and her women of accomplishment asserted. Mrs. Lawrence Fletcher, whose life was a whirl of volunteer leadership positions, stated, "I refuse to let anything I do carry over to the hours before my husband leaves in the morning or after he gets home." No matter how busy a woman was, she always had time for family, and her "home life was as important . . . as her professional life." Working women were as "efficient" in the home as out of it, Wahl proclaimed each week, addressing worries that the domestic sphere would suffer as middle-class women increasingly stepped beyond it, simultaneously buttressing the belief that women maintained sole responsibility for the work at home.[8]

Although most interviewees were married women with children, Wahl incorporated single women in her campaign to domesticate the image of the career woman. By virtue of what Wahl saw as inborn feminine interests, her gender gave the career woman an edge in life over a man. To Wahl, Katherine Towle, a dean at the University of California, Berkeley and a former marine, demonstrated "that a career woman has an advantage over a man — she still has that homemaking instinct to bring happiness to her leisure time." According to Wahl, unmarried women made their own homes, entertained, and led satisfying lives. But Wahl was not above doing her part to improve a single woman's social life. About another unmarried academic administrator whose recipe required filling dried fruit with cream cheese, she admonished, "Don't be afraid of a date with a dean!" Women were homemakers with or without marriage; careers in no way diminished this interest. Wahl both domesticated and championed women with careers.[9]

By positing a homemaking instinct impervious to the supposedly diluting influences of careers, Wahl made "She Also Cooks" a forum for women's views on the special contribution their sex brought to their employment and activities. Work — volunteer, part- or full-time, professional or artistic — became an extension as well as an alternative to domesticity in Wahl's vision, legitimizing women's increasingly expanding roles. Each week's column provided additional evidence for individual women's successful management of busy lives outside the home.

Wahl used the experiences of the women she featured in her column to articulate a mid-twentieth-century expression of maternalism: that is, a set of values, interests, and strengths related to women's nurturing, which women employed outside of the home as well as within it. She and many of those whose praises she sang believed that women brought special female qualities to their professions. For example, fifteen of the women she interviewed held jobs in teaching, nursing, or public health — jobs that women had dominated for most of the century. This Wahl explained easily by referencing women's affinity for and ability in "human relations" and children's needs especially. "A helpless child," Wahl wrote, "is always closest to a woman's heart, and its care her most compassionate task."[10]

Those queried shared this tenet, although they referred more vaguely to intangible feminine influences. They believed that women contributed a female sensibility at work, making their input important. A woman investment broker thought the financial world of stocks and bonds required a "woman's point of view." In advertising there was always the "woman's angle" to tout, according to one Oakland advertising executive: "We can write copy and think of sales angles that appeal to a woman — not that men can't do this, but sometimes we hit the nail on the head a little better. There are more women in the advertising field when it comes to food and clothing and anything that has to do with home economics or homemaking."[11] For Wahl and the prominent women that she spotlighted, a connection to homemaking or mothering could be found whether the woman was a real estate agent, architect, business-woman, or even a pharmacist (which, after all, she pointed out, simply required following an exact recipe). Feminine skills served women in their roles outside the home, allowing them to contribute in ways that men could not, these women attested. As Mrs. Miller, coordinator of industrial education for a junior college, declared, "We exert a different kind of influence than men ever could in whatever field, because of the way we look at life." Like the social feminists of the turn of the century, who organized around the notion of female difference, Wahl and her fellow Bay Area professional women used mothering as a platform from which to expand opportunities for women.[12]

While emphasizing traditional female qualities on one level, on another, Wahl's column served as evidence that women's lives were changing, and she and many of the women she interviewed emphatically endorsed these changes. Nonetheless, Wahl acknowledged ambivalence and allowed women to speak for themselves. When they said they put home, husband, and children first, she printed it, but never without pointing out how much else the self-defined homemaker had also accomplished. When Cecilia Bartholomew, an author, expressed those sentiments, Wahl concluded, "But in 20 or so years of adhering to this conviction she has established a national reputation as a short story writer — and will see her first novel published this summer." It was the combination of domestic and public activity that provided a woman with the fullest life, Wahl opined, and the accomplished women she queried on the topic agreed. When she saluted her colleague at the *Tribune*, Nancy Mavity, Wahl commented, "In private life Mrs. Edward Rogers . . . is a visible proof of her argument that a home and career not only can but should be combined for a woman." In a dizzying list of occupations Mavity was described as a writer, author, college instructor, mother of two, grandmother of four, as well as the possessor of a doctorate. Women could manage the "double life," and they thrived when they did so, according to Wahl.[13]

If one scans the comments from "She Also Cooks," a consensus emerges, perhaps best expressed by pianist and mother of two, Marie St. Gaudens (a descendant of the sculptor) when she told Wahl, "I don't feel women's place is just in the home. . . . If she has a particular talent, it's really a shame to let it go." Women had a need and an obligation to pursue a talent. They had a duty to use an education or skill. As citizens, they were obligated to serve their community. Their families, society, and they themselves gained when they committed themselves to something outside of the home. Wahl and the East Bay women she showcased expressed these views again and again. Home life itself would be improved. Novelist Alice Hobart told Wahl, "A woman who goes out and gets a new viewpoint and brings something back into the home is better than one who stays home all day and has very little to talk about either to her husband or children except food." Just over 11 percent of the women Wahl interviewed stated that outside interests and activities made women better wives and mothers.[14]

Not only did she hale their accomplishments outside the home, however. Wahl celebrated their abilities within it and, in particular, their culinary talents. A survey of the 104 recipes reveals important tidbits of information about women and cooking in the late 1950s, at least among this small sample of women. Nearly a third of the recipes were for desserts, and the most frequent sorts were custards and cakes. Next in frequency of appearance were, not surprisingly, given that these were women dividing their time between work and home, that 1950s standby—the casserole. More sparingly sprinkled through the recipes were appetizers or dishes with an ethnic flavor, appearing with roughly equal frequency. Eight women shared old family recipes, and four told how to preserve or pickle fresh produce, something American women of the 1950s turned to mass production for more commonly. In fact, over 40 percent of the recipes relied on mass-produced prepared foods as either supplement or base.

The casserole trend of the 1950s reflected the no-nonsense, practical approach women brought to cooking for their families. With women's busy lives as family managers, volunteers, or careerists, time spent cooking had to be minimized. Thus, ironically, a food trend born of Depression-era deprivation and wartime rationing—when home cooks employed eggs, beans, and cheese to stretch meager budgets or supplies—was revived in an era of affluence. The beauty of casseroles was that they were easily expanded, making them "useful for all sorts of buffet entertaining." A cook only had to "throw together" leftovers, a starch, canned soup or vegetables, perhaps some cheese, and scatter breadcrumbs, cornflakes, or potato chips, another popular topping, across the top. Once the dish was assembled and in the oven, the cook merely kept track of the time. Casseroles made easy, hearty, one-dish suppers, and the ability to whip up a tasty one qualified as a culinary skill that accomplished women around the East Bay were pleased to share.[15]

As they described their favorites, Wahl and her contributors focused mainly on the recipes' quick and easy preparation, their palatability for children, and their style for entertaining. But, hands down, "easy" was a recipe's biggest selling point. Recipes based on processed food had become ubiquitous enough by the late 1950s for Betsy Fitzgerald Rahn to remark that her "family's favorite birthday dessert, Golden Date Cake," was not a "package recipe but still pretty easy." Busy women like Marjorie Benedict, a Republican National Committee member and Berkeley homemaker, confessed, "I don't have much time for my cooking these days." Frances Hickey, a "wife, mother, and grandmother" who also "has a full-time career as director of volunteers" for the regional Children's Home Society, was happy to share her recipe for "chicken breasts picant," one she thought appropriate for the column because "It's very easy to fix which is an item for a busy person." Others provided ideas for a "fast meal at night" or easy salads to prepare for company. Leota Moulton, an artist and president of the San Francisco Women Artists, boasted that her "busy housewife dish," handy for "when unexpected company arrives for dinner," meant that "honestly, I'm only in the kitchen about 10 minutes." Jerry Washburn was an "unsung" "career-woman-for-free" who volunteered with the Camp Fire Girls and taught folk dance at the school for the blind. Volunteer work was "a must" for Mrs. Washburn. "If you just do your work at home, it becomes such a small world," she said. Mrs. Washburn confided that she read Wahl's column herself. "I like your recipes from active women. I always think, 'She's busy. This will be a practical and easy recipe.' And I've tried many of them without a failure." For lack of time, many women in the 1950s eschewed the fancy for the practical. Efficiency and love of cooking could still go hand in hand. From their perspectives, the kitchen had a place in these women's lives, rather than their place being in the kitchen. Extrapolating from this small East Bay sample, it would seem that postwar American women wanted to reduce the drudgery and time devoted to cooking, but that they still derived satisfaction from concocting combinations of ingredients, even if their components came from packages.[16]

Recipes composed mainly of processed foods, while they may have cost more than the original unprocessed ingredients, claimed to save the homemaker's time. One featured recipe relied almost exclusively on commercially prepared ingredients. Nydine Latham's "specialty for quick preparation when unexpected guests arrive" was "crab bisque." The recipe went on to call for "one can each asparagus soup, mushroom soup, tomato soup, and split pea soup," to which the rushed "cook" was to add a can of crab meat. As Wahl wrote, the "main requirement is a can opener." Othelia Lilly pronounced herself "first assistant" to her husband, "who loves to operate on the stove," while she herself was "very good at opening cans." Not surprisingly, the electric can opener was introduced to consumers in 1956. Today the appliance seems a waste of counter space, but after reading recipes that call for opening three or four cans, their appeal in the 1950s becomes clear.[17]

Modern and convenient, packaged foods also constituted a blank canvas upon which the busy woman could still imprint her individual whim. A woman whose cupboard was chock-full of cans might also grow her own herbs with which to doctor them without seeing a contradiction. As Mrs. Atrocchi put it, "The secret is spices, not time. You can add curry to mushroom soup and make an East India dish. You can add sherry and minced clams to mushroom soup. . . . I find cooking very creative." Here, the home cook followed the lead of cookbook authors who recommended "spiking" prepared foods to dress them up. American women tinkered with recipes to their own liking, turning spring scallion soup into clam soup with the twist of a wrist, or transmuting baked chicken into chicken stroganoff with a container of sour cream. Despite or perhaps because of a love of shortcuts, experimenting in the kitchen was important to women in the 1950s. While the popularity of and reliance on cookbooks indicates to some scholars the spread of ignorance and the decline of experiential knowledge in the kitchen, these women felt comfortable using ingredients in new ways on their own. For example, Helen Mason's favorite recipe was a curry dish that was "actually a combination of several." Combining recipes was also how another of Wahl's women created her special version of strawberry pie.[18]

Perhaps because cooking had, for many, been reduced to heating up processed foods, these women focused on the creativity that remained essential to getting satisfaction out of the task. It is not clear whether technology and labor-saving packaged foods really did reduce the housewife's day of toil in the 1950s. In fact, some studies suggest that by raising the standards of the possible, technological improvements — home appliances, for example — increased their workload. But even when operating an electric can opener was the main skill called for in a recipe, women staked a claim to artistry in the kitchen. Many called themselves "inexact cooks" who whipped things up without reference to a book. Cooking by smell or taste, they had a difficult time giving a quantifiable recipe to Wahl and proudly told her so. Emphasis on their inexactness when it came time to provide a recipe suggests that these women saw cooking as creative and intuitive, even if preparation had been simplified.[19]

"She Also Cooks" also provided women with a community conversation on cooking. Even employed women and civic volunteers were isolated in the home when it came to the task of preparing family meals. Swapping recipes and tips through the forum of Wahl's column and sharing their opinions about cooking were ways of ameliorating that isolation. The tone that Wahl and the women she interviewed took when discussing cooking — casual and conversational — echoed that of a book which in its many revised editions enjoyed phenomenal success in the 1950s and continues to do so today: Irma Rombauer and Marion Rombauer Becker's *Joy of Cooking*. According to Rombauer biographer Anne Mendelson, what made this recipe compendium especially appealing to midcentury women was that Rombauer did not "tell other people how they should cook, but how she cooked and what a bang she got out of it." What *Joy of Cooking* offered readers and users was "camaraderie" and information for women who, once married, took on a lifelong job of preparing meals with little help or guidance. In Wahl's column, women swapped both time-saving tips and time-honored knowledge, reflecting the contradictory place of cooking in women's lives as an arduous chore and a point of pride. The preponderance of simple recipes suggests that this was a conversation that Oakland women who would never appear in *Who's Who* might still enjoy — without necessarily trying — some of the more elaborate and time-consuming dishes. Even these, the cooks in question were careful to point out, were a special occasion dish in their homes.[20]

A cooking column that stressed quick and easy recipes, featured career women, but was called "She Also Cooks," encapsulates the ambiguities and tensions that surrounded the transformation of women's roles in the postwar years. How did Wahl deem it best to defend the femininity of women active in the public sphere and their right to be there? By associating them with women's primary activity in the private one: "She *Also* Cooks." For example, Wahl introduced Mrs. Gerald Whitaker (whose first name is not mentioned), "So that her public won't get the false idea that all she has done is be president of the state club federation, chairman of national events for the general federation, a Berkeley city council woman . . . and this year's choice for . . . the Most Useful Citizen of the Year — Mrs. Whitaker declares, 'I'm a GOOD cook.' " Wahl wrote that a musician "makes beautiful music — not just on the concert stage, but in the kitchen," while an attorney "after the trial has recessed . . . dons her apron." Wahl described Cora Riser as "at home in both places." A teacher and member of the Oakland Board of Education, Riser was "still well acquainted with the workings of her kitchen stove." Author Beverly Cleary was "as skillful with the skillet as with the typewriter." Historian Harvey Levenstein observes that in the 1950s, Americans though that "food preparation was central to women's role binding family ties." Home cooking was, he writes, a female "monopoly." Cooking provided Wahl with a convenient symbol through which to associate working women with femininity. Wahl called the career woman a cook, defining her as feminine, and simultaneously broadened the scope of femininity.[21]

Week after week, in her recipe column Wahl introduced East Bay residents to women who in action and in words challenged the domestic ideal by demonstrating there was more to a woman's life than homemaking: public involvement, she insisted, benefited the family, the community, *and* the individual woman. Mrs. O'Brien told Wahl that "outside activities are 'the most important part of life. . . . In spite of the fact that for a woman her home should come first. But if she wants to have a full and interesting life she should have both.' " An assistant public defender for Alameda County encouraged women's careers outside the home: "Unless a woman is allowed to develop her own abilities, she has a frustrated feeling and no sense of fulfillment. She's not happy and when you're not happy you don't do anybody any good who is near you." Five years before *The Feminine Mystique* appeared, these women endorsed self-fulfillment as a worthy and necessary ingredient in married women's lives and pointed to full-time domesticity as a potential problem. Postwar women may have had a monopoly on cooking, but these women refused to allow cooking to monopolize them.[22]

Wahl occasionally interwove parenthetical feminist comments into her interviews that challenged the fairness of this monopoly. She observed, "How much easier it still is for a man to develop his 'particular talent' without so much of his creativeness demanded by his home!" Cloaking feminist content in cookery, Wahl extolled women's equality and homemaking skills, inserting nascent criticism of traditional women's roles.[23]

In supporting the right of the individual woman to follow her ambition to its full fruition, Oakland women in the 1950s presaged liberal feminism. By justifying their presence in the public sphere with maternalist ideology, they echoed progressive era reformers and feminists. Wahl's women articulated a vision of women's opportunity and fulfillment buttressed by a staunch faith in individualism. They believed that women with talents, desires, or interests beyond homemaking deserved the opportunity to explore them. Basic fairness, intellectual ability, and maternalism legitimized this broadened scope. In other words, midcentury women combined equality and difference-based justifications as they made their case for expanding women's roles.

Unlike the feminist movements that bookended these midcentury women, however, neither Wahl nor her subjects proposed collective political action specifically on behalf of women or displayed grave concern for less-privileged women, despite their charity work. Opportunities, they believed, were there for the ambitious woman's taking. Accommodating family responsibility involved individual solutions, cooperative husbands, hired help, and, perhaps, subordinating career to child rearing until later in life. Wahl did not address the problems women might face at work, the difficulties of balancing it all, or women who worked as a matter of course, not choice.

Wahl showcased women who augmented their family roles without questioning them. Insisting on the central place of domesticity in women's lives, these Oakland women also assumed that problems arising from juggling home and work were each individual woman's to solve. And they exuded, by their very success, the confidence that their solutions were simple and available to all. For example, Othelia Lilly, a poet, favored careers for women, even if they neglected the housework a little in order to achieve success. After all, "their gifts are far more important than the things anyone can be hired to do." When children entered the picture, Lilly thought the balance became more challenging: "If they have families, each has to solve her own problems in that respect." These women advocated choice. The middle-class women that Wahl interviewed had that luxury. The belief that married women deserved the opportunity for public activity ignored the very real need that drove less affluent women to pursue employment. Berkeley City Councilwoman Bernice May, however, did recognize that economic need denied many women the choice of combining home and career: "Many a woman works to keep her home together — and we have to consider what would be the alternative if she didn't." But even she neglected to mention any alternative forms of child care for working mothers. These prominent, privileged women had waited until children were of school age, hired caretakers, or found work that did not encroach on children's lives. They found private solutions to what they saw as individual problems.[24]

Wahl proposed an alternative to the feminine mystique's version of female fulfillment, but one still grounded in domesticity. Thus she constructed a mystique of her own. In her column, musicians, authors, and attorneys proudly accepted accolades and shared culinary tips. As they did so, they made what a later generation would call "having it all" sound effortless. Intended as comfort and company for busy career women, the column may well have left female readers feeling inadequate. Wahl set the bar high—success, good cooking, and acceptance of the status quo—and left ordinary working women out of her vision in the process. Indeed, the column functions as an early expression of the superwoman syndrome, elevating women who had found individual success as role models and ignoring the underlying need for structural changes. Wahl sought to legitimate women's public activity by affixing her good cooking seal of approval.

Wahl's column created an idyllic vision of women's fulfillment though both domestic and public activity. Yet it offered an important alternative to the competing ideal of full-time domesticity by collecting female lore on combining work and family. Wahl summed up her second year of interviewing "successful" women by saying, "Each of them is convinced that woman's duty includes more than housekeeping, but that it never excludes her home. And few of them have any bitterness about the fact that having a career, for a woman, means having two."[25]

Wahl's column is a transitional text from a transitional time in American women's history. By spotlighting women's embrace of convenience food *and* their continued creativity in the kitchen, Wahl hoped to clear the way for women to apply skills outside the home. She championed traditional womanly traits and simultaneously argued for their applicability in public life. Wahl provided role models for getting ahead in the business world, formulas for fusing homemaking and career, and recipes for gracious entertaining or quick suppers for children. She accepted the primacy of family, the double burden of the career woman who had a job at home and one at the office, and conceded that women might have to work harder than men to succeed. Her acerbic asides, however, convey impatience with the gender status quo even as she showed women successfully navigating it. That undercurrent of impatience illustrates that the roots of feminism flourished alongside domesticity in the 1950s. While it may have fallen to Betty Friedan to legitimize "open protest against 'the housewife trap,' " middle-class women in the 1950s had, without collective public protest, loosened the ties of domestic "entrapment," and in Oakland, at least, they found a public forum that openly celebrated them and attempted to ease their redefinition of the possible in women's lives.[26]

Notes

1. Kay Wahl came to the *Oakland Tribune* from the *Post-Inquirer*. "She Also Cooks" appeared weekly from 1957 to 1964. Wahl was from a prominent East Bay

and California family, the Eshelmans. She wrote about women like herself, both affluent and accomplished. Thanks to Floyd Tucker, formerly of the *Oakland Tribune*, for background information on Kay Wahl.

2. Joanne Meyerowitz, "Beyond the Feminine Mystique: A Reassessment of Postwar Mass Culture, 1945–1960," 231, in Meyerowitz, *Not June Cleaver: Women and Gender in Postwar America, 1945–1960* (Philadelphia: Temple University Press, 1994), 229–62. Meyerowitz's groundbreaking collection of essays extended beyond the middle-class stereotype of the unhappy homemaker to include discussion of the activism and experiences of women in diverse communities during the 1950s and also questioned what had for the most part become a historical given: feminist author and activist Betty Friedan's version of postwar women's history, *The Feminine Mystique*. American women were, Friedan wrote, stifled by housewifery and media exhortations to forsake everything, including themselves, for home, husband, and children. But when Meyerowitz investigated a broader spectrum of magazine sources than those Friedan drew on, she found a greater variety of views about women and domesticity. Betty Friedan, *The Feminine Mystique*, 10th anniversary ed. (New York: Dell Publishing, 1973). Eugenia Kaledin provides a thorough survey of women's activities during the supposedly domestic decade. Kaledin, *Mothers and More: American Women in the 1950s* (Boston: Twayne, 1984).

3. The nine remaining columns made no mention of education. This project will ultimately cover the entire run of the column; however, for the purposes of this chapter, the first two years have been analyzed.

4. The demographics of her column reflect more on a nostalgic image of Oakland's prewar past than an accurate portrait of the postwar Oakland reality. Wartime migration transformed the San Francisco Bay Area and particularly the East Bay region, bringing hundreds of thousands of migrants who sought defense work and economic opportunity. World War II was the crucible of multicultural Oakland. For more on the social and political struggles that accompanied ethnic and residential transformation, see Marilynn S. Johnson, *The Second Gold Rush: Oakland and the East Bay in World War II* (Berkeley: University of California Press, 1993).

5. With regard to marital status and number of children, I draw solely on what Wahl reported. If children or husbands went unmentioned, I assume that they did not exist, since she was careful to note them in most columns. She rarely mentioned age, so my use of the term *over forty* is based on contextual comments about year of college graduation, tenure at a particular job, last anniversary celebrated, and number and age of children or grandchildren.

6. Nor was Wahl alone in her propaganda effort on behalf of the working wife. Historian Susan Hartmann has pointed to two national organizations that worked to foster "change in popular attitudes and in institutional practices" regarding female employment during the 1950s. (See "Women's Employment and the Domestic Ideal in the Early Cold War Years," in Meyerowitz, *Not June Cleaver*, 85). For a discussion of married women's work and postwar family life, see Jessica Weiss, *To Have and to Hold: Marriage, the Baby Boom, and Social Change* (Chicago: University of Chicago Press, 2000).

7. Kay Wahl, "She Also Cooks," *Oakland Tribune*, 3 Nov. 1957; 10 Nov. 1957; 1 Dec. 1957. Wahl's column appeared in "The Feminine Sphere" or section "S." For a discussion of the cultural importance of home and family life as a defense against communism during the cold war, see Elaine Tyler May, *Homeward Bound: American Families During the Cold War* (New York: Basic Books, 1988).

8. Wahl, 8 Dec. 1957; 29 Dec. 1957; 12 Jan. 1958.

9. Wahl, 15 Dec. 1957; 13 April 1958.

10. "Human Relations, and the Problems They Create, Are Her Special Interest." Wahl, 29 Dec. 1957; 2 Feb. 1958.

11. Wahl, 11 May 1958.

12. Wahl, 29 Sept. 1959; 11 May 1958; 1 Feb. 1959; 4 Oct. 1959.

13. Wahl, 23 Feb. 1958; 15 June 1958.

14. Wahl, 10 Aug. 1958; 26 Oct. 1958.

15. Gerry Shremp, *Kitchen Culture: Fifty Years of Food Fads* (New York: Pharos Books, 1991), 12, 40–41. Wahl, 3 Nov. 1956; 2 Feb. 1958; 23 Mar. 1958.

16. Wahl, 29 Dec. 1957; 1 Dec. 1957; 6 April 1958; 13 Jul. 1958; 27 Jul. 1958; 24 Aug. 1958; 5 April 1959; 12 April 1959; 2 Aug. 1959. Such recipes were popular; in the 1950s, author Poppy Cannon created a cookbook dynasty beginning with her 1952 best-seller, *The Can Opener Cookbook*. Shremp, *Kitchen Culture*, 40.

17. Wahl, 24 Dec. 1958. Shremp, *Kitchen Culture*, 42. Wahl, 30 Aug. 1959. Beginning in the 1930s, canned soups were prevalent in American home cooking. Anne Mendelson writes that in *The Joy of Cooking*, "Condensed tomato soup appears as the basis of a soufflé, a medium for poaching eggs, the liquid for thinning Braunschweiger sausage into a canapé spread, the tomato element in a seafood sauce for spaghetti, and the chief flavor accent in an aspic salad." Mendelson, *Stand Facing the Stove: The Story of the Women Who Gave America "The Joy of Cooking"* (New York: Henry Holt, 1996), 131. For a thorough discussion of the postwar processed food industry, see Harvey Levenstein, *Paradox of Plenty: A Social History of Eating in Modern America* (New York: Oxford University Press, 1993), 101–13.

18. Wahl, 1 Nov. 1959; Shremp, 40, 42; Wahl, 16 Nov. 1958. The homegrown herb/canned food paradox is an American one. Mendelson writes, "Arbiters of taste who go to *The Joy of Cooking* looking for one masterly dish after another will find that the recipes in any edition from 1931 on present a picture of American cooking filled with wild inconsistencies — the inconsistencies of real people's real food preferences, from canned soup sauces to homemade noodles" (5).

19. Ruth Schwartz Cowan, *More Work for Mother: The Ironies of Household Technology from the Open Hearth to the Microwave* (New York: Basic Books, 1983), 199. As Levenstein points out, "Longer shelf-lives, more processing, precooking, and packaging all had one great justification: to liberate 'Mrs. Consumer' from the drudgery of the kitchen" (108).

20. From Betty Friedan on, a constant theme in the discussion of the twentieth-century housewife is her isolation. See also Ellen M. Plante, *The American Kitchen, 1700 to the Present: From Hearth to Highrise* (New York: Facts on File, 1995), 282.

21. Wahl, 17 Nov. 1957; 29 Dec. 1957; 22 June 1958; 5 Oct. 1958. Levenstein, 103.

22. Wahl, 15 Nov. 1959; 31 Aug. 1958.
23. Wahl, 10 Aug. 1958.
24. Wahl, 30 Aug. 1959; 15 Nov. 1959; 2 Aug. 1959.
25. Wahl, 11 Jan. 1959.
26. Meyerowitz, "Beyond the Feminine Mystique," in *Not June Cleaver*, 252.

"My Kitchen Was the World"

Vertamae Smart Grosvenor's

Geechee Diaspora

DORIS WITT

The question I was most often asked was why didn't I consider myself a "soul food" writer. Over and over I would try to explain my philosophy on the nonracial aspects of blackeyed peas, watermelon, and other so-called soul foods on TV, radio, and in lectures. It seemed to me while certain foods have been labeled "soul food" and associated with Afro-Americans, Afro-Americans could be associated with all foods.
I would explain that my kitchen was the world.
— Vertamae Smart Grosvenor, introduction to the
second edition of *Vibration Cooking*, 1986

In her critically acclaimed 1991 film *Daughters of the Dust*, Julie Dash explores the lives of Gullah peoples on the Sea Islands off the coast of South Carolina and Georgia. Brought from Africa to the United States as slaves, they cultivated indigo and later cotton while creating "a distinct, original African-American cultural form" because of their relative isolation from outside influences (Creel 69). Dash's film focuses on a single day in 1902, when members of the Peazant family are planning to leave their home on Ibo Landing to begin a new life on the mainland. Family "matriarch" Nana Peazant cannot understand why her relations would want to abandon the land and the cultural traditions that, in her opinion, constitute their rightful heritage. Throughout the day, many of the Peazant women are shown engaging in one of those traditions, the preparation of food for a feast the family will share before taking leave. Images of fresh okra, shrimp, rice, and other island delicacies contribute to the film's somewhat nostalgic portrayal of Ibo Landing as a site of authentic pleasure outside the realm of commodity capitalism. The women's labor is presented not as alienating or oppressive but rather as a natural accompaniment to their socializing.

At the center of these culinary rituals is the "hair braider," a character portrayed, fittingly, by South Carolina native and "Geechee" popularizer Vertamae Smart Grosvenor. A longtime commentator on National Public Radio (NPR) and host in the mid-1990s of the Public Broadcasting Service (PBS) series *The Americas' Family Kitchen*, Grosvenor was one among at least two dozen African Americans who published nationally distributed cookbooks during soul food's peak years from 1968 to 1971.[1] Previously, the foods associated with black slavery and black poverty — inexpensive pork and corn products in particular — had sometimes been viewed with disdain by middle-class or upwardly mobile African Americans. As the integrationist, southern-based civil rights movement evolved during the 1960s into a northern-based, separatist drive for Black Power, however, many black nationalists began using the term *soul* to valorize the cultural forms created through a history of black oppression. Soul was most commonly associated with a popular style of black music that had evolved from gospel traditions, but as the decade progressed it was increasingly used to refer to a broader array of black cultural practices, including foodways. Yet the celebration of what was understood to be a primarily black mother/daughter tradition — soul food cooking — was fraught with ideological contradictions, since the Black Power era was also structured by extreme hostility toward black women as "slave" mothers and castrating "matriarchs" (Dubey 1–32).

It perhaps should come as no surprise, then, that in her underground classic *Vibration Cooking, or the Travel Notes of a Geechee Girl* (1970), Grosvenor negotiated this contradiction by disavowing "soul" while proselytizing for many of the foods associated with it. The dishes she included in her cookbook ranged from the standard chitterlings, watermelon rind preserves, and hoppin' john to by no means typically soul fare such as feijoadas, Irish potato soup, salade niçoise, and stewed Jerusalem artichokes. On a generic level, moreover, *Vibration Cooking* is memorable as a hybrid of cookbook, autobiography, and travelogue similar to *The Alice B. Toklas Cook Book* (1954) — which, Grosvenor acknowledged in a 1971 *Ebony* interview, she used as a model for her own writing (Garland 90). Recipe gives rise to anecdote, and anecdote to recipe. Both are integral to the text. *Vibration Cooking* thus stands out from many contemporaneous African American cookbooks in its attempt to disrupt normative categories of racial identity and textual genre alike. Indeed, the book's generic plasticity might be viewed as an analogue to Grosvenor's formulation of what I will call a protodiasporic model of black American culture.[2]

Since the publication of Paul Gilroy's *The Black Atlantic* in 1993, scholars of race have been giving renewed attention to the ramifications of black migration for our understanding of how the nation-state has developed in tandem with ideologies of racial difference. Working to critique the exclusionary logic that renders whiteness the normative condition of Western citizenship, Gilroy formulates an alternative theorization of black modernity as a phenomenon of transatlantic, cross-cultural exchange. Movement and music operate as privileged terms in *The Black Atlantic*, the latter providing for Gilroy perhaps the exemplary manifestation of the former. Whereas traditional conceptions of the black diaspora are preoccupied with movement from east to west, primarily from Africa to Europe and the Americas, Gilroy's understanding of the term offers up a more complicated dynamic in which black Americans and Europeans talk back, as it were, to Africa. He explores, for instance, the influence of black American musical styles on black British and African cultures.

This essay will work from Gilroy's model in order to investigate the often vexed relationship between black women and soul food. Having presented her first cookbook as a "travel" narrative and having hosted a television series devoted to "Afro-Atlantic" cookery, Grosvenor provides an especially apt opportunity to consider the ramifications for feminist work on race of a critical theory that celebrates cultural syncretism over cultural isolation. At issue will be the interplay between Grosvenor's attempt to lay the groundwork for a nonessentializing study of African American culinary history and her personal mutability — her somewhat ambiguous positioning between poverty and affluence, between black nationalism and white feminism, even between the historically isolated Sea Islands and the small town of Fairfax, South Carolina, located at least forty-five miles inland, where she was born.

Grosvenor might be understood to have embraced a diasporic aesthetic not only to subvert the equation of African American culinary traditions with southern black poverty, but also to undermine stereotypical representations of African American women as domineering mammies and emasculating matriarchs. Yet the seeming paradox is that in the process of critiquing soul's positioning of black women as paradigmatic threats to the boundaries of the self, Grosvenor represents herself as the abject.[3] What I will speculate is that this paradox is actually foundational to the discourses of diasporic black identity. And to the extent that the cultural logic of (maternal) abjection does continue to underwrite even progressive conceptualizations of the diaspora, African American women such as Grosvenor will indeed find it necessary to engage in a series of complex negotiations of position to find a psychically and politically liberatory "home" in a theory of black homelessness.

"The Truth Will Out"

Born Verta Mae Smart in 1939, Grosvenor actually grew up not in South Carolina but in North Philadelphia, where her paternal grandmother, Estella Smart, had migrated after being widowed (*Vibration* 11).[4] Referring to herself as "one of those 'key' children" (*Vibration* 31), Grosvenor says that she would often amuse herself while alone after school by putting on plays: "I was actor, director and audience all in one" (*Vibration* 30). As she matured from a frail, premature infant into a robust and precocious adolescent, Grosvenor feared that she would never be able to fulfill the first and foremost expectation of her gender: "I knew that I was destined never to marry. What man would want a six-foot-tall woman?" (*Vibration* 54). Accordingly, after finishing high school she decided to travel to Paris to become a "bohemian" and pursue her love of the theater. While there she became acquainted with Robert Strawbridge Grosvenor, a white sculptor-to-be from a prominent and wealthy U.S. family. They were married and eventually settled in New York City. By the time the marriage ended around 1964, Grosvenor had given birth to two daughters, Kali and Chandra. Shortly after *Vibration Cooking* was published, she was married again, this time to African American artist Ellsworth Ausby (Garland 94).

During the late 1960s, Grosvenor — who has published works as "Verta Mae," "Verta Grosvenor," "Vertamae Grosvenor," "Vertamae Smart Grosvenor," and "Vertamae Smart-Grosvenor" — worked at a variety of jobs while trying to succeed as an actress. She was a cook known as "Obedella" at Pee Wee's Slave Trade Kitchen (*Vibration* 89); she was "a clothing designer and seamstress, creating bizarre six-legged and four-armed outfits for advertising photographers" (Garland 88); and she was a "space chantress" and "cosmic force" with the musician Sun Ra and his Intergalactic Solar Myth Science Arkestra (Garland 88). The only occupation she always avoided was domestic labor, which not coincidentally was her mother's occupation. After having worked briefly in that capacity for one of her high school teachers, a job that ended when her "father found out" (Grosvenor, *Thursdays* 9), Grosvenor was determined to steer clear of the main employment opportunity traditionally open to African American women. Although her largely un-fulfilled theatrical aspirations had already made her known among many avant-garde musicians, artists, actors, and writers in New York and abroad, she did not achieve wider notice until after *Vibration Cooking* appeared.

The catalyst for its publication was her elder daughter, Kali, herself a precocious writer. After seeing Kali's poetry displayed in their apartment, one of Grosvenor's friends asked to show it to his agent at Doubleday. The result, *Poems by Kali* (1970), was published when its author was only eight years old. Meanwhile, Grosvenor had been doing some writing of her own:

While reading the Alice B. Toklas Cookbook, I'd been impressed with the way she had captured the feeling of her times in Paris during the 20s and people she had known, of Gertrude Stein, the salon and Picasso. So I thought I'd do a little cookbook for the people *I* knew in Paris, New York, and even back home in South Carolina and Philadelphia. Maybe I'd have a couple hundred copies printed up myself and give them to my friends so we could remember the experiences we'd shared. I'd tell them about the food, but I'd also tell them about what went down. But the people who were doing Kali's book seemed to think it could sell and that's the way it all happened. (qtd. in Garland 90)

Part autobiography, part travelogue, part culinary anthropology, part social history, part political commentary, *Vibration Cooking* undertook the para-doxical task of attempting to parody the genre of the standard cookbook even as it emulated Toklas's famous text. Whereas Fannie Farmer's domestic sci-ence classic, *The Boston Cooking-School Cook Book* (1896), had been orga-nized under rubrics such as "Cereals," "Eggs," "Soups," "Soups with Meat Stock," "Soups with Fish Stock," and "Soups without Stock," Toklas offered up "Murder in the Kitchen," "Food to Which Aunt Pauline and Lady Godiva Led Us," and "Food in the Bugey during the Occupation." The stakes were thus high for Grosvenor, but she clearly held her own: *Vibration Cooking* con-tained a memorable series of set pieces, including "The Demystification of Food," "Birth, Hunting and Gator Tails," "The Smarts, the Ritters and Chief Kuku Koukoui," "First Cousins and the Numbers," "Forty Acres and a Jeep," "Taxis and Poor Man's Mace," and "White Folks and Fried Chicken."

Albeit somewhat derivative of Toklas's, Grosvenor's approach to writing a cookbook was, in other words, still idiosyncratic. As a result, *Vibration Cooking* developed a strong word-of-mouth following, and its author's career quickly began to flourish. Her brief essay "The Kitchen Crisis" was included in *Amistad 1* (1970), a collection of "Writings on Black History and Culture" by a group of prominent (and otherwise all-male) black intellectuals and artists; a lengthy article about her was featured in *Ebony* magazine (Garland); she appeared on television with, among others, the Galloping Gourmet, Barbara Walters, and Dick Cavett (*Vibration* 1992 ed., xv); and she published a second book, this one a stinging indictment of the exploitation of African American women as domestic servants, called *Thursdays and Every Other Sunday Off* (1972). The late 1970s and early 1980s witnessed an explosion of attention to African American women writers such as Toni Morrison, Ntozake Shange, and Alice Walker. Perhaps not coincidentally, Ballantine issued a revised and expanded edition of *Vibration Cooking* in 1986, and Marian Burros profiled Grosvenor in the *New York Times* in 1988. By then she had established a career as a commentator with NPR and was involved in the filming of *Daughters of the Dust*. The year after Dash's film was released, Ballantine brought out the third edition of the now-legendary cookbook, this time under its "Many Cultures, One World" imprint. "There is," as Grosvenor acknowledged in the introductions to both the 1986 and the 1992 editions, "nothing like having a book published to change your life" (xiii; xiv). In her case, at least, she was right.

Of course, there is also nothing like having a book republished to tempt one to change the story of one's life. In the 1986 edition, for instance, Grosvenor disavowed the influence of Toklas on her initial conceptualization of *Vibration Cooking*, asserting in the new introduction: "The only thing I have in common with Alice B. Toklas is that we lived on the same street in Paris" (xv). She repeated this disclaimer in the 1992 edition (xvi). As the epigraph to this chapter illustrates, moreover, by 1986 Grosvenor was also maintaining that at the time she first published *Vibration Cooking* she did not "consider" herself to have been "a 'soul food' writer." Although her attitude toward soul food was clearly far more complicated than was that of many of her peers, Grosvenor's writings from the early 1970s reveal her to have been rather less equivocal in her estimation of the term than she has later wanted to allow. Indeed, the last sentence of "The Kitchen Crisis" was the thoroughly unambiguous pronouncement "Long Live Soul Food" (300).

Grosvenor's conflicted willingness to capitalize on the widespread interracial fascination with black dietary practices during the Black Power era, even while censuring its racist underpinnings, is exemplified by an article called "Soul Food" that she published in *McCall's* magazine in September 1970.[5] Clearly intended for a white female audience, the article begins with the observation that "[e]verybody talking about what soul food is; fore we even get into that lets talk about what it aint" (72):

> Soul food aint frozen collard greens.
> Soul food aint fresh turnip greens and smoked pigs tails cooked together for three hours. Thats tasteless.
> Soul food aint when you are white and you invite the token negro from your job to guest for dinner on thursday (black maid's night out) and when he arrives you serve portuguese sardines on crackers, south african rock lobster tails, greek wine, and california grapes. Thats bad taste. (72)

After dismissing most of what constituted the "radical chic" perception of soul food and ridiculing the discrepancy between the public posturing and the private lives of many white liberals, Grosvenor proceeds to enumerate examples of what soul food is: "Soul food is onions chopped up on collard greens" (72); "Soul food is plantain served with bacalao and ackee" (72); "Soul food is vanilla wafers" (72); "Soul food is farina de manioc" (73). Much of the interracial male fascination with soul food during the 1960s had fixated on chitterlings as the "stone" soul food ("Eating"). Because of their association with excrement, chitterlings could be used by whites to foreground the traditional racist association of blackness with filth, while simultaneously allowing many proponents of Black Power to parody white America's obsession with (racial) purity. But in contrast to this common, if divergently motivated, privileging of chitterlings as the sine qua non of soul food in popular discourses of the era, Grosvenor's expansive listing of foods to be associated with soul clearly operates as a strategy for disrupting racist stereotypes about black culture. Carefully distancing her understanding of soul food from commodified interest in the "slave" diet, she relocates African American dietary practices in the context of the culinary history of peoples of color around the world.

This information about Grosvenor's early investments in soul food should remind us, moreover, to be skeptical of her claim in the 1986 edition of *Vibration Cooking* that she devoted much time to explaining her "philosophy on the nonracial aspects" of soul food when the book first appeared. In the 1970 essay "The Kitchen Crisis," Grosvenor had, in fact, offered precisely the opposite culinary philosophy, proclaiming with characteristic dramatic flair that "the truth will out. Yes! Food is colored. Peaches are Chinese. Watermelons are African. Mangos is Indian. Avocado is Mexican. Carrots are Arab. If you check it out, ain't too many things, food or people, REAL WHITE-AMERICANS" (299). She invokes "natural" foods to signify the "unreality" of whiteness as a racial designation that is equated with a lack of color. By "outing" peaches, watermelons, mangos, avocados, and carrots, Grosvenor foregrounds the quixotic impossibility of white America's pursuit of racial purity via the consumption of chemically "processed" foods.[6]

Outing, of course, is structurally connected to the practice of "passing" in that both rely on the ontologization of (what I take to be) socially constructed identities. As Amy Robinson has explained, passing generally operates in a triangulated social field: "Three participants — the passer, the dupe, and a representative of the in-group — enact a complex narrative scenario in which a successful pass is performed in the presence of a literate member of the in-group" (723). Alternatively, outing becomes meaningful when the member of the in-group successfully enlightens the dupe. Not unlike the joke, as Freud has defined it, both passing and outing require the presence of a third party to reach completion (*Jokes* 171–93). In thinking about Grosvenor's motivations in claiming to tell the "truth" about culinary history even while repeatedly contradicting herself, it seems worth paying attention not only to the question of whom she views as members of the in-group and whom as dupes, but also to the possibility that she herself is the one engaged in a complex performance of passing.

The (Dis)Guises of a Geechee Girl

Grosvenor's early references in *Vibration Cooking* to her desire to become an actress set the stage, as it were, for one of the book's recurrent themes: her penchant for theatricality and self-dramatization. As Quandra Prettyman has succinctly put it: "One doesn't know whether to speak of Grosvenor or Verta Mae, the writer or the crafted persona. Sometimes she poses, sometimes she poses at posing" (132). Grosvenor's recollection of being "actor, director and audience all in one" in her childhood play productions presents this aspect of her personality as an individual idiosyncrasy. However, many of the stories Grosvenor recounts instead seem intended to situate her performances as a strategy for disrupting the typecasting of black women as mammies.

For instance, in *Thursdays and Every Other Sunday Off*, Grosvenor describes an occasion in 1965 when she had gone to a "citadel of white supremacy" to pick up Kali, "who was visiting a little girl in her class" (12). Despite being dressed in the "first Vogue Couturier pattern" that she had ever sewn, Grosvenor was directed to the servants' entrance and subjected by a "middle-aged white woman" to the inevitable question: "Going in late today, aren't you?" (12). Taken aback by her realization that bourgeois clothing was insufficient to counter the woman's ingrained prejudices, Grosvenor offered the following response: "I am not a maid. . . . All of us aren't maids, you know" (12). Through anecdotes such as this, Grosvenor mobilizes her fascination with clothing and performance as a strategy for critiquing the demeaning stereotypes imposed on African Americans by racist whites. She insinuates that, regardless of their class status, all black women are subject to being perceived as servants and therefore associated with the "dirt" which must be abjected from proper (white) bourgeois society.[7]

For Grosvenor, dirt structures the relationship between white and black women. The former generate it; the latter clean it up. At one point in *Thursdays and Every Other Sunday Off*, she fantasizes about inverting this scenario, announcing to the reader that "when I move in my new apartment, I'm gonna get me a white cleaning lady. That may seem strange to some of yall, but after all the years my mama spent on her knees, it would make me sick to have anyone in her image cleaning my house" (11).[8] But even as she envisions employing a white woman who would bear the cultural burden of being associated with dirt, Grosvenor also suggests that overly "clean" women are not to be trusted. In *Vibration Cooking*, for example, she recalls being invited for dinner by a white actress, "now a leading young ingénue in the theater" (99). Immediately upon arriving, Grosvenor realized that "something was wrong. No smells of food cooking or having been cooked. The kitchen was spotless. My daddy always told me that you had to watch those people who never dirtied the kitchen. He said if they don't make a mess in the kitchen they ain't cooking nothing fit to eat" (*Vibration* 100). The un-dirtied kitchen clearly signifies the white woman's artificiality, her lack of "soul." But, of course, having a dirtied kitchen puts black women at risk of being labeled "nasty" (*Vibration* 163).

Men, however, turn out to be central to this catch-22 ideology of dirt. Though Frank Smart had warned Grosvenor as a child to be wary of overcleanliness in the kitchen, her own scrupulous adult sanitation practices resulted in an offer of marriage. The prospective mate "said that he had a thing for girls who get on their hands and knees to scrub floors (I never use a mop) and who can cook. The dude asked me to marry him but I didn't" (*Vibration*

19). To be her father's honorary son, she must embrace the "filth" of soul. To be her suitor's wife, she must bear the ongoing burden of keeping the race clean. Rather than face this contradiction, Grosvenor indicts the more immediate symbol of oppression, the person who most obviously benefits from the oppression of women of color. "Is there enough money to send for a girl from the South or the Islands, or, as of late, South America, to keep house for you, mind your overindulged brat, while you go to Women's Lib meetings?" she asks rhetorically of white women in *Thursdays and Every Other Sunday Off* (9).

Needless to say, Grosvenor was only one among many African American women who were critical of second-wave feminism as it emerged during the Black Power era. Toni Morrison had perhaps most famously articulated this position in a 1971 *New York Times Magazine* essay called "What the Black Woman Thinks About Women's Lib." After pointing out black women's skepticism about the class biases of the early movement, she condemns white feminists for talking about liberation while delegating "the management of the house and the rearing of children to others. . . . The one great disservice black women are guilty of (albeit not by choice) is that they are the means by which white women can escape the responsibilities of womanhood and remain children all the way to the grave" (64). At least in this early essay, Morrison fails to question her presuppositions about why the "responsibilities" of housework and child rearing should fall on the shoulders of women and not men. When she refers to how black women servants have moved white women's "dirt from one place to another" (64), it seems clear that she, like Grosvenor, is holding white women responsible for the "dirt" generated by white men and white children as well.

If Morrison did equate "housework" with "drudgery," even when done in one's own home (63), Grosvenor, by contrast, initially seems much less ambivalent in her adherence to traditional gender role ideologies within African American communities. Cooking and cleaning were only problematic for her if done for a white family. Moreover, like one of her contemporaries, soul food cookbook writer Princess Pamela, Grosvenor locates food preparation within a heterosexual matrix of desire. Whereas Princess Pamela had insisted, "Every woman should learn / to cook for her man / 'cuz love and indigestion / don't mix" (190), Grosvenor observes, "Cooking for a man is a very feminine thing, and I can't understand how a woman can feed her man TV dinners" (*Vibration* xiv–xv). Similarly, in the *McCall's* article, Grosvenor idealizes women's labor in the kitchen as a tactic for creating male sexual as well as gastronomic desire:

Soul food is when a fine brother hurts his back playing basketball and a fly sister comes to bring him a jar of homemade oxtail soup and another brother is there and he eats two bowls and the next day he calls the first brother asking for the sisters phone number and the first brother is mad cause he only offered the brother to be polite and give the illusion of solidarity anyhow. He say "hell no" cause he impressed that she cooked the oxtails for two hours, let them cool, stripped the meat off the bones, took off the excess grease, added barley, noodles, potatoes, whole tomatoes and frozen mixed vegetables and he decide to hit on her himself. (75)

In this scenario, women who rely on modern food technologies are seen as failing to fulfill their normative role in establishing heterosexuality. Male desire is stimulated by labor-intensive soul food cooking, not by opening a can. Readers of the 1992 edition of *Vibration Cooking* will not, however, be privy to Grosvenor's most explicit alliance with the heterosexism of early 1970s black nationalism—a homophobic deployment of the term *faggot* (150)—since this was another aspect of the text that was subsequently altered.

Grosvenor's embrace of her African heritage, her hostility to second-wave white feminism, her refusal to question assumptions about women's responsibility for domestic labor, and her homophobia all clearly mark her affiliation with the prevailing black nationalist ideology of the early 1970s. In fact, *Vibration Cooking* is riddled with allusions to her close ties with prominent proponents of the Black Aesthetic. The book's epigraph, for example, is a poem by Amiri Baraka, whom Grosvenor would eventually count among her good friends. But, notwithstanding her intimacy with the Black Arts scene in New York and abroad, if we read *Vibration Cooking* as a precursor to fiction published by black women during the 1970s—such as Toni Morrison's 1973 novel *Sula*—Grosvenor's position with respect to the prevailing black nationalist aesthetic emerges as more complicated than is otherwise readily apparent.

In her work on black women novelists and the Black Aesthetic, Madhu Dubey explores strategies through which novelists such as Toni Morrison, Gayl Jones, and Alice Walker resisted the compulsion to present a unified vision of blackness that elided differences of sexuality, gender, and class. She suggests that "black feminist theorizations of identity" need to combine "a continuing appreciation of the cultural history that has produced the black writer's strong investment in the model of a whole, cohesive self" with "a vigilant attention to the differences within the black experience that confound any totalized, unitary definition of black identity" (4). If we extrapolate from Dubey's analysis, Grosvenor's penchant for inconsistency and disguise might be read as part of a strategy she deployed with considerable skill to negotiate a place for herself, for *Vibration Cooking*, and even for her female forebears within the black-male-dominated terrain of the Black Arts movement. Thus, when Morrison had written that Sula's "was an experimental life" (*Sula* 118), she could easily have been describing the author of *Vibration Cooking*.

Grosvenor's critique of Black Aesthetic ideology is not difficult to discern. For example, though black nationalists generally viewed black mothers as mired in the past and therefore a barrier to black men's revolutionary pursuits, Grosvenor announces early in *Vibration Cooking* that her paternal grandmother, Estella Smart, "is avant-garde. . . . Last year she was engaged and I had already bought the fabric to make her wedding dress to this dude but she broke it off. I don't think she is ready to give up her freedom" (11). Even more tellingly, Grosvenor begins *Vibration Cooking* with a section called "Birth, Hunting and Gator Tails," which describes the scene of her birth. Weighing in at three pounds, she was half the size of her twin brother, and she was not expected to live. Her parents deposited the tiny newborn in a makeshift incubator, a shoe box, on the wood-stove oven door. According to Grosvenor's mother, "it was a case of touch and go for a while, cause she got the childbirth fever" and nearly threw her daughter into the fireplace. But whereas Grosvenor lived to grow into a healthy, self-sufficient woman, her six-pound brother died at birth, having reputedly "stayed in the womb too long" (*Vibration* 3).[9] Through this anecdote, Grosvenor vividly rewrites prevailing Black Arts and Black Power ideologies according to which the domineering black mother imprisons the male child in her womb. The death of her twin brother results from his own fetal inertia.

Grosvenor's efforts to reconfigure the masculinist biases of the nationalist aesthetic also emerge through her formal experimentation with the (already feminized) genre of the cookbook. Perhaps most notably, while much of *Vibration Cooking* seems to be addressing black men as well as black women, by the end of the book Grosvenor takes as her actual reader a specific African American woman, her friend Stella. As would *Sula*, *Vibration Cooking* concludes by affirming the value of solidarity between African American women. The ending of the 1970 edition of *Vibration Cooking* finds Stella narrating her adventures via letters as she travels through South America and Africa while Grosvenor remains at home in New York. It is Stella, not Grosvenor, who broadens the book's horizons beyond the United States and Europe. It is Stella who sends Grosvenor the climactic message: "Child, after 350 years, I am home. Africa, the motherland. . . . It is not true that the Africans don't like or want us. Biggest lie the white man ever told. He told the Africans that we didn't like them either. Divide and conquer is his game but it is over" (175).

Yet despite her affinities with Afrocentrism, Grosvenor herself had already attached the label "Home" to the first section of *Vibration Cooking*. It describes her relatives in South Carolina, her childhood in Philadelphia, and her successful but finally fraudulent "pass" as Princess Verta. Africa is clearly a part but not the whole of her identity and hence the likely purpose of her attribution of Afrocentric selfhood to Stella: the Geechee Girl cannot be so narrowly defined.[10]

Travel Notes

Of all the inconsistencies and ambiguities in Grosvenor's persona, of all the ways in which she worked to construct a place for African American women within the political and cultural scene of early 1970s black nationalism and white feminism, perhaps the most intriguing is her deployment of the self-description "Geechee Girl." Often used interchangeably with "Gullah," the term *Geechee* refers to the inhabitants of the Sea Islands, as well as to the creole language they speak (Major 194, 216). It is also a term of derision applied to dark-skinned blacks (Major 194). But in *Vertamae Cooks in the Americas' Family Kitchen* — a cookbook Grosvenor published in 1996 as an accompaniment to her PBS television program — she explains her continuing terminological preference by identifying Geechee as an "in-group" designation: "They call us Gullah, but 'we call weself Geechee' " (14).

Whichever label one applies, the Sea Islands have long been of interest to students of black American culture. Not surprisingly, of course, the early studies tended to offer a derogatory representation of the Gullah peoples. In his 1930 book *A Social History of the Sea Islands*, Guion Griffis Johnson explained that the Sea Island Negroes "spoke a garbled English, imperfect words and expressions which they and their parents and grandparents had learned from the few whites with whom they came in contact" (127). But even as Johnson was rendering such judgments, other scholars were beginning to question the assumption that enslaved Africans had carried with them to the New World no viable cultural traditions. In particular, Melville Herskovits's study *The Myth of the Negro Past* (1941) contributed to the explosion of scholarly work on African retentions in the Americas. Decades of often acrimonious debate over his thesis ensued, but by 1980 the *Journal of Black Studies* devoted an entire issue to the topic of "Sea Island Culture." Guest editors Mary Twining and Keith Baird carefully pronounced in their preface: "As far as the Sea Islands are concerned it may perhaps be safely asserted that the issue now is not so much the debate over the existence of Africanisms but the continuation of research to determine just where and how much material exists" (385).

In figuring herself as a Geechee, therefore, Grosvenor was participating in a much broader movement to reinterpret and revalue the African heritage of black Americans. If the Sea Island peoples had previously been seen as pariahs, Grosvenor paraded her Geechee relatives as a badge of honor. Of course, the two difficulties in this scheme, as I have already mentioned, are her move to Philadelphia "when she was 9 or 10" (Burros C6) and, more intriguingly, her failure to have been born on the Sea Islands in the first place. In *Vibration Cooking*, Grosvenor does refer to a first cousin named Queen Esther who is "from out by Beaufort way" (42), but most of the relatives she describes are from the inland counties of Allendale and Hampton—just like herself. In discussing her family background, Grosvenor does not take time to distinguish island from inland Geechee culture, nor does she refer to herself as hailing from the coast. Once the book was reissued in 1986, though, the public construction of her origins began to undergo some shifts.

To wit: the *New York Times* profile of Grosvenor by Marian Burros was accompanied by a photograph of a coastal scene—marshland lined with palm trees—which itself contained inset photographs of Grosvenor and a plate of food. The photographs' caption announces that "Vertamae Smart-Grosvenor, who is from the coastal region of South Carolina, makes her Frogmore stew with shrimp, sausage and corn" (C1). In the article's opening paragraph, Burros pursues this less-than-precise representation. Referring to Charleston as "not far from where [Grosvenor] was born," she fails to mention that this unnamed "where" lies over sixty miles west of Charleston, on the far side of what is now Interstate 95. Two other photographs accompanying the article are of St. Helena Island, at whose famous Penn School Grosvenor was a writer-in-residence during the 1970s (C6). Burros invokes this information, along with Grosvenor's work-in-progress as a technical director for and actress in *Daughters of the Dust*, as a way of further associating her subject's background with Sea Island culture. Thus, she quotes Grosvenor using the first-person plural to explain the importance of Dash's film: "We have to preserve what remains of our African socioreligious beliefs and culture" (C1). Given that Burros also writes about how Grosvenor was forced to learn English from a "radio soap opera" after moving to Philadelphia (C6), readers lacking familiarity with *Vibration Cooking* (and South Carolina) would have every reason to infer from the article that Grosvenor was truly a child of the Sea Islands.

Ballantine soon joined in by illustrating the cover of the third edition of *Vibration Cooking* with a map of southeastern South Carolina (fig. 10.1). The map is positioned to include the coastal area stretching from Charleston to Beaufort. Grosvenor's birthplace is just barely visible on the far left edge of the book. Even so, the reader must be satisfied with locating "airfax" since, at least on my copy, the "F" did not quite survive the crop. The towns of Luray and Estill, home to Grosvenor's relatives the "Ritters and the Myerses and the Smarts" (*Vibration* 3), lie farther south but also farther west, and thus do not make an appearance on the cover at all. By the time *Vertamae Cooks in the Americas' Family Kitchen* appeared four years later, Grosvenor was reminiscing in detail about how, when she was a schoolchild in Philadelphia, she had informed a teacher: "E teif me pinders n e hand een ain onrabel e mout!" (14). Failing to understand that "a boy stole [her] peanuts and ran off without saying a word," the teacher demanded that Grosvenor "speak English!" (14). Oddly, though, memories of language barriers had not found their way into Grosvenor's recollections of her childhood in *Vibration Cooking*. There she uses southern black vernacular to represent the speech patterns of herself and her family.

My aim in raising these concerns is not to imply that Grosvenor has lied in "passing" herself off as a Geechee. As Sea Island historian Charles Joyner has explained, "On the coastal mainland adjacent to the Sea Islands are black people who share [the] folk culture and [the] creole language" of the Gullahs (x). Acknowledging that these mainland dwellers "are not — strictly speaking — Sea Islanders," Joyner further observes that the story of the Sea Islands is "in many ways . . . their story too" (x). Migration patterns from the islands to the mainland would readily account for Grosvenor's Gullah heritage. Rather, I aim to use this discussion of Grosvenor's ambiguous positioning in relation to the more typical island-oriented perception of Gullah peoples as a way of critiquing some problematic aspects of scholarly and now popular fascination with the Sea Islands. Whether or not Grosvenor recognized in 1970 that the emergent interest in Gullah culture would privilege as most "authentic" those people born and raised offshore, by the time Burros conducted her interview with Grosvenor, the standards for what it meant to be a Geechee Girl had clearly been raised.

The paradox in which Grosvenor has become implicated, it seems to me, is that Gullah culture is valorized for inscribing both motion and stasis. Scholars have looked to the Sea Islands as a site where remnants of the "originary" displacement of Africans to the Americas can be identified. In this sense, the Sea Island peoples are understood to code movement, but only

Fig. 10.1. Cover of the third edition of *Vibration Cooking* (1992). Reproduced by permission of Random House. Photograph courtesy of the University of Iowa Audiovisual Center Photo Service.

a movement that is always already completed, always already in the past. As an almost inevitable result, much of our cultural romance with Gullah peoples has been structured by a desire for the Sea Islands to remain henceforth a site of cultural inertia. Having learned to recognize and value their encoding of the African diaspora, we necessarily bemoan continued creolization as a loss of authenticity. And this is the issue, it seems to me, which is at the heart of the obfuscations over Grosvenor's place of origin. Grosvenor offered herself up as a traveling Geechee Girl to a world that has become increasingly fascinated with Gullah isolation.

Yet this is also the reason why I finally find Grosvenor's deployment of the trope of the "travel" book so compelling in its insistence on her right to ongoing cultural and personal hybridization. Despite having been born miles from the coast, despite having grown up in Philadelphia, despite having studied in France, despite having married a white sculptor and moved to Greenwich Village, despite having visited numerous countries and continents, Grosvenor has still claimed her identity as a Geechee. Far from weakening her sense of her heritage, her travels have expanded and fortified it. "I was a grown girl and across the ocean before I, as folklorist Zora Neale Hurston has described it, looked at home through the spyglass of anthropology and began my exploration into Afro-Atlantic foodways," she recalls in *Vertamae Cooks in the Americas' Family Kitchen* (17).[11]

As I explained at the outset of this chapter, because of her emphasis on the importance of travel and her often contradictory political orientation toward black internationalism as well as black nationalism, Grosvenor's writings on food resonate in a variety of ways with Paul Gilroy's influential theorization of the black diaspora. "The worth of the diaspora concept," he writes, "is in its attempt to specify differentiation and identity in a way which enables one to think about the issue of racial commonality outside of constricting binary frameworks — especially those that counterpose essentialism and pluralism" (*Black* 120). But whereas Gilroy tends to privilege music as the central cultural form through which the countermodernity of the black Atlantic has been articulated, I would suggest that Grosvenor's writings on black culinary history serve as a useful supplement to Gilroy's oppositional model. Most obviously, work on food provides scholars of the black Atlantic with a paradigm in which black women and questions of gender are not — or at least should not be — automatically marginalized. No less important, work on food encourages us to recognize barriers to, and even assumptions about the gender of, movement that discussions of black music can sometimes seem to skirt. We should not allow music's seeming evanescence to prevent us from recognizing the ways in which black women have been associated with the stationary "soul" harbor that enables black male diasporic movement.

This concern is actually quite easy to explain. In his work on black musical traditions, Andrew Ross observes that "soul was something that *happened to the body as it was moving*, and therefore it was nowhere more apparent than in the response to musical rhythms, whether carried in the head, or heard through the air" (100). But soul food's implicit inscription of black women as (slave) mothers would lead me to respond that, at least during the Black Power era, soul was perhaps more accurately understood as something that happened to black male bodies as they moved both toward and away from presumptively inert black female ones (Witt 90–101). Had this not been the case, Grosvenor might not have chosen to deploy a jazz rather than a soul aesthetic in conceptualizing her work on black culinary history. Herself a veteran of Sun Ra's Solar Myth Science Arkestra, Grosvenor alludes frequently in *Vibration Cooking* to jazz musicians such as Archie Shepp and jazz-influenced writers such as Amiri Baraka. In keeping with this thematization of jazz, the original book ended with a section called "To Be Continued." The 1986 and 1992 editions fulfilled this promise by altering the section's name to read "Continued" and adding several new vignettes. Her anticipation in the first edition of the book of a subsequent variation hearkens less to the repetitive rhythms of soul than to the citational "spontaneity" of jazz. To the extent that she affiliated herself primarily with the latter, more black male-dominated, musical mode, Grosvenor disassociated her cookbook from the taint of slave maternity with which the majority of Black Arts practitioners were obsessed.

One of her anecdotes in *Vibration Cooking* seems intended to foreground precisely the difficulties she was facing in negotiating this tension between jazz and soul. In a section called "Collards and Other Greens," Grosvenor reports: "Collard greens almost caused me and Archie Shepp to break friendship. His play was being presented at the Chelsea Theatre and for the opening night party they were going to have a 'soul food party.' They asked me to cook the greens. Peggy and I cut up fifteen pounds of greens. We got calluses on our fingers. I called a friend of mine (an actor in the play) to ask him to drive me to the theater, and he said, 'Didn't they tell you the show is not opening tonight? It's opening Thursday'" (131–32). Although she ends up including a recipe for "Collard Greens a la Shepp" (132), Grosvenor makes clear her irritation at having her time-sensitive culinary labors taken for granted by someone whose profession celebrated idiosyncratic usage of time.

What disturbs me, obviously, are the moments when discourses of black music revert to "constricting binary frameworks" in which black women's traditional association with the kitchen undermines the very possibility of figuring them in terms of movement. And this is a problem that seems to inhere in discourses of diasporic black identity as well. Gilroy again offers a perceptive reading of the sources of this tension. "The need to locate cultural or ethnic roots and then to use the idea of being in touch with them as a means to refigure the cartography of dispersal and exile is perhaps best understood," he argues, "as a simple and direct response to the varieties of racism which have denied the historical character of black experience and the integrity of black cultures" (*Black* 112). The question this raises, though, is whether black men and black women are positioned in comparable ways with respect to this compulsion to be "in touch with" black roots.

Consider, in this context, Puerto Rican bibliophile Arthur Schomburg's proposal for a book on transatlantic black culinary traditions, probably written in the 1920s. In one of the few spots in the proposal where Schomburg specifically addresses the role of African American women in the development of these traditions, he writes that he plans to "maintain along with the traditional mammy cooks of the South that the exact formula for any but the most ordinary dishes, cannot be written down — that a pinch of this and a handful of that may be more ex[p]ressive than level tablespoonfuls in giving the feel of a dish. That no matter how ingredients are measured they must be combined with a sort of magic in order [to] achieve the perfect blend" (6). Because Schomburg otherwise fails to discuss the role of black women in his conception of Afro-Atlantic culinary history, one finishes reading this dynamic prospectus with the distinct impression that, for him, diasporic black culinary exchange is fundamentally anchored by ahistorical and immobile black mammies in the South.

Given such assumptions, the apt ambiguity of Victor Cruz's 1969 tribute to Grosvenor's culinary abilities — "en la casa de verta" — is difficult to miss:

> for on monday in 1969 on the streets
> was diamonds. downtown society bodegas one
> right after the other. avocado & tomato juice
> spaceships parked in front of vertas house / sparkling
> yellow metal with stickers from Venus Airlines
> Moon Shuttle Jupiter Car Service Mars heliport
> & all on monday by a bridge. 1969 year of the rooster
> hot sauce / street beans. . . .
>
> > caribbean rice on the fire

with african beans warming
wow
the centuries & centuries
of sea exploration & mixing.
but here we all are
in vertas soul space kitchen
taking off. (*Vibration*, third edition, 221)

Construing Grosvenor's kitchen as both a restful haven from "centuries & centuries / of sea exploration" and also a spaceship about to embark on a voyage of its own, Cruz's poem—which serves as the conclusion to all three editions of *Vibration Cooking*—recapitulates the complex undertaking through which Grosvenor balanced her traveling Geechee Girl persona with an homage to her forebears, who, lacking the wherewithal to "move," have divided their time between "miss ann's kitchen" and their own. For this reason, if *Vibration Cooking* ends with Cruz's romantic invocation of an intergalactic black diaspora, elsewhere in her work Grosvenor still foregrounds the local interactions that have historically structured the day-to-day lives of many working-class African American women.[12] Grosvenor's importance for the history of women and food surely lies in her effort to negotiate the imperatives of race, gender, and class difference in a way that speaks to black women's historical experience of subordination in U.S. society while also locating their lives and cultural innovations in a broader, potentially more liberatory, global framework.

Notes

This essay is a condensed version of chapter 6 from my book, *Black Hunger: Food and the Politics of U.S. Identity* (New York: Oxford University Press, 1999).
1. See the appendix of *Black Hunger* for a (doubtless partial) listing of cookbooks published during this era.
2. For wonderful discussions of Grosvenor's manipulation of "masking" as a strategy for subverting stereotypes about African American women, see Prettyman 131–33 and Zafar 75–78.
3. Julia Kristeva's well-known theorization of the terms *abject* and *abjection* in *Powers of Horror* has influenced my usage here. Abjection, for Kristeva, refers to the (always inherently unsuccessful) process by which we attempt to differentiate self from other. Food, eating, and birth are central to Kristeva's conceptualization of this process. For more information, see Kelly Oliver's helpful essay on Kristeva, "Nourishing the Speaking Subject."

4. Unless otherwise specified, all page references are to the 1970 edition of *Vibration Cooking*.

5. An uncredited 1969 *Time* magazine article called "Eating like Soul Brothers" memorably depicted white fascination with black culinary practices during the Black Power era. The following year, Tom Wolfe famously satirized white patronage of soul food in *Radical Chic and Mau-Mauing the Flak Catchers* (31).

6. In making this claim, I am implicitly relying on work on "whiteness" that attempts to theorize the underpinnings of binaries equating whiteness with artificiality, standardization, and civilization and blackness with naturalness, improvisation, and primitivism. See, for example, Dyer 67–139.

7. Here I am drawing on Mary Douglas's important theorization of pollution rituals, as well as Peter Stallybrass and Allon White's influential discussion of the position of servants in the bourgeois social order (149–70).

8. For excellent sociological work on the relation of black servants and white female employers, see Rollins.

9. Morrison's better known presentation of the reasoning behind Eva's decision to kill her son Plum in *Sula* follows a similar logic. She simply "had to keep him out" of her womb, Eva explains (72).

10. See Collins 155–83 for a fuller explication of why Afrocentrism can be problematic for those interested in gender analysis.

11. In this context, it is worth noting, moreover, that "travel" is actually a central concept of Sea Island religious experience, signifying the voyage undertaken by a seeker prior to conversion to the religious community (Creel 80).

12. Sun Ra's obsession with outer space — as amply illustrated by John Szwed in his biography of the controversial jazz musician — doubtless influenced both Grosvenor and Cruz in adopting this metaphor.

Works Cited

Burros, Marian. "Gullah Cooking: Improvising on Cultures Past." *New York Times* 4 May 1988, late ed.: C1+.

Collins, Patricia Hill. *Fighting Words: Black Women and the Search for Justice.* Minneapolis: University of Minnesota Press, 1998.

Creel, Margaret Washington. "Gullah Attitudes Toward Life and Death." *Africanisms in American Culture.* Ed. Joseph E. Holloway. Bloomington: Indiana University Press, 1990. 69–97.

Daughters of the Dust. Dir., writ., and prod. Julie Dash. Perf. Cora Lee Day, Alva Rodgers, Adisa Anderson, Kaycee Moore, Barbara O, Eartha D. Robinson, Bahni Turpin, Cheryl Lynn Bruce, and Vertamae Smart-Grosvenor. 1991. Videocassette. New York: Kino on Video, 1992.

Douglas, Mary. *Purity and Danger: An Analysis of the Concepts of Pollution and Taboo.* 1966. London: Ark-Routledge, 1984.

Dubey, Madhu. *Black Women Novelists and the Nationalist Aesthetic.* Bloomington: Indiana University Press, 1994.

Dyer, Richard. *Heavenly Bodies: Film Stars and Society*. New York: St. Martin's, 1986.

"Eating like Soul Brothers." *Time* 24 Jan. 1969: 57.

Farmer, Fannie Merritt. *The Original Boston Cooking-School Cook Book*. New York: Weathervane, n.d. Rpt. of *The Boston Cooking-School Cook Book*. Boston: Little, 1896.

Freud, Sigmund. *Jokes and Their Relation to the Unconscious*. 1905. Ed. and trans. James Strachey. 1960. New York: Norton, 1989.

Garland, Phyl. "Vibes from Verta Mae: 'Double-O Soul' Chef Authors Fascinating Guide to 'Vibration' Cooking." *Ebony* Mar. 1971: 86–94.

Gilroy, Paul. *The Black Atlantic: Modernity and Double Consciousness*. Cambridge: Harvard University Press, 1993.

Grosvenor, Kali. *Poems by Kali*. Garden City, N.Y.: Doubleday, 1970.

Grosvenor, Vertamae Smart [Verta Mae; Vertamae Smart-Grosvenor]. "The Kitchen Crisis: A Rap." *Amistad I: Writings on Black History and Culture*. Ed. John A. Williams and Charles F. Harris. New York: Vintage-Random, 1970. 293–300.

——. "Soul Food." *McCall's* Sept. 1970:72–75.

——. *Thursdays and Every Other Sunday Off: A Domestic Rap by Verta Mae*. Garden City, N.Y.: Doubleday, 1972.

——. *Vertamae Cooks in the Americas' Family Kitchen*. San Francisco: KQED Books, 1996.

——. *Vibration Cooking, or the Travel Notes of a Geechee Girl*. Garden City, N.Y.: Doubleday, 1970. 2nd ed. New York: Ballantine, 1986. 3rd ed. New York: One World-Ballantine, 1992.

Jackson, George. *Soledad Brother: The Prison Letters of George Jackson*. New York: Bantam, 1970.

Johnson, Guion Griffis. *A Social History of the Sea Islands*. Chapel Hill: University of North Carolina Press, 1930.

Joyner, Charles. Foreword. *When Roots Die*. By Patricia Jones-Jackson. Athens: University of Georgia Press, 1987.

Kristeva, Julia. *Powers of Horror: An Essay on Abjection*. 1980. Trans. Leon S. Roudiez. New York: Columbia University Press, 1982.

Morrison, Toni. *Sula*. 1973. New York: Plume-Penguin, 1982.

——. "What the Black Woman Thinks About Women's Lib." *New York Times Magazine* 22 Aug. 1971: 14–15+.

Neal, Larry. "Some Reflections on the Black Aesthetic." 1970. *The Black Aesthetic*. Ed. Addison Gayle Jr. New York: Doubleday, 1971. 12–15.

Oliver, Kelly. "Nourishing the Speaking Subject: A Psychoanalytic Approach to Abominable Food and Women." *Cooking, Eating, Thinking: Transformative Philosophies of Food*. Ed. Deane W. Curtin and Lisa M. Heldke. Bloomington: Indiana University Press, 1992. 68–84.

Prettyman, Quandra. "Come Eat at My Table: Lives with Recipes." *Southern Quarterly* 30 (Winter-Spring 1992): 131–40.

Princess Pamela. *Soul Food Cookbook*. New York: Signet-NAL, 1969.

Robinson, Army. "It Takes One to Know One: Passing and Communities of Common Interest." *Critical Inquiry* 20.4 (1994): 715–36.

Rollins, Judith. *Between Women: Domestics and Their Employers*. Philadelphia: Temple University Press, 1985.

Ross, Andrew. *No Respect: Intellectuals and Popular Culture*. New York: Routledge, 1989.

Schomburg, Arthur A. Untitled typescript. [Proposal for a history of African American cooking.] Arthur A. Schomburg Papers, Activities, and Writings. Folder 7, Box 12. SC Micro 2798, Reel 7. New York Public Library's Schomburg Center for Research in Black Culture, [c. 1920s?].

Stallybrass, Peter, and Allon White. *The Politics and Poetics of Transgression*. Ithaca: Cornell University Press, 1986.

Szwed, John. *Space Is the Place: The Lives and Times of Sun Ra*. New York: Da Capo, 1998.

Toklas, Alice B. *The Alice B. Toklas Cook Book*. New York: Harper, 1954.

Twining, Mary A., and Keith E. Baird, eds. "Sea Island Culture." Special issue. *Journal of Black Studies* 10.4 (June 1980): 379–492.

Witt, Doris. *Black Hunger: Food and the Politics of U.S. Identity*. New York: Oxford University Press, 1999.

Wolfe, Tom. *Radical Chic and Mau-Mauing the Flak Catchers*. New York: Farrar, 1970.

Zafar, Rafia. "Cooking Up a Past: Two Black Culinary Narratives." *GRAAT* 14 (1996): 73–84.

"If I Were a Voodoo Priestess"
Women's Culinary Autobiographies

TRACI MARIE KELLY

For years I have perused old recipes, collected recipes, hoarded cookbooks, and idled over pictures of tables perfectly set in mail-order catalogs. I am drawn to the ceremonies of the daily table. I remember with pride my mother's table when it was set for special occasions, set with the silver she purchased one piece at a time when she worked as a soda jerk in Ketchum, Idaho. Her embroidered tablecloth, begun by her mother and finished by my mother upon Grammy Peg's death, is cream linen sprayed with colorful flowers. The table is finished off with the wedding china, white with silver rims. My mother's holiday table has looked that way for as long as I can remember. It's steady, familiar. On holidays we children know to get out the extra leaves for the table, leaves that do not match the rest of the set because my father never got around to finishing the project, and whatever stemware my mother has ten matching pieces of that year.

There were other things that center on the table and food at our house. Certain women were responsible, always, for bringing certain items to holiday feasts. Grandma Purr was in charge of the marshmallow salad. Grammy Peg came with sugar cookies and mincemeat pies. Aunt Ruth was in charge of the rolls. It was the women who held this table and its traditions together. It was the women of various last names (Kelly, Brown, Langwith, Wallington) who kept the family returning to the table, reminding us that we should all get together more often.

For many women, sitting around a table or standing around a kitchen counter becomes the space where their stories are told. For generations, oral storytelling has brewed while dinners have simmered. Not only do we learn the secrets to a good piecrust or the special ingredients in Hunter's Stew as we listen in the kitchen, but we also learn the important stories that make up the lives of these women. There is a power that we get from telling our stories through our recipes. Pearl Bailey, entertainer and cookbook author, tells us of her deep connection with the kitchen: "I don't like to say that my kitchen is a *religious* place, but I would say that if I were a voodoo priestess, I would conduct my rituals there" (21). While Bailey is speaking tongue-in-cheek, there is no mistaking how integral the kitchen is when she is revealing her own life.

A literary extension of this kitchen storytelling, the culinary autobiography, has increasingly appeared on bookstore shelves. The culinary autobiography is a complex pastiche of recipes, personal anecdotes, family history, public history, photographs, even family trees. Bailey, whose book falls into this broad category of autobiography, recognizes that her cookbook is different from what is expected: "Sitting here thinking of yesterday and cooking for tomorrow, I have written this book. It is a cookbook, but not a typical one. . . . I want to try to communicate *why* I cook. . . . I cook because emotionally it is necessary for me to cook, and I want to explore this mystical satisfaction, this meaning and joy that comes from my activities in the kitchen" (ix–x). A culinary autobiography like Bailey's is more than quaint or nostalgic; it is an intensely expressive forum where women share their lives, relationships, and their recipes. They seem to be saying of life and food, "Here are the ingredients. And here is how to put them together successfully."

These recipes-with-memories are a natural extension of storytelling, with the recipes acting as a kind of "cue card" giving the memoir a structure and a template to embellish. Some women have appreciated the "canvas" of the kitchen, using that space to create nourishing meals, memories, and art. These works are rich sources for autobiographical assertion because they present the lives of women through their own voices, rendered from a room that has been, truly, a room of their own. Mary Maples Dunn, former director of the Schlesinger Library on the History of Women, puts the study of women and culinary history into perspective: "If you're going to understand where women were coming from . . . you're going to have to understand what their lives were like, and a heck of a lot of their time was spent in the kitchen" (qtd. in Willoughby C4).

This chapter explores the three main types of culinary autobiographies that I have been able to discern: the culinary memoir, the autobiographical cookbook, and the autoethnographic cookbook. I will discuss how outside influences, the need for veracity, and the need for friends also influence the construction of these kinds of autobiographies. I have studied many nationally published book-length culinary autobiographies upon which I base my ideas. Some that are rewarding are Alice B. Toklas' *The Alice B. Toklas Cook Book*; Pearl Bailey's *Pearl's Kitchen*; Norma Jean Darden and Carole Darden's *Spoonbread and Strawberry Wine: Recipes and Reminiscences of a Family*; Elizabeth Ehrlich's *Miriam's Kitchen*; Ruth Reichl's *Tender at the Bone*; Debby Bull's *Blue Jelly: Love Lost and the Lessons of Canning*; Laurie Colwin's *Home Cooking: A Writer in the Kitchen* and *More Home Cooking: A Writer Returns to the Kitchen*; Simone Beck's *Food and Friends: Recipes and Memories from Simca's Cuisine*; Mimi Sheraton's *From My Mother's Kitchen: Recipes and Reminiscences*, and Carrie Young's *Prairie Cooks: Glorified Rice, Three-Day Buns, and Other Reminiscences*.

More than Cookery Books: The Importance of Culinary Autobiography

In a culinary autobiography, the division between functions of cooking, history, and storytelling blur; the reader may wonder in some cases whether the recipes are the primary texts and the other devices incidental, or the reverse. But why should we look at the culinary autobiography as a distinct form at all? Once we realize that a cookbook is more than a collection of instructions — that it may be an expression of the self — we have another avenue to explore in the ongoing effort to reclaim the words with which women have organized their lives and values.

Estelle Jelinek, a literary theorist who works with autobiography, has commented that women's life stories often appear fragmented in comparison with men's stories. Because women's lives are often interrupted by outside demands and domestic duties, that atmosphere spills into the written representation of their lives. As a form, culinary autobiography simultaneously resists and evokes Jelinek's assertion; while it may appear that the recipes interrupt the stories or vice versa, the combination of the two elements actually provides a strong framework for organized recollection—it's just not a form we are accustomed to seeing. The recipes provide verisimilitude for the stories, and the stories explain the food.

The important initial move is to recognize the validity and significance of culinary literature. Cookbooks that are also memoirs should be studied with the same sense of urgency as other genres. That has not been the case thus far. Anne Goldman states, "We do not often perceive cookbooks as literature" (170), and she is correct. It is essential, if we are going to understand the lives of women, to think seriously of this genre as both a literary and historical form. Jeanne Schinto remarks on the need for cookbooks in the women's literary tradition: "Women searching for a subject of scholarly pursuit often sidestep culinary history. . . . But culinary history, a lively but still relatively new academic field, isn't only the study of old recipes and ways of cooking. In fact, that is a minor—some in the know would say insignificant—part of the work. Culinary scholars take into account the social, family, and women's history imbedded deep in the story of food and its preparation. Cookbooks are just one source of this research" ("Dinner Roles" 16). Culinary autobiographies function on several levels. While food critics or cookbook collectors might see culinary autobiographies as merely of local interest, if we apply the critical strategies for reading autobiographies to reading the culinary autobiography, a large collection of helpful theoretical assertions can be transferred.[1]

For example, in her introduction to *American Women's Autobiography*, Margo Culley asserts that this literary practice, in general, has its roots in the Puritan practice of conversion narratives, and autobiographies that appear to be entirely secular in nature also have their roots in the Puritan tradition (10). She states that the "individual autobiographical act was ultimately an act of community building. . . . [T]he positioning of the autobiographical act within a social context in the expectation that one will be judged but also in the hope that *one's life story will be useful to others and will strengthen the community* [has its] roots in the earliest practice of autobiography in America" (10, emphasis added).

We can see how her theory of purpose behind women's autobiography also plays into forms of the cookbook.[2] One's life story—combined with family and community storytelling as well as the recipes that keep those communities together—falls neatly into Culley's assertion about the Puritan-based didactic tendencies of many American autobiographies. She goes on to explore the idea that "the autobiographical act continues to be socially positioned as women begin to write explicitly for other women . . . writing for other women in the hopes that one's narrative *might be useful to them*" (11, 13). When women's autobiographical acts are combined explicitly with elements that are "useful" (in this case, recipes), the appeal of that work is enhanced.

Forms of the Culinary Autobiography: An Attempt at Categorization

In these books, I have discerned three main manifestations in form and purpose with variations. After reading many of these stories, I feel compelled to attempt to categorize them to better understand how they conformed to or rebelled against the literary genres that I had been taught to recognize. I could have continued to subdivide each of these three categories, but my aim was more general. I merely wanted to begin seeing the patterns and suggesting ways that we might start to think about them. And while I group them largely under the term "culinary autobiography," each variant is distinct in purpose and presentation.

The first that I explore are the culinary memoirs, which present a personal story interlaced with reminiscences about cooking, dining, and feasting. These are autobiographical gestures that have an emphasis on food, but they may or may not provide recipes. The second are the autobiographical cookbooks, which intertwine practices of autobiography and cookery books. The last are the autoethnographic cookbooks, which are documents written by a community or family members, presenting information intended to educate an outside audience about personal or group activities and values. If we can begin to think about the differences in intent and presentation in these works, we may begin to understand how the authors want their readers to interpret the personal information provided.

The Culinary Memoir

Two recent publications, Elizabeth Ehrlich's *Miriam's Kitchen* (1997) and Ruth Reichl's *Tender to the Bone* (1998), fall into the category of culinary memoir. Both authors attempt to capture the essence of their mothers who cooked (either well or not so well) and the younger generation (the authors). Erhlich describes the traditions and rhythms of cooking in a kosher kitchen. Her female relatives guide her path in this spiritual and physical realm. Reichl describes her mother, who is the antithesis of a good cook. In fact, Reichl's brother calls their mother a "menace to society" (9) because she often served food that had begun to rot. Reichl writes, "She had an iron stomach and was incapable of understanding that other people did not. . . . My mission was to keep Mom from killing anybody who came to dinner" (4–5).

In culinary memoirs like these two, the main purpose is to set forth the personal memories of the author. Food is a recurring theme, but it is not the controlling mechanism. Within the text, there may or may not be recipes. What sets this kind of culinary autobiography apart from the others is that if recipes are included in the book, they are not indexed. While this may seem a minor point, when recipes are not indexed, the author is decidedly emphasizing the importance of the *story* in contrast to the recipes. If the recipes were important to the author *beyond* casting verisimilitude (influenced by the recipe-sharing tradition), the recipes would be indexed. When the recipe index is missing, the intent is for the reader to focus on the life story, not to carry the book into the kitchen and pull out the pans. The recipe is part of a deep description, a Proustian gesture (from the viewpoint of the cook), wherein the reader can read the recipe, imagine the cooking, but then keep reading.

A recipe index is significant because it is a signal to the reader that the recipes can be used outside of the story; the intent is for the reader to read *and* cook. When the index is absent, we can make a certain assumption as to why that recipe was included in the life story: these un-indexed recipes are incidental, not integral, to the understanding of the moment, illuminating a memory while perpetuating the recipe-sharing tradition. Often, recipes in this kind of culinary autobiography are separate from the flow of the prose, set apart in tone and appearance from the rest of the text.

Both *Miriam's Kitchen* and *Tender at the Bone* include recipes, clearly removed from the surrounding autobiographical narrative by white space, changes in font, and changes in writing style. In each case the structure of the text makes it apparent that understanding the food and the impetus to make certain dishes is important if we are to understand the personalities of the women who produce it.

In some cases, it may *appear* that the recipes are indexed; for example, in Ehrlich's *Miriam's Kitchen*, the table of contents states "Potato Pudding" and gives a page number. Yet if we turn to the page indicated, we do not get the recipe; rather, we receive a story wherein the potato pudding is the theme. We learn much about the authors and their mothers and mothers-in-law, recipes and all, but the readerly signal (a recipe index) that provides quick access while working in the kitchen is absent. In the larger literary tradition of describing a momentous meal, we understand that the food is only a part of what we need to comprehend about the personal recollections of the author. The difference here is that these are the recollections of women who know the intricacies of cookery. Therefore, it is appropriate that we understand the importance of food *and* the methods of preparing it. Much effort is put into preparing meals, and the inclusion of recipes displays the talent, labor, and imagination of the cook and her culinary tradition.

Another signal of the balance of importance between story and recipes is the table of contents. In these examples, the chapters are organized by theme, event, or tradition. Missing is the traditional practice of dividing food by its role: baked goods, main dishes, soups. The practice in culinary memoirs of employing alternative divisions reinforces the implication that we are reading about a life with cookery traditions observed. And while the recipes work (at least the ones that I have tried), these books are not primarily cookery books; they are memoirs.

The Autobiographical Cookbook

The autobiographical cookbook is a complex intermingling of both auto-biographical and cookery traditions. Works that belong in this category include *The Alice B. Toklas Cook Book* and Pearl Bailey's *Pearl's Kitchen*. Such texts do not necessarily favor one element or the other; rather, the authors try to balance and illuminate the inter-elemental nature of how the recipe reveals the life story.

The background on *The Alice B. Toklas Cook Book* gives us insight into how Toklas conceptualized the purpose of her book. An American publisher (presumably Simon Michael Bessie, who wrote a "Note" to the new edition), approached Toklas about writing the story of her life. Toklas declined at first, stating, "Gertrude did my autobiography and it's done" (vii).[3] Poppy Cannon also wrote about the symbiotic relationship between the Stein and Toklas: "Miss Stein wrote and talked, Miss Toklas cooked and talked" (vii). In their writing lives, when Gertrude Stein wrote and Alice B. Toklas edited and cooked, the act of separating food, fact, fiction, and friends would be impossible.

When Toklas finally began to ponder the possibility of writing, she realized, "What I could do . . . is a cookbook. . . . It would, of course, be full of memories" (Bessie vii). Long after Stein's death, Toklas broached again the idea of the cookbook with memoirs. In 1951, she wrote to Louise Taylor, thanking her for the use of some cookbooks. In that letter, Toklas noted, "I enjoyed them immensely. The ones I liked the best naturally had the most extravagant recipes, nothing one could possibly afford but that made reading it more romantic and more of an adventure. It has given me an idea for my own humble effort. A cook book to be read. What about it?" (*Staying On Alone* 221–22). We can see how Toklas viewed the literary format. Her book was to be used not only for cooking but also for reading. She was always self-effacing when it came to her own writing. Remembering her own response to the friends who prompted her to write a cookbook, Toklas concludes her work with a single line: "As if a cookbook had anything to do with writing" (280).

In that cookbook, Toklas's style of writing suspends the action in order to give detailed instructions for preparation of the food that is associated with that memory. (Pearl Bailey follows much the same writing method.) Schinto, in her essay "The Art of Eating Words," remarks: "The author's own idiosyncratic way of writing about food may well be the book's unique ingredient. . . . *The Alice B. Toklas Cook Book* . . . is described by its author as a 'mingling of recipe and reminiscence.' And it is pleasantly unclear whether the recipes are Toklas' excuse to write the memoirs, or vice versa, so successfully does she entwine the two" (491). This interaction between action and recipe may be a bit unsettling for a reader looking for a memoir or a cookbook in the common understanding of those literary forms. Toklas reintroduces or reinvents the much older practice of coexisting recipes and stories enhancing each other. Such interplay makes perfect sense to the reader who understands that Toklas wanted to write a cookbook to be read for enjoyment; she wanted to write the memoirs of her years with Stein; and that those two elements (the cookery instructions and the memories) could not be separated. Not only are her intentions toward her readership multiple (read, savor, create, ingest) but her plural narrative voices (moving between storyteller, culinary instructor, and history teacher) reflect her complex objectives for the text.

In autobiographical cookbooks, recipes play an integral part in the revelation of the personal history. Because they are part of the self that is being revealed in the prose, the recipes are not removed from the prose flow.[4] As well, the recipes are indexed, conveying the notion that the author wants the book and its reader to move readily between the reading room and the kitchen. The text can be read as autobiography alone, it can be used as a cooking reference alone, or it can be used for both simultaneously.

The recipes may be embedded into the prose text of the memoirs, but they are not separate from the flow of the prose. Toklas moves directly from the recollection into the directions for the dish at hand. For example, when Stein and Toklas traveled throughout the United States for Stein's speaking tour, they spent time in California with Toklas's friend Señora B., and Toklas recalls:

Señora B. made a simple Spanish sweet of which *Panoche* is the coarse Mexican version. She made it like this and unpretentiously called it
DULCE (I)
In a huge copper pan put quantities of granulated sugar, moisten with cream, turn constantly with a copper spoon until it is done. Then pour into glasses. (132–33)

In the chapters that cover events pertaining to her life with Stein, Toklas employs this practice of suspending or augmenting the action or memory with instructions for the dish.[5] Her style of moving from prose to the name of the dish to the instructions back to prose memoirs reflects the high interest she had in food and its place in their daily lives. For Toklas, memorable incidents and the food associated with them are inextricable from each other. Like Proust's flood of memories at the taste of a madeleine, Toklas's memory hinges on meals and their recipes.

The Autoethnographic Cookbook

Finally, another manifestation of the autobiographical in cookery books is the autoethnographic cookbook. Books such as Norma Jean and Carole Darden's *Spoonbread and Strawberry Wine* and Carrie Young's *Prairie Cooks: Glorified Rice, Three-Day Buns, and Other Reminiscences* are good examples. These texts include recipes with indexes as well as autobiographical or autoethnographic detail. Typically, recipes are indexed, but that indexing is combined with other elements (family members, seasons, traditions). An autoethnography has been defined in several ways; I use the term to mean a document written by a community or family member, presenting information intended to educate an outside audience about private personal or group activities and values. Françoise Lionnet defines autoethnography as the "defining of one's subjective ethnicity as mediated through language, history, and ethnographical analysis; in short, that the book amounts to a kind of 'figural anthropology' of the self" (383). In another essay, Mary Louise Pratt describes the form and function of the autoethnographic text as a work in "which people undertake to describe themselves in ways that engage with representations others have made of them. . . . [They] involve a selective collaboration with and appropriation of idioms . . . merged or infiltrated to varying degrees with indigenous idioms to create self-representations intended to intervene" (445). The culinary autobiography, then, in its auto-biographical assertion combined with the task of illuminating the practices of community and family, can appropriately be called an autoethnography. It uses a familiar form (the cookbook) to reinvent the perception of the author and her family or community for those outside her immediate realm to challenge or alter preconceived notions.

Autoethnography shows itself to be particularly apparent in some cook-ery books that contain family photographs, biographical information, anec-dotes, prayers, and family trees. The intent is to provide the recipes to others in the recipe-sharing tradition, but the author also intends to teach people outside of her particular family, community, or region. We learn how to pre-pare the food; we also learn the traditions that mark the food as exceptional or ritual.

By the inclusion of nonrecipe items, the author leads us further into her life and community by making available other documentation of lifestyle and history. This is an essential step in contributing to the idea of veracity in the stories, biographies, and the recipes themselves. By including intimate ar-tifacts, the author is trying to sidestep the problems of narrative associated with autobiography (Is this really how it happened?) while also providing vital context for the foods presented in the recipes. The recipes gain from the autobiographical or autoethnographic gesture because when food is presented contextually — surrounded by the words of the people who create and treasure their foods — it becomes more than an appropriated artifact of a culture being represented in text. That food now has meanings presented with it, embodying values, patterns of behavior, and community standards. The recipe becomes signifier of self and community position.

As an example of an autoethnographic cookbook, the Dardens' *Spoon-bread and Strawberry Wine* serves us well. The Dardens skillfully present the reader with far more than a collection of family recipes. The family recipes are the backbone of the project, but the elements that set this particular project apart from others are apparent in the preface, introduction, and the details within the chapters themselves. We begin to understand that this book also functions as an autoethnography. And while this is *their story*, the detailed focus is on the individual family members and traditions that make them who they are.

What is noticeably different in this case is that each relative has his or her own individual section. Before we progress to the main text of the cookbook, we understand to a certain degree that if we are looking for bread recipes, then we will get Aunt Artelia's version of those foods, that Uncle J. B.'s recipe files have contributed instructions for meat and potatoes, and that Uncles C. L., Arthur, Russell, and Charlie had a penchant for seafood.

This cookbook was meant to do far more than sing praises and show the hardships of one black family in the South. In the biographies of the individuals, the Dardens instill history by giving examples and explanations of customs and rituals. By this act, the Dardens reveal that their cookbook was meant to reach a wider audience than cooks of the southern United States. Upon presenting the New Year's Day traditions as the Dardens still celebrate them, the authors include a small lesson in black southern folklore. "Black folklore has it that Hoppin' John brings good luck and greens bring monetary blessings in the coming year, so we always serve this traditionally Southern meal with all the essential trimmings" (259). This explanation would be unnecessary to anyone familiar with black southern folkways, but the explanation here serves two purposes. First, it elaborates on why the Dardens include the dishes in their celebration. Second, it explains in plain terms the significance of the dishes' inclusion at that particular feast for those readers who might be unaware of the tradition; the recipe provides the opportunity for the folklore.

In the "Funerals" chapter, the Dardens explain that as "granddaughters, nieces, and cousins of morticians, we have attended our share of funerals and wakes" (271). It is at these rituals of grieving that "the best Southern cooking is to be had." This, in and of itself, is not an uncommon phenomenon, for often people observe that family and neighbors outdo themselves in providing the grieving family with foodstuffs; however, the Dardens take this opportunity to transmit a history lesson: "The custom of caring for the bereaved in this manner goes back to ancient Africa, where the family of the deceased was given not only food but items of value, including clothing and household items by the entire community in an effort to offset the loss in a practical manner. This was particularly important if the deceased was the head of a household and the continuation of family stability was a concern. In the antebellum South, churches, fraternal orders, and burial societies took over a similar function, and to a significant extent this continues today" (271). The Dardens do not give any scholarly reference to this assertion nor does it seem that they have to. The phenomenon of a feast associated with caring for the bereaved could simply be considered a human instinct. They have provided a contextual framework for the continuing tradition of the funeral feast within their own culture.

In the autoethnographic cookbook, a culinary code is set forth that details both the food methods and the foodways of a particular culture, using the self and the family as the autoethnographic template for recipe sharing. As readers and cooks, we learn more than just some recipes or one person's life story; the text reveals and decodes traditions and rituals for people who are not familiar with them. These kinds of autobiographical assertions reveal aspects of culinary traditions, as manifested within the author's range of experience. At the same time, we learn culinary skills and methods particular to that culture.

The questions for the reader when approaching culinary autobiographies are many and varied. Are the recipes authentic, or have they been altered so that a more general readership can use them? Are specialized food items included in order to set boundaries between authentic and nonauthentic reproductions of a food item?[6] When recipes are included, is that a simple manifestation of the recipe-sharing tradition, or is it more complicated because the recipient is unknown (whereas, traditionally, the giver knows the receiver of a recipe and there is an immediate reason for the sharing)? When given to the reader, recipes assume a life of their own and are thus perpetuated. The recipes, as retellings of the stories, are transformed. They assume new meanings in each and every kitchen where they are reproduced.

The Hash Fudge Factor: Friends and Their Recipes

When recounting a life, friends are also an important factor in how we see ourselves. Often, in culinary autobiographies, recipes and advice are included that have been donated by various acquaintances. Sometimes this can be problematic. Sometimes it can be enlightening. For Toklas, one recipe proved to be a headache. For Debby Bull, advice from friends permeated the very manner in which she produced her food.

For me, *The Alice B. Toklas Cook Book* was the gateway to thinking about texts that combine recipes and autobiography. I found this cookbook by accident; I was supposed to be researching Gertrude Stein for a graduate course. But in an article about Stein, an interesting passage about Toklas's cookbook and the fury over the marijuana fudge recipe sent me to the cookbook section. Written by Alice B. Toklas and published in 1954, it contains an interesting mingling of recipes and remembrances about Gertrude Stein and their famous circle of friends.

When Toklas began to run out of steam while creating her cookbook, she asked for contributions, and she created a chapter called "Recipes from Friends." It is in this chapter that trouble started for Toklas. Brian Gysen, a man Stein had met only once and Toklas hardly knew, submitted a recipe for fudge made with marijuana. This recipe was printed in the European edition of the cookbook, but it was edited out for the American audience. The appearance of the recipe in the cookbook raised quite a response from her European audience; Toklas claimed that she did not know the meaning of the botanical terms *cannabis sativa* when she decided to include the recipe in her collection (Simon 218). Toklas was incensed that the public could have the impression that "Gertrude had been indulging in haschich all these years and . . . [might] think that the resulting state of mind might account for Gertrude's writing" (Simon 218–19). Because of her exhaustion near the end of writing the book, Toklas claimed she did not "notice" the recipe, but her dear friend Thornton Wilder chided her that it "might well be the publicity stunt of the year." Toklas did not see much humor in the situation. She guarded the image and the memory of Stein fiercely and was uncomfortable with the implications that the drugged fudge could have had regarding Stein's reputation as a literary artist.

Upon closer inspection, it appears that Toklas had probably given the recipe a bit more attention than she claimed. If we look at some of the characteristics of the recipe as printed, we can see similarities to other recipes that she included in the "Recipes from Friends" chapter. For example, underneath the title of "Haschich Fudge" there is a note in parentheses remarking "(*which anyone could whip up on a rainy day*)" (259). This subtitle, in both its form and tone, is like many other subtitles that are included with the other recipes from contributors in this section. Also, the use of a dash in the first paragraph of the recipe is strikingly similar to her use of the dash in other recipes of her own throughout the cookbook, as is the diction and tone; the diction for the rest of the recipe is unlike Toklas's in any other part of the book, so we can probably assume that Toklas did not alter the recipe's instructions after that first paragraph and thus, more than likely, did not know or did not pay attention to the ingredients. And while this close reading of one small anomaly may prove nothing more than haphazard proofreading on Toklas's part, the entire incident still leaves questions. We are left wondering, even after reading her biography and letters, whether she understood the recipe's ingredients. Toklas was known for her meticulous editing and proofreading of Stein's texts, yet when she submitted her manuscript for the cookbook to the publisher, it was full of errors. It "set a record, one of the staff thought, in sloppiness" (Simon 219). This may also shore up the hypothesis that Toklas missed the implication of the ingredients in the fudge.

Friends like Brian Gysen can be problematic in a recipe collection, but other kinds of friends can also make their way into recipes. In *Blue Jelly*, an autobiographical cookbook, Debby Bull recounts her struggle to recover from an especially bad breakup. While she is busy throwing out everything that belonged to her ex-boyfriend, she runs across a bag of huckleberries in the freezer. She cannot toss out perfectly good berries, but she can't bear to keep them around either. So she transforms them into jelly. The preciseness of the canning ritual comforts her, and the rest of her book details her road back to a positive self-image while she cans and pickles the abundance of her life.

In the chapter titled "Raspberry Jam," Bull realizes that her roadblock in getting over her boyfriend is that she formulated all of her ideas about love from rock and roll songs. At the end of her exploration about this personal dynamic, she provides the recipe and methodology for raspberry jam. Suddenly, we get a recollection about a friend's advice on self-image:

Simmer for half an hour or so until the berries are really soft, stirring to keep it all from frying on the bottom. I filled up lots of free time, like when there's nothing to do but stir, thinking about how everything would've turned out perfectly and nobody would have left me if I were prettier. I tried to force myself to think about something Tina Turner had told me. "You cannot put me in the pile with the pretty ones, but I do not go in the pile with the ugly ones either," she'd said. "And I like it here in the middle. There's a lot more freedom." Meanwhile, sterilize the jars for 10 minutes in boiling water. (36–37)

Much like Toklas, remembrances and recipes are so intertwined in the author's mind as to be inseparable. While Bull's conversation with Tina Turner is in no way relevant to the production of raspberry jam, that piece of advice *is* an important step in Bull reclaiming her sense of self.

And that is the whole point of presenting a life with recipes. When the food cannot be separated from the friend or memory, we come to realize that life itself is a recipe. Sometimes it is a recipe that we should throw out, but sometimes the recipe should be filed away and kept for when we have more than we know what to do with.

Recipes Inside and Outside Storytelling: Telling the Truth

In *Tender at the Bone: Growing Up at the Table*, Ruth Reichl tells the reader from the very first line that storytelling was prized in her family. A trip to the store could turn into a grand adventure when told by her mother. Her father would "rearrange" what happened at work that day in order to tell a better tale. Reichl writes, "If this required minor adjustments of fact, nobody much minded: it was certainly preferable to boring your audience" (ix). She highlights the fact that her book falls into the same kind of storytelling: "Every-thing here is true, but it may not be factual. . . . I have occasionally embroi-dered" (x).

What is understood or implied is that the *recipes are real*. As discussed earlier, the recipes in Reichl's book appear on their own pages, removed from the narrative. The recipes are unaffected by the storytelling practices that make "facts" ambiguous. Reading the recipes themselves is also an exercise in decoding the author's intentions. We must heed how the recipe is printed, but the tone of the recipe can be of interest, too. Does the author default to the traditional command tone of the mainstream cookbook? Stir in, add two eggs, cool at room temperature. Or does the author's voice permeate the instruc-tions, overriding a strong tradition of command-style cookery writing? What-ever the presentation of the recipe, a reader can further interpret the author's willingness to share a life and to imbue the notion that food and its stories are intertwined.

The idea that recipes in these books are "real" is key. Recipes can't be fiction. The concept that recipes reproduced in a book are ones that *work* is an essential element of the implied contract between the reader and the author of cookery books. Intriguing questions begin to arise when we look at the culin-ary autobiography functioning like any other autobiography.

Philippe Lejeune in his work *On Autobiography* has an interesting asser-tion that when the autobiography is signed by the author, that person has entered into a kind of contract with the reader. With the signature comes an assurance of "telling the truth," and assertion of veracity by the author that events and particulars are as faithfully represented as possible. This contract with the reader quickly falls apart when elements such as subjectivity, point of view, and "truth" itself are examined closely. Representation of the self is necessarily a selective process, and that process is no less edited when writing an autobiography than in any other self-revealing activity. Therefore, any autobiographical act is necessarily suspect in its representation of the truth or reality. As with most texts, the cookbook (or even the recipe card) has a space for authorial signature — a place for the author to proceed with the contract of veracity. By signing the text — whether a book, a cookbook, an autobiography, or a recipe card — the author promises that this is the "truth." This might be especially important in the context of cookbooks and recipes, for if the "truth" is not given, a dish will fail. Susan Leonardi notes that to share recipes "is an act of trust between women," and the trust assumed is that the recipe is "real" (346). To share a recipe is to share a part of one's self, and writing one's own name, signifying authorship or ownership, is an assertion on the part of the giver. She wants to be recognized for the dish. It is a bow to the past and a marker for the future. Thus, when an autobiography is enhanced by recipes from author to reader, the trust implied by the recipe-sharing tradition affects the reception of the autobiographical offering.

Recipes, when included with autobiographical assertions, transform the autobiography. If we believe that the recipes will work (that they are "real"), will we have more faith that the autobiography is a faithful recounting of a life? Recalling the layers of narrative frameworks that use recipes in fictional works, we may have many of the same concerns with the culinary autobiography. Is this a "real" recipe? Is this how events in this person's life really happened? Who is giving these recipes and stories and to what end? Is this a book for reading or for using in the kitchen or both?

Altering the Ingredients: Reading Beyond the Recipes

Other culinary writings do not fall conveniently into the categories that I have provided. How could the copious works of M. F. K. Fisher ever fall neatly into just one of these categories? Other kinds of cookbooks compile recipes with short biographies of numerous cooks (such as *The Secret to Tender Pie: America's Grandmothers Share Their Favorite Recipes* by Mindy Marin or *In Nonna's Kitchen: Recipes and Traditions from Italy's Grandmothers* by Carol Field). Yet another form are the anthologies of culinary stories (some with recipes, some without) like *Through the Kitchen Window* (edited by Arlene Voski Avakian) or *We Are What We Ate* (edited by Mark Winegardner). We are just beginning to understand that culinary writing, in all its manifestations, is also a valid arena for interpreting women's lives.

If, as ethnographers and sociologists assert, women are the keepers of traditional or ritual foods for a family or group, it only makes sense that the culinary autobiography would eventually come about. Part of the reason for this type of book being produced is a sense of urgency in documenting the fading familial and societal traditions that once held groups together more strongly.[7] If women are the keepers of family and group history, and if women are also largely responsible for daily food production and presentation, the culinary autobiography combines those elements that need recording within a genre that historically privileges women's voices and opinions.

The autobiographical self that is represented in the culinary autobiography claims for herself a sense of place, heritage, and history that may not be otherwise articulated. Using recipes as a framework for a discourse of the self allows the author to construct milieu for others as she sees fit. It allows her to present her heritage as she knows it (whether that be a rewriting of generally known history or a challenge to cultural practices), and it gives a place to articulate alternative voices and viewpoints. If read as such, the culinary autobiography can be a site of multiple textual assertions that need to be read beyond the recipes. The culinary autobiography is unique because it is almost a natural extension of an oral storytelling tradition that has been playing itself out for generations in our very own kitchens.

Notes

1. For my purposes, I define an autobiography as the attempt to tell one's life story from beginning to end, while the memoir is a fraction of the life history, chosen for representation by the author by criteria that may or may not be articulated. Both are autobiographical expressions with differing lengths, forms, and purposes.

2. In discussing the parameters of autobiographical studies, Culley writes, "While repeating the truism that autobiography is the most democratic of genres, and making occasional gestures that autobiography indeed might include precontact Indian cave drawings, photo albums, narrative quilts and cookbooks, most critics have focused on a narrow group of highly 'literary' texts and/or texts of writers known for their public achievements" (5).

3. Gertrude Stein, Toklas's life partner, wrote *The Autobiography of Alice B. Toklas*, wherein she took on the voice of Toklas. *The Autobiography* does not have any recipes in it. In fact, it hardly mentions cooking at all.

4. The recipes in autobiographical cookbooks do, however, follow the recipe-writing tradition of coded language with specific formatting and language use. For more on the specific language practices in recipes, begin with Diane Massam's "Recipe Context Null Objects in English" and Janet Theophano's "A Life's Work: Women Writing from the Kitchen."

5. The chapters that depend heavily on the memoirs are "Dishes for Artists," "Murder in the Kitchen," "Food to Which Aunt Pauline and Lady Godiva Led Us," "Food in the United States," "Servants in France," "Food in the Bugey During the Occupation," and "The Vegetable Gardens at Bilignin." The other chapters cover more historical or cultural aspects of the dishes, relying less on the pattern of introducing recipes that she establishes in the memoir chapters.

6. See Anne Goldman's "I Yam What I Yam"; she addresses the practice of enacting food boundaries in order to set author apart from reader.

7. The Dardens, who wrote *Spoonbread and Strawberry Wine*, make this assertion directly. Others, like Carrie and Felicia Young, allude to the need to document family history, but do not state it forthrightly.

Works Cited

Avakian, Arlene Voski, ed. *Through the Kitchen Window: Women Explore the Intimate Meanings of Food and Cooking*. Boston: Beacon, 1997.

Bailey, Pearl. *Pearl's Kitchen*. New York: Harcourt Brace, 1973.

Beck, Simone. *Food and Friends: Recipes and Memories from Simca's Cuisine*. New York: Viking, 1991.

Bessie, Simon Michael. "A Happy Publisher's Note to the New Edition." *The Alice B. Toklas Cook Book*. 1954. New York: Perennial, 1984.

Bull, Debby. *Blue Jelly: Love Lost and the Lessons of Canning*. New York: Hyperion, 1997.

Cannon, Poppy. Introduction. *Aromas and Flavors of Past and Present*. By Alice B. Toklas. New York: Harper, 1958. vii–xxxii.

Colwin, Laurie. *Home Cooking: A Writer in the Kitchen*. New York: HarperPerennial, 1993.

———. *More Home Cooking: A Writer Returns to the Kitchen*. New York: HarperPerennial, 1993.

Culley, Margo. "What a Piece of Work Is 'Woman'! An Introduction." *American Women's Autobiography*. Ed. Margo Culley. Madison: University of Wisconsin Press, 1992. 3–31.

Darden, Norma Jean, and Carole Darden. *Spoonbread and Strawberry Wine: Recipes and Reminiscences of a Family*. 1978. New York: Doubleday, 1994.

Ehrlich, Elizabeth. *Miriam's Kitchen: A Memoir*. New York: Viking, 1997.

Field, Carol. *In Nonna's Kitchen: Recipes and Traditions from Italy's Grandmothers*. New York: HarperCollins, 1997.

Goldman, Anne. " 'I Yam What I Yam': Cooking, Culture, and Colonialism." *De/Colonizing the Subject: The Politics of Gender in Women's Autobiography*. Ed. Sidonie Smith and Julia Watson. Minneapolis: University of Minneapolis Press, 1992. 169–95.

Jelinek, Estelle C. *Women's Autobiography: Essays in Criticism*. Bloomington: Indiana University Press, 1980.

Lejeune, Philippe. *On Autobiography*. Minneapolis: University of Minneapolis Press, 1989.

Leonardi, Susan J. "Recipes for Reading: Summer Pasta, Lobster à La Riseholme, and Key Lime Pie." *PMLA* 104.3 (1989): 340–47.

Lionnet, Françoise. "Autoethnography: The An-Archic Style of Dust Tracks on a Road." *Reading Black, Reading Feminist: A Critical Anthology*. Ed. Henry Louis Gates, Jr. New York: Meridian, 1990. 382–414.

Marin, Mindy. *The Secret to Tender Pie: America's Grandmothers Share Their Favorite Recipes*. New York: Ballantine, 1997.

Massam, Diane. "Recipe Context Null Object in English." *Linguistic Inquiry* 20.1 (1989): 134–39.

Pratt, Mary Louise. "Arts of the Contact Zone." *Ways of Reading: An Anthology for Writers*. Ed. David Bartholomae and Anthony Petrosky. Boston: Bedford, 1993. 442–56.

Reichl, Ruth. *Tender at the Bone: Growing Up at the Table*. New York: Random House, 1998.

Schinto, Jean. "The Art of Eating Words." *Yale Review* 72.3 (1990): 489–502.

———. "Dinner Roles." *Women's Review of Books* 10.1 (1992): 16–17.

Sheraton, Mimi. *From My Mother's Kitchen: Recipes and Reminiscences*. New York: Harper and Row, 1979.

Simon, Linda. *The Biography of Alice B. Toklas*. New York: Doubleday, 1977.

Stein, Gertrude. *The Autobiography of Alice B. Toklas*. 1933. New York: Vintage, 1990.

———. *Tender Buttons. Selected Writings of Gertrude Stein*. Ed. Carl van Vechten. New York: Modern Library, 1962.

Theophano, Janet. "A Life's Work: Women Writing from the Kitchen." *Fields of Folklore: Essays in Honor of Kenneth S. Goldstein*. Ed. Roger D. Abrahams. Bloomington: Trickster Press, 1995. 287–99.

Toklas, Alice B. *The Alice B. Toklas Cook Book*. 1954. New York: Perennial, 1984.

———. *Staying On Alone: The Letters of Alice B. Toklas*. Ed. Edward Burns. New York: Liveright, 1973.

Willoughby, John. "Feminists Find History in the Kitchen." *New York Times* 10 May 1995: C4.

Winegardner, Mark, ed. *We Are What We Ate: Twenty-four Memories of Food*. New York: Harcourt Brace, 1998.

Young, Carrie, with Felicia Young. *Prairie Cooks: Glorified Rice, Three-Day Buns, and Other Reminiscences*. Iowa City: University of Iowa Press, 1993.

Contributors

Alice A. Deck is associate professor of English and Afro-American studies at the University of Illinois at Urbana-Champaign. Her research interests include African American and modern African literature, women's autobiography, black feminist theory, and media representations of American minorities. She is the author of "Autoethnography: Zora Neale Hurston, Noni Jabavu, and Cross-Cultural Discourse" in *Black American Literature Forum* (1990) and " 'Whose Books Is This?' Authorial vs. Editorial Control of Harriet Brent Jacobs's *Incidents in the Life of a Slave Girl; Written by Herself* " in *Women's Studies International Forum* (1987). Her work in progress includes *Against the Tyrannies of Silence: Black Women's Autobiography in Africa and the United States* (contracted with Indiana University Press) and an interdisciplinary study of the black Mammy as an American icon.

Jane Dusselier is a Ph.D. candidate in American Studies at the University of Maryland — College Park. She is the recipient of the Helzberg Award with Outstanding Merit from the Women's Council at the University of Missouri. She is writing a dissertation on the cultural history of the candy industry from a gendered perspective.

Erika Endrijonas holds a joint appointment as assistant dean and professor at the Union Institute. She earned her Ph.D. in American history at the University of Southern California. Her current research interests include how food scarcity during the Depression shaped the appetite and attitude of an entire generation, many of whom still view and treat food differently from the generations that have followed.

Sherrie A. Inness is associate professor of English at Miami University. Her research interests include gender and cooking culture, girls' literature and culture, popular culture, and gender studies. She has published eight books: *Intimate Communities: Representation and Social Transformation in Women's College Fiction, 1895–1910* (1995), *The Lesbian Menace: Ideology, Identity, and the Representation of Lesbian Life* (1997), *Tough Girls: Women Warriors and Wonder Women in Popular Culture* (1999), *Nancy Drew and Company: Culture, Gender, and Girls' Series* (editor) (1997), *Breaking Boundaries: New Perspectives on Regional Writing* (coeditor) (1997), *Delinquents and Debutantes: Twentieth-Century American Girls' Cultures* (editor) (1998), *Millennium Girls: Today's Girls Around the World* (editor) (1998), and *Running for Their Lives: Girls, Cultural Identity, and Stories of Survival* (editor) (2000).

Traci Marie Kelly is assistant professor of composition and literature at the University of Minnesota, Crookston. She also teaches for the Women's Studies Department at the University of North Dakota. Her research interests include culinary literature, autobiography, women writers, and technology and writing. She is currently working on a book-length study titled "Burned Sugar Pie: Women's Voices in the Literature of Food."

Jessamyn Neuhaus received her Ph.D. in history from the Claremont Graduate University. Her research interests include twentieth-century American history, cultural studies, and the history of sexuality. An excerpt from her dissertation on cookbook and gender ideology in the United States, 1920–1963, has been published in the *Journal of Social History*. Neuhaus has taught in the humanities department at the New College of California, San Francisco.

Katherine Parkin is a Ph.D. candidate in history at Temple University. Her research interests include women's history, cultural history, and political history. She teaches at Temple University in the History and American Studies Departments and in the School of Social Administration.

Christopher Holmes Smith is a Ph.D. candidate in media and cultural studies at the University of Wisconsin — Madison. His primary research interests include ethical perspectives on African American subject formation, modern and postmodern philosophy and social theory, and cultural studies. His investigation of contemporary hip-hop culture, "Method in the Madness: Exploring the Boundaries of Identity in Hip-Hop Performativity," was published in *Social Identities: Journal for the Study of Race, Nation, and Culture*. He also coauthored, with John Fiske, "Naming the Illuminati," which appears in Ronald Radano and Philip V. Bohlman, eds., *Music and the Racial Imagination* (1999).

Janet Theophano is associate director of the College of General Studies and adjunct assistant professor at the University of Pennsylvania. She is coeditor of *Diet and Domestic Life in Society* (1991), author of *Household Words: Women Write for and from the Kitchen: An Exhibition Catalog of the Esther B. Aresty Rare Book Collection on the Culinary Arts* (1996), "A Life's Work: Women Writing from the Kitchen" in Roger Abrahams, ed., *Fields of Folklore: Essays in Honor of Kenneth S. Goldstein* (1995), "I Gave Him a Cake: An Interpretation of Two Italian American Weddings" in Stephen Stern and John Allan Cicala, eds., *Creative Ethnicity: Symbols and Strategies of Contemporary Ethnic Life* (1991), "Expressions of Love, Acts of Labor" in *Pennsylvania Folklife* (Autumn 1995), and other essays.

Jessica Weiss is an assistant professor of women's history at California State University, Hayward. Her research interests are in the areas of gender and women's history with a particular focus on the postwar era. She is the author of "Making Room for Fathers: Men, Women, and Parenthood, 1950–1980," in Laura McCall and Donald Yacovone, eds., *A Shared Experience: Men, Women, and the History of Gender* (1998), "A Drop-In Catering Job: Middle-Class Women and Fatherhood, 1950–1980," *Journal of Family History* (Spring 1999), and *To Have and to Hold: Marriage and Family in the Lives of the Parents of the Baby Boom* (2000).

Doris Witt is an assistant professor at the University of Iowa where she teaches twentieth-century American literary and cultural studies. She is the author of *Black Hunger: Food and the Politics of U.S. Identity* (1999).

Index

Acknowledgments

I would like to thank a number of people who have read chapters included in the anthology, among them Faye Parker Flavin, Lowell Inness, Stephanie Levine, and Whitney Womack. I am especially grateful for Faye Parker's help in reading every chapter; she is an excellent critic of my work and much more. Parker makes me a better writer and — the more difficult task — a better person. Whether she is preparing soup for a sick friend or purchasing a birdbath so the birds will have a place to splash around in her backyard, Parker shows me every day what it means to have a kind heart. I respect and admire her deeply, and I am fortunate to have her in my life. I only hope that I can return a small amount of all that she has given me.

I also appreciate the advice and feedback given to me by a number of food scholars, including Arlene Voski Avakian, Amy Bentley, Paul Christensen, Lisa Heldke, and especially Warren Belasco, Jane Dusselier, and Janet Theophano. In addition, I am thankful for all my contributors' efforts on behalf of this collection. Even with tight deadlines, they never failed to be considerate and conscientious. I owe them all a great deal.

Many friends have provided support during this project, including Barbara Emison, Julie Hucke, Stephanie Levine, Michele Lloyd, Gillian O'Driscoll, Lisa Somer, Barbara Spaulding, Wendy W. Walters, and Liz Wilson. I am blessed to have such dear friends. They know how much I appreciate their help and how thankful I am for their presence. In this group of friends I would also like to include my Miami University colleagues. These people contribute greatly to my life; I couldn't have a better group of colleagues, and I appreciate each of them.

I also wish to thank my dear mother, Ruth Ebelke Inness (1920–98). "Thanking" her is such a weak term for what I feel. My mom's spirit pervades this work, my life. She is impossible to separate from me — my debts to her are immeasurable. She is sorely missed.

Finally, I wish to thank everyone at the University of Pennsylvania Press, including Noreen O'Connor. This book is dedicated to Patricia Reynolds Smith, my editor at the Press. The job an editor has at an academic press is monumental. She must juggle a wide number of book projects that are nearing completion; she must also constantly search for new projects. She must deal with daily interruptions as authors call her, seeking encouragement or support for a new project. She must serve as a rigorous editor, but she must also be psychologist, friend, and coach as she works with authors. Although Pat's responsibilities are many, she always makes time to provide the bit of encouragement to her authors when they most need it. She finds precious minutes to help an author fine tune a new project. And, most important, she finds the time to offer words of wisdom about the often murky and mysterious ways of academe. I dedicate this work to her.

For permission to include a revised version of a previously published work, I wish to acknowledge the following book: Doris Witt, " 'My Kitchen Was the World': Vertamae Smart Grosvenor's Geechee Diaspora," in *Black Hunger: Food and the Politics of U.S. Identity* (New York: Oxford University Press, 1999).